Praise for Randall Kennedy's

FOR DISCRIMINATION

"Meticulously argued. . . . An illuminating, detailed argument in favor of affirmative action and its application via race-based methods. . . . Kennedy vividly portrays Supreme Court decisions as malleable, subject to reinterpretation and even reversal not only because of the makeup of the court but because of the changing tide of political circumstances and public opinion."
—*The Boston Globe*

"Kennedy's *For Discrimination* provides supporters of affirmative action with the penetrating, concise, coolheaded arguments for racial justice they've been waiting for."
—*Vanity Fair*

"Remarkably astute and tough-minded. . . . Should be required reading for anyone interested in genuine equal opportunity in the United States." —*Florida Courier*

"This is an important book. Kennedy, who admits to having benefitted from affirmative action, will force a lot of long-needed conversations with his opinions, conversations for which he includes abundant, solid fodder." —*Times Weekly*

"Provocative. . . . Important. . . . *For Discrimination* offers a thorough analysis of the topic and leaves the reader feeling as though he or she has just left a lawyer's office having been briefed on the many perspectives on affirmative action within in the United States, and is now ready to testify in court."

—*PopMatters*

"This is arguably the most clearheaded defense of affirmative action ever written. Kennedy's incisive analysis includes a compelling critique of a range of arguments by legal experts and social scientists on the pros and cons of affirmative action. In clear prose *For Discrimination* advances powerful arguments for sensibly defined affirmative action. This thoughtful book is a must-read for all Americans devoted to addressing past and current injustice."

—William Julius Wilson, Lewis P. and Linda L. Geyser University Professor, Harvard University

"Required reading. . . . Kennedy knows where the nerve endings are in discussing the complexities of race in America. . . . Admirably balanced and provocative."   —*Publishers Weekly*

"A probing and well-considered look at the complexities of race relations and the continuing controversial issues of affirmative action in contemporary America."   —*Booklist*

Randall Kennedy

FOR DISCRIMINATION

Randall Kennedy is the Michael R. Klein Professor of Law at Harvard Law School. He received his undergraduate degree from Princeton and his law degree from Yale. He attended Oxford University as a Rhodes Scholar and is a former clerk to Supreme Court Justice Thurgood Marshall. The author of six books, he won the Robert F. Kennedy Book Award for *Race, Crime, and the Law*. A member of the bars of the Supreme Court of the United States and the District of Columbia, a member of the American Philosophical Society and the American Academy of Arts and Sciences, Kennedy is also a Charter Trustee of Princeton University and the proud father of Henry William Kennedy, Rachel Elizabeth Lové Kennedy, and Thaddeus James Kennedy.

FOR
DISCRIMINATION

Race, Affirmative Action,
and the Law

RANDALL KENNEDY

VINTAGE BOOKS
A Division of Penguin Random House LLC
New York

The Library of Congress has cataloged the Pantheon edition as follows:
Kennedy, Randall, [DATE]
For discrimination : race, affirmative action, and the law /
Randall Kennedy.
pages cm
Includes bibliographical references and index.
1. Affirmative action programs—Law and legislation—United States.
2. Race discrimination—United States. I. Title.
KF4755.5.K46   2013   342.7308'73—dc23   2013001471

Vintage Books Trade Paperback ISBN: 978-0-307-94936-3
eBook ISBN: 978-0-307-90738-7

Author photograph © Martha Stewart
Book design by M. Kristen Bearse

www.vintagebooks.com

In Praise of Eric Foner and Sanford Levinson

I have been blessed to know wonderful teachers. This book is dedicated to two who stand out as extraordinary models, mentors, and friends. Professor Eric Foner is the preeminent interpreter of the history of the United States. Professor Sanford Levinson is the most adventurous, independent, and wide-ranging intellectual in the American legal academy. For more than three decades they have encouraged me unstintingly. I thank them for the tremendous positive difference they have made in my life.

Contents

FOR DISCRIMINATION

Introduction

Growing Up with Affirmative Action

I can clearly recall watching the Jerry Lewis version of the film *The Nutty Professor* from a balcony set aside for African Americans in a theater in Columbia, South Carolina, in the summer of 1963. Ironically, as a nine-year-old, I perceived that Jim Crow arrangement as *favoring* blacks; it was far easier for us to throw candy down on the whites seated below than for them to throw things up at us. Back then, I thought that Americans were divided into teams designated by complexion. State authorities fed this perception with a chain in the middle of the road that separated whites and blacks in the area where my aunt lived, the choice to close rather than desegregate public parks, and ordinances requiring racially separate bathrooms (especially memorable for me were the signs differentiating "white ladies" from "black women").

I was born in Columbia in 1954, the year the Supreme Court invalidated racial segregation in public schools. I visited frequently but did not live there. Fleeing racism like many millions of other Southern black refugees, my parents raised me and my siblings in Washington, D.C. My father once told me he feared that if he remained in the Deep South, he would kill or be killed in a racial altercation. He was a postal clerk who attended a couple of years of college at two black institutions: Dillard University, in New Orleans, and Southern University, in Baton Rouge.

My mother was a schoolteacher who earned an undergraduate degree from South Carolina State College, an institution created for Negroes in order to "protect" the state's white university. When she sought a higher degree, she learned that that sort of study was unavailable to her in her home state. To fulfill what they perceived as their obligation under "separate but equal," state authorities subsidized her tuition so that my mother could study "abroad" at some institution that would accept blacks.* That is how she wound up as a student at New York University, where she earned a master's degree.

Throughout the late 1950s and early 1960s, I enjoyed a happy childhood in a loving household. By moving north, my family did not wholly escape racism; anti-black attitudes and practices were (and are) a national phenomenon. But what we encountered in D.C. paled in comparison with what my extended family faced in South Carolina; one of my cousins was at the civil rights protest at South Carolina State College in which three undergraduates were murdered by state police in an episode of racially motivated violence that, while the subject of a fine book, has never received the attention it warranted.†

In my house, discussion about the civil rights movement was constant. From my parents I learned to revere well-known heroes and heroines—Martin Luther King, Jr.; Rosa Parks; Fannie Lou Hamer—as well as lesser-known figures like James Hinton, Modjeska Simkins, and Matthew Perry. Subsequently, I have

* Previously, the Supreme Court had held that paying tuition for blacks to attend out-of-state schools that accepted them failed to satisfy a state's obligation to provide racially equal educational opportunities. See *Missouri ex rel. Gaines v. Canada*, 305 U.S. 337 (1938). As has often been the case, a long lag separated the Court's ruling and realities on the ground.
† See Jack Bass and Jack Nelson, *The Orangeburg Massacre* (second edition, revised and enlarged, 1984).

come to appreciate with ever-deepening gratitude the benefits they pried open and that I have enjoyed as a matter of course. For one thing, I have had the privilege of attending an extraordinary array of schools that became accessible to more than a negligible number of black students only after the late 1960s: St. Albans School for Boys (1968–73), Princeton University (1973–77), and Yale Law School (1979–82). An affirmative action ethos played a role in my admittance and flourishing at each of these selective, expensive, and powerful institutions. This ethos consists of a desire to make amends for past injustices, a commitment to counter present but hidden prejudices, a wish to forestall social disruption, and an intuition that racial integration will enrich institutions from which marginalized groups have largely been absent.

Of course, I encountered invidious racial discrimination in these schools periodically, but, luckily for me, the balance of my encounters along the race line were positive. I have often been shown special attention in competitive settings in which my blackness was perceived as a plus. I am quite certain that my race played a role in prompting teachers at St. Albans—the most formative of the schools I attended—to be especially helpful to me during my days as a student there. The same was true at Princeton, where I enjoyed the solicitude of William Bowen, who was then the president of the university, and Neil Rudenstine, the university provost (and later the president of Harvard). Their generosity was due, in part, to the mysterious alchemy of friendship. It was also due to their self-conscious, systematic efforts to lend special aid to promising scholars of color in America and indeed around the world. Throughout their distinguished careers, Bowen and Rudenstine have been highly effective practitioners of the affirmative action ethos.[1]

When I was a senior in college, considering law school, I attended a gathering that featured the Yale Law School dean of admissions. He distributed a document that included a chart noting the range of Law School Admission Test (LSAT) scores of the students in the most recent entering class. I had just received my LSAT results. My score was disappointing—low enough that it did not even appear on the chart. I waited until the dean had fielded all of the other students' questions before I bashfully approached him and asked whether, given my score, I should still apply. He asked what sort of grades I had earned. When I told him that I had an A-minus average, he urged me to proceed. I won admission to Yale, Harvard, and every other school to which I applied. I had the profile of a hard worker, and I also had a halo over me, having just won a Rhodes Scholarship. In other words, without affirmative action I would surely have gained admission to a fine law school. But in its absence, and in the face of that spectacularly mediocre LSAT score, would I have gained admission to Yale and Harvard? Maybe not.

I attended Yale Law School (YLS) in the aftermath of *Regents of the University of California v. Bakke* (1978). In that landmark ruling, the Supreme Court invalidated a particular affirmative action program but upheld affirmative action in university admissions in general, if structured in a certain way and pursued for the sake of "diversity." At YLS, virtually all black students supported affirmative action. Doing so was seen as a sacred communal obligation. A memorable dinnertime discussion with black peers in my first year involved the question of what to do when *Bakke* became the subject of inquiry in class. One upperclassman (who has subsequently distinguished himself in government service and business) argued passionately that the case allowed for only one defensible outcome: he maintained that we ought not allow *Bakke* to be debated, because our presence at the school should not be subject to debate. He recommended that we walk out of class if opposition to affirmative action was voiced. I recall thinking at the time that that advice was silly. How else were we—aspiring lawyers—to master the arguments and counterarguments regarding affirmative action other than by engaging antagonists? But I also remember biting my tongue; as a newcomer, I thought it prudent to be quiet until I got a better sense of my surroundings.

Affirmative action figured, too, in another episode that remains vivid for me decades later. In my second year, in the introductory course on taxation, a black student was the first person called on. There were only two or three other black students in that class, and I made it a point to speak with them afterwards. I wanted to know whether they had felt as anxious as I had when our black classmate was called upon and whether they had felt as relieved as I had when she displayed mastery of the relevant material. They told me that they, too, had felt personally implicated by her performance and that they, too, had cheered silently when she answered commendably, putting "the race" in a good light. The perception of linked fate and that feeling of being always on the spot as a representative of the race, at least in mixed company, are features of African American life that predate affirmative action and arise outside of its presence. They are accentuated, however, in settings in which affirmative action is salient.

In law school, I earned the respect of professors and served on the editorial board of *The Yale Law Journal.* My most instructive and inspiring experience during law school was working at the National Association for the Advancement of Colored People (NAACP) Legal Defense and Educational Fund (LDF). There

I had the good fortune of meeting an array of wonderful attorneys, including Jack Greenberg, who offered me a position at LDF. I would have accepted the offer but for the intervention of James Vorenberg, dean of Harvard Law School. He called me near the end of my final year at Yale to ask whether I had considered a career in legal academia. I told him that I had not but that I was open to thinking about it. Dean Vorenberg invited me to Harvard to talk with him, and I did so on several occasions during the postgraduate years when I served as a law clerk for Judge J. Skelly Wright of the United States Court of Appeals and Justice Thurgood Marshall of the United States Supreme Court. Vorenberg and his colleagues convinced me that a career as a law school professor would be fun and fulfilling.

This recruitment was highly unusual. Rarely does Harvard seek to persuade someone to apply for a faculty position. Dean Vorenberg and his colleagues did so in my case because influential professors at Yale had touted me, because I had written essays that appeared in a number of national publications, and because of the prestige in academic circles of the judges for whom I was clerking. They also took extra steps to recruit me because they wanted to add some color to a faculty that, in the mid-1980s, included only one African American and no Latinos, Native Americans, or Asian Americans. During the two years before my arrival, in 1984, the campus had been beset by highly publicized protests in which a substantial number of students and a small number of faculty members accused the law school administration of discriminating against minority academics of color or failing to reach out sufficiently to recruit them.[2]

Affirmative action played a role not only in eliciting my candidacy; it played a role, too, in the ultimate determination to make me an offer. Was I "qualified"? Sure, I was. Indeed, I was highly qualified. But so, too, were still stronger candidates, probably all of whom were white. Top law schools search not merely for those who are highly qualified; they search for the most outstanding among the best qualified. I doubt that I measured up to that standard. To obtain an offer, I needed and received a boost from affirmative action. A race-sensitive desire to assist a promising black scholar, along with my own hard-earned skills and credentials, helped me gain admission to a faculty that otherwise would probably have been outside my reach.*

Affirmative action has also buoyed my professional career. In 1998, I was inducted into the American Academy of Arts and Sciences and the American Philosophical Society, two of the country's most prestigious honorific academic societies. By that point I had built a record of which I could justly be proud, including articles in leading law reviews and an award-winning book. Still, racial considerations explain in part why I was honored ahead of others, senior to me, who had deeper, more distinguished records than mine. Having snubbed outstanding black scholars in previous eras,† the American Academy and similar organizations are using blacks like me to make amends and to serve other functions.

I do not feel belittled by this. Nor am I wracked by angst or

---

* My experience is by no means unique. For recollections of similar experiences, see William Julius Wilson, "Race and Affirming Opportunity in the Barack Obama Era," *DuBois Review,* Spring 2012; Harry T. Edwards, "The Journey from *Brown v. Board of Education* to *Grutter v. Bollinger*: From Racial Assimilation to Diversity," *Michigan Law Review* 102 (2004): 944, 955–58. See also Stephen L. Carter, *Reflections of an Affirmative Action Baby* (1992).

† I think of these organizations' failure to honor, among others, W. E. B. DuBois (author of *The Souls of Black Folk, Black Reconstruction in America* and *The Philadelphia Negro*); Carter G. Woodson (inaugurated the celebration of Negro History Week, founded the Association for the Study of Negro Life and History, established the *Journal of Negro History,* and wrote scores of articles and books); Benjamin Quarles (author of *The Negro in the American Revolution, Lincoln and the Negro, The Negro in the Civil War,* and *Black Abolitionists*); or Charles Hamilton Houston (distinguished lawyer and educator who reinvigorated the Howard University School of Law and inspired scores of civil rights attorneys including Thurgood Marshall).

guilt or self-doubt. I applaud the effort to rectify wrongs and extend and deepen desegregation in every aspect of American life.

There will be those, I suspect, who will put a mental asterisk next to my name upon learning that my race (almost certainly) counted as a plus in the process of selecting me for induction into these organizations. If they do, then they should also insist upon putting a mental asterisk next to the name of any white person who prevailed in any competition from which racial minorities were excluded.* The distinguished historian Eric Foner highlights this point nicely, noting that when he graduated from Columbia College at Columbia University in 1963, his class was all male and virtually all white. "Most of us," he writes, "were young men of ability, yet had we been forced to compete for admission with women and racial minorities, fewer than half of us would have been at Columbia." Still, he observes, "none of us . . . suffered debilitating self-doubt because we were the beneficiaries of affirmative action—that is, favored treatment on the basis of our race and gender."[3]

Many Americans misconceive achievement, attributing it entirely to individual effort and talent.† In reality, though, achievement stems from many sources: individual effort, to be sure, but also luck (the good fortune to have a healthy body and mind) and social support (family, schools, parks, libraries, labora

---

* They should be willing, for instance, to put an asterisk next to baseball great Babe Ruth, whose home run record was produced in the absence of black pitchers. See Larry Tye, *Satchel: The Life and Times of an American Legend* (2009).
† A vivid illustration of this misconception emerged in the presidential election of 2012, when Mitt Romney and his supporters took umbrage with President Barack Obama's observation that collective investments such as public schooling and road building play a role in every successful business enterprise. See, e.g., "You Didn't Build That," *Wall Street Journal*, July 17, 2012; James Taranto, "You Didn't Sweat, He Did," *Wall Street Journal*, July 18, 2012.

tories). In assessing my own record, I try to maintain equanimity, knowing that on account of race I have sometimes been penalized and sometimes been preferred. I do my best and hope that my work meets high standards. I realize, though, that judgment is social, contingent, and subject to forces beyond my control.

Does my status as a beneficiary of affirmative action oblige me to support it? Absolutely not. Mere benefit from a policy imposes no obligation to favor or defend it. Warren Buffett should not be precluded from condemning an unwise tax provision that favors the wealthy simply because he was assisted by it. If a policy is wrong, one should speak out against it. Reasonable affirmative action, however, is not wrong.

I champion sensibly designed racial affirmative action not because I have benefited from it personally—though I have. I support it because, on balance, it is conducive to the public good. It is a continuation and intensification of an egalitarian and democratic impulse in American race relations that has been gathering momentum, albeit fitfully and with dramatic reversals, since at least the Civil War. Racial affirmative action partially redresses debilitating social wrongs. Racial minorities, and blacks in particular, have long suffered from racist mistreatment at the hands of the federal government, state governments, local governments, and private parties. This oppression has produced a cycle of self-perpetuating problems that will not resolve themselves without interventions that go beyond prospective prohibitions on intentional racial mistreatment. Past wrongs have diminished the educational, financial, and other resources that marginalized groups can call upon, and have thus disadvantaged them in competition with whites. Hence, it is not enough simply to end racist mistreatment. Reasonable efforts to rectify the negative legacy of past wrongs are also morally required.

Compensatory justice is not the only strong basis for racial affirmative action. It can also be defended as an adjunct to antidiscrimination measures, countering hard-to-identify racial biases that continue to impede racial minorities. Antidiscrimination norms are notoriously underenforced, given the difficulty of discerning violations, loopholes in the law, and the expense of litigation. Working as a discrimination-blocking prophylactic, affirmative action indirectly counteracts misconduct that would otherwise be left unhindered.[4]

Affirmative action also usefully integrates marginalized groups. While compensatory affirmative action works on behalf of groups that have suffered historical mistreatment, integrationist affirmative action can work on behalf of any group that is wrongly alienated from the main currents of American life, no matter what the cause of its isolation or estrangement. Resuscitating aims and sentiments that animated key sectors of the civil rights movement, integrative racial affirmative action, in the words of Professor Elizabeth Anderson, "helps people learn to cooperate across racial lines, breaks down racial stigmatization, interracial discomfort, and habits of segregation, makes decision makers more aware of and accountable for the impact of their decisions on all racial groups, and invigorates democratic exchange in civil society."[5]

Affirmative action can also serve a pedagogical function, by facilitating the creation of environments in which, aided by racial diversity, enriched learning and wiser decision making ensue. Close observers of various types of organizations—universities, firms, juries, etc.—maintain that diversity often enhances their overall performance. The diversity rationale is a relative newcomer among justifications for affirmative action. It did not attain prominence until the *Bakke* decision and has been viewed with skepticism ever since, even among strong proponents of affirmative action. I used to disdain the diversity rationale, and I continue to think that some of the claims made on its behalf are excessive.* Still, there is something true and powerful in the message that concerted efforts to include marginalized groups in society's key forums are not only abstractly virtuous but concretely productive, not only good for beneficiaries but good for the institutions to which they contribute.

Like all policies, affirmative action entails costs. It risks instilling excessive race-mindedness, stoking resentments, and diverting attention from those whose needs are even greater than those typically benefited by positive discrimination. Affirmative action also creates, or at least exacerbates, stigmatic harms, calling into question the ability, or even the capacity, of putative beneficiaries. In these pages I will say much about these costs, which are substantial. I maintain, though, that the net benefits generated by affirmative action justify its continued existence.

I also argue that affirmative action, in its typical design and implementation, is in accord with the federal Constitution. There is nothing in the Constitution's text, in the intentions of its framers, or in the logic of its mission that should be seen as precluding racial affirmative action. The Supreme Court has cast a heavy pall over affirmative action because it runs afoul of what it claims is a mandate of constitutional color blindness. The Court is wrong. The Constitution does not compel color blindness and should not be seen as harboring an aspiration for color blindness. The Fourteenth Amendment directs states to offer all persons "the equal protection of the laws"—a malleable formulation that is sufficiently capacious to accommodate affirmative action.

Constitutional color blindness threatens policies that are

* See pages 94–106.

assisting to create a multiracial polity in which previously oppressed peoples participate as productive, equal actors in every sphere of American life. Constitutional color blindness is thus a destructive jurisprudence. The Constitution should be construed as prohibiting only *invidious* racial discrimination, by which I mean conduct undertaken for racial considerations not merely despite hurtful consequences but because of its hurtfulness.[6] Other sorts of racial distinctions, including racial affirmative action, should be regulated by regular majoritarian politics.

While controversy over affirmative action arises in a variety of settings, including employment, housing, electoral districting, and the selection of jurors, the struggle over higher education is the context on which I concentrate. I do so mainly because, as Professor Glenn C. Loury observes, "elite education is the primary site in American life where access to influence and power is rationed."[7] The intense interest in the affirmative action controversy at the top public and private colleges and universities, where seats are scarce and competition savage, stems from their positions as key gateways to opportunity, socialization, and certification. Selective institutions of higher education are far-reaching training grounds for the power elite.* That largely explains why the struggles at these sites have given rise to the most significant judicial rulings, the most influential writings in the affirmative action literature, and the most important of the electoral campaigns against so-called reverse discrimination.

---

* The strategic importance of higher education, including professional schools, is shown by Justice Sandra Day O'Connor's observation, still true today, that "individuals with law degrees occupy roughly half the state governorships, more than half the seats in the United States Senate, and more than a third of the seats in the United States House of Representatives." *Grutter v. Bollinger,* 539 U.S. 306, 332 (2003). Underlining the remarkable influence of the most selective institutions is the fact that, as of 2012, *every* member of the Supreme Court attended law school at either Harvard or Yale.

———

Affirmative action's foreseeable future is likely to mirror its present confusing condition. Consider, for example, that many proponents of color blindness support so-called race-neutral affirmative action programs that use nonracial criteria such as income or class rank with the expectation that doing so will yield larger numbers of successful racial minority candidates. Many such programs are race-conscious right beneath the patina of their apparently raceless packaging. Some color-blind constitutionalists attack such programs, charging that they are illicitly race-sensitive even if, textually, they are silent as to race. That attack, though, will fail to resonate anytime soon. The affirmative action ethos has become deeply rooted. The social forces that created it, combined with changes it has wrought, have made racial homogeneity unacceptable in most key public forums. Even many conservatives who decry affirmative action accord enhanced value, because of race, to like-minded people of color who integrate their ranks, such as Clarence Thomas, Thomas Sowell, Condoleezza Rice, Herman Cain, Susana Martinez, Michelle Malkin, Marco Rubio, Allen West, Tim Scott, Ben Carson, and Shelby Steele. The diffusion of the sentiments that have generated affirmative action will prevent its extinction, though it will probably be increasingly constrained. For now, affirmative action is like an injured bear: too strong to succumb to its wounds but too hurt to attain full vitality.[8]

Before proceeding, a word needs to be said about the problem of defining "affirmative action." It is a slippery term even when one is trying to be clear and straightforward. Often, though, antagonists in the affirmative action wars care little about clarity, in that what they most desire is to score a propaganda victory for their side by whatever means necessary. This is the reality that prompted a California judge to observe aptly that "the term 'affirmative action' . . . is rarely defined . . . so as to form a common base for intelligent discourse."[9] Indeed, the term itself has been a subject of litigation. Organizers of the ballot initiative that ultimately banned affirmative action in public education, contracting, and employment in California decided to omit any mention of "affirmative action" from the text of their proposal, Proposition 209. They did so upon learning that while many voters reacted negatively to the term "preferences," these same voters reacted positively to "affirmative action." The authors of Proposition 209 responded accordingly: they designed their ballot initiative so that it expressly banned "preferences" while saying nothing about "affirmative action." Opponents of Proposition 209 sought a clarification that would inform the public that outlawing preferences would entail the outlawing of affirmative action. They sought a court order to force the state attorney general to note on the ballot that ratification of the initiative would prohibit both "affirmative action" and "preferences." They prevailed before a trial court but lost on appeal.[10] As a result, many voters who actually supported keeping at least some form of "affirmative action" nonetheless helped to erase it altogether.[11]

Supporters of affirmative action are not the only ones who have complained about deceptiveness; opponents have complained as well, charging that backers of affirmative action systematically hide the nature of the pro-minority racial favoritism that operates within affirmative action programs. Professor Lino Graglia remarks scoffingly that " 'affirmative action' is simply a euphemism for racial discrimination," while Professor Brian Fitzpatrick derides "diversity" admissions protocols as a "lie."[12] Others charge that affirmative action is a constantly changing shell game governed by nothing more elevated than perceptions of what will be good for beneficiary groups.

When first used in a racial context, "affirmative action" referred to efforts to enforce prohibitions against invidious discrimination. Hence, in the first state proscription of racial discrimination in employment, New York's law of 1945,[13] the legislation authorized a commission to order that a culpable defendant "cease and desist" from its unlawful practice and "take such affirmative action," including hiring, reinstating, or upgrading employees as warranted. Later, President John F. Kennedy directed that all federal contracts include a provision requiring contractors to "take affirmative action to ensure that applicants are employed . . . without regard to their race, creed, color, or national origin."[14] Kennedy meant to endorse vigorous enforcement of antidiscrimination norms—nothing more. It is this version of affirmative action—we might call it the old affirmative action—that was, according to some commentators, underhandedly supplanted by a new affirmative action that entailed granting group-focused preferences to racial minorities.[15] Charges of betrayal and dishonesty are often excessive.* Many who broadened the scope of the old affirmative action, adding to it an enhanced boost for racial minorities, openly did what has been done repeatedly throughout history: they adapted

---

* Professor Carl Cohen claims, for example, that "the phrase 'affirmative action' was kidnapped. That honorable expression, originally denoting efforts to *eradicate* all preference by race, had its meaning *inverted*. In the good name of what had been designed to *uproot* preference, preference was now formally incorporated and made often obligatory." See Carl Cohen and James P. Sterba, *Affirmative Action and Racial Preference: A Debate* (2003), 20.

an existing term and idea to changing circumstances to reach ends illuminated by new knowledge.

The charge of disingenuousness, however, is not wholly baseless. Wrongly denying that there is any element of "preference" or "discrimination" in the new affirmative action, some of its proponents have hurt their own cause. Surely one of the most influential defenders of affirmative action over the past decade has been Barack Obama. Acutely sensitive to charges that he supports racial favoritism that discriminates against whites, Obama defines affirmative action in a fashion meant to drain it of controversy. "Affirmative action programs," he writes, "when properly structured, can open up opportunities otherwise closed to qualified minorities without diminishing opportunities for white students."[16] But how can that be? If a campus or work site is at all constrained by scarcity, as all selective ones are, special efforts made on behalf of racial minorities will necessarily diminish opportunities for whites, even if only minimally. Obama is simply obscuring the inescapable dilemmas that affirmative action poses. Racial affirmative action *does* distinguish between people on a racial basis. It *does* discriminate.* It *does* redistribute resources. It *does* favor preferred racial categories of candidates, promoting some racial minorities over whites with

---

* A law in South Africa requires universities there to take "appropriate measures for the redress of past inequalities" but declares that they "may not unfairly discriminate in any way." That the law prohibits "unfair" discrimination suggests an implied recognition and permission for "fair" discrimination. Because "discrimination" in America has come to be associated only with evil practices, friends of affirmative action often attempt to dissociate it from any form of "discrimination." I understand this strategy but decline to follow it. I use a number of synonyms in referring to affirmative action, including "positive discrimination" and "fair discrimination." See Judith February, "From Redress to Empowerment: The New South African Constitution and Its Implementation," in David L. Featherman, Martin Hall, and Marvin Krislow, eds., *The Next Twenty-five Years: Affirmative Action in Higher Education in the United States and South Africa* (2010), 77.

superior records. It *does* generate stigma and resentment.[17] These issues cannot usefully be hidden for long behind verbal tricks. To properly and decisively convince the public of the value of affirmative action, proponents will have to grapple candidly with its dilemmas.[18]

Struggles for terminological advantage, the passage of time, the inevitable fuzziness that accompanies popular usage, and desires to avoid making choices that might cost support are not the only obstacles to clarity in defining affirmative action. Problematic, too, is that "affirmative action" refers to a spectrum of interventions from "soft" to "hard." One soft form is outreach affirmative action—targeted recruitment to elicit applications from those who might otherwise refrain from applying for an opening because of unfamiliarity or because of knowledge that applicants from certain groups were unwelcome in the past.* Another soft form of affirmative action is defining "discrimination" in a way that requires a decision maker to use a selection process that will minimize the extent to which it adversely affects already disadvantaged groups. Under this "disparate impact"

---

* Many opponents of "racial preferences" were once willing to overlook outreach affirmative action. As the struggle has worn on, however, ideological clarity has generated a more exacting view. Courts have ruled, for instance, that California's Proposition 209 bars racially selective outreach. See, e.g., *HiVoltage Wire Works, Inc. v. City of San Jose,* 24 Cal.4th 537 (2000). See also Eugene Volokh, "The California Civil Rights Initiative: An Interpretive Guide," *UCLA Law Review* 44 (1997): 1335, 1340–53. For traces of the earlier, more relaxed view, see Thomas Sowell, *Affirmative Action Reconsidered* 3 (1975); Richard Posner, "The *Bakke* Case and the Future of Affirmative Action," *California Law Review* 67 (1979): 171, 188. ("The practice of simply searching harder for black applicants . . . is racial discrimination . . . [But] it seems unlikely that . . . 'unequal search' will be held unconstitutional. Its adverse effects on whites are probably too slight and attenuated to constitute a denial of equal protection.") But see Roland Fryer, Jr., and Glenn C. Loury, "Affirmative Action and Its Mythology," *Journal of Economic Perspectives* 19 (2005): 147, 150. ("Targeted outreach will generally lead to an equilibrium in which the targeted applicants . . . enjoy wider job options, more bargaining power, and consequently greater remuneration than comparable nontargeted applicants.")

theory of discrimination, a selection scheme that disproportionately excludes racial minorities may be deemed illegal even in the absence of racial intent.[19]

Hard forms of affirmative action include setting aside opportunities exclusively for those affiliated with designated groups or selecting persons affiliated with a designated group over competitors with superior credentials, or negating seniority to protect junior hires who hail from certain groups. The form of the affirmative action policy in question affects the intensity of the conflict surrounding it; typically, the harder the policy, the more resistance it provokes.

In the end, two points are clear. The first is that, however defined, "affirmative action" is a contested term that is unlikely to be described in a fashion that will garner a consensus. The second is that I must nonetheless posit a definition. From now on, unless otherwise noted, when I refer to "affirmative action," I mean policies that offer individuals deemed to be affiliated with a beneficiary group a preference over others in competitions for employment, education, or other valued resources.*

---

* Below are other ways in which commentators have defined "affirmative action."

    Affirmative action "refers to a wide array of measures . . . which grant preferential treatment in the allocation of scarce resources . . . to the members of underrepresented, ascriptive groups formerly targeted for racial discrimination." Daniel Sabbagh, *Equality and Transparency: A Strategic Perspective on Affirmative Action in American Law* (2007), 2.

    "By 'affirmative action,' I refer to any policy that aims to increase the participation of a disadvantaged social group in mainstream institutions, either through 'outreach' (targeting the group for publicity and invitations to participate) or 'preference' (using group membership as criteria for selecting participants)." Elizabeth Anderson, *The Imperative of Integration* (2010), 135.

    "Racial affirmative action is the race-conscious allocation of resources . . . that is motivated by an intent to benefit racial minorities." Girardeau A. Spann, *The Law of Affirmative Action* (2000), 3.

"[Affirmative action] seeks to remedy the significant underrepresentation of members of certain racial, ethnic or other groups through measures that take group membership or identity into account." Paul Brest and Miranda Oshige, "Affirmative Action for Whom?" *Stanford Law Review* 47 (1994): 855–56.

Affirmative action is "a program in which people who control access to important social resources offer preferential access to those resources for particular groups that they think deserve special treatment." Peter Schuck, *Diversity in America: Keeping Government at a Safe Distance* (2003), 136.

" 'Affirmative action' is a phrase that refers to attempts to bring members of underrepresented groups, usually groups that have suffered discrimination, into a higher degree of participation in some beneficial program." Kent Greenawalt, *Discrimination and Reverse Discrimination* (1983), 17.

"Affirmative action [programs are those in which] members of minority groups receive a preference in the award of jobs, admissions to selective colleges and universities, or government contracts." Richard H. Fallon, Jr., *The Dynamic Constitution: An Introduction to American Constitutional Law* (2004), 124.

Affirmative Action in the History of American Race Relations

Federal Civil Rights as "Discrimination" Against Whites: Reconstruction

Every major step toward undoing racial oppression in America has been met with the charge that it constitutes reverse discrimination against whites and unfair preference for people of color. Consider America's first federal civil rights law. The Civil Rights Act of 1866 declared all persons born in the United States citizens. It also clothed all persons with the same rights as whites for purposes of suing or being sued, contracting, owning property, or serving as witnesses. Prior to this legislation, the Supreme Court, pursuant to the notorious *Dred Scott* decision, had ruled that blacks, whether free or enslaved, were not citizens of the United States. The federal government and many states, moreover, had openly barred blacks and other racial minorities from exercising even the most elementary civil rights.[1]

President Abraham Lincoln's successor, President Andrew Johnson, vetoed the Civil Rights Act, charging that it represented "special legislation."[2] He disliked the citizenship provision, because it would immediately make citizens of native-born blacks while European-born immigrants had to wait several years in order to qualify for citizenship via naturalization. According to Johnson, this "propose[d] a discrimination against large numbers of intelligent, worthy and patriotic foreigners and in favor of the negro." Johnson similarly disliked the provision that authorized federal judicial enforcement of rights that, for some purposes (contracting, owning property, suing, and testifying), placed blacks on the same plane as whites.* This part of the bill, Johnson complained, affords "discriminatory protection to colored persons." According to Johnson, these arrangements "establish[ed] for the security of the colored race safeguards which go infinitely beyond any that the General Government has ever provided for the white race. In fact, the distinction of race and color is by the bill made to operate in favor of the colored and against the white race."

The Civil Rights Act and Johnson's veto (which was eventually overridden) highlight two important points. One has to do with overlooked complexities regarding what counts as "race-sensitive" as opposed to "race-blind" policy. Johnson characterized the Act of 1866 as illicitly race-sensitive insofar as it contained, in his view, a "distinction of race . . . made to operate in favor of the colored and against the white race." Was this charge racial demagoguery? Partly. The act did simply stipulate that, with respect to the activities named, parties shall merely have the same rights "as [are] enjoyed by white citizens." On the other hand, Johnson was correct in observing that this exertion of federal power was unprecedented and that the dominant purpose behind it was to elevate the legal status of African Americans. Many observers today consider the Act of 1866 to be "race blind." But textually, the act is explicitly attentive to race, and

---

* Note the limited nature of the Civil Rights Act. It says nothing about voting or jury service. Blacks and other targets of racial discrimination would have to await subsequent legal protection, most notably the Fourteenth and Fifteenth Amendments to the Constitution (in 1868 and 1870, respectively), for relief from state-enforced racial exclusions in these areas.

its framers were moved primarily by a desire to help a particular sector of the populace: colored Americans. The Act of 1866 can thus be seen as a race-sensitive precursor of "affirmative action."[3]

A second point accentuated by the Act of 1866 and Johnson's veto of it is the alacrity with which many have deployed the rhetoric of "reverse discrimination" in attacking reforms that diminish white privilege.* Those who sought to abolish slavery, a Florida slaveholder fumed, were determined to "give the 'nigger' more privileges than the white man."†[4] With the abolition of slavery only a year old, President Johnson was already claiming that blacks (and their allies) were seeking racial favoritism. In 1874, disapproving of federal legislation prohibiting racial discrimination in the provision of public accommodations, the *Chicago Tribune* asked (in an editorial entitled "The Nigger School?"), "[i]s it not time for the colored race to stop playing baby?"[5] In 1883, in the course of invalidating parts of that same legislation, the Supreme Court accused blacks of seeking preferential treatment by demanding the end of caste-like exclusions. Impatiently lecturing the black plaintiffs in *The Civil Rights Cases,* the Court declared that "when a man has emerged from slavery . . . there must be some stage in the progress of his elevation when he takes the rank of a mere citizen and ceases to be the special favorite of the laws."[6]

---

* This is *not* an attempt to preemptively label as racist all opposition to racial affirmative action. Opponents include people who have been demonstrably anti-racist in attitude and action. (See, e.g., Charles Fried, Nat Hentoff, Richard Kahlenberg, Michael Lind, John McWhorter.) I do mean to show, however, that racism has long been among the variety of motivations behind antagonism to policies deemed to constitute "racial favoritism" or "reverse discrimination" on behalf of colored folk. This is a fact that all participants in the debate should face.

† Similarly, Senator John C. Calhoun warned that if abolitionists succeeded in emancipating the slaves, "the next step would be to raise the negroes to a social and political equality with whites; and that being effected, we would soon find the present condition of the two races reversed. [Blacks] and their northern allies would be masters, and [white southerners] the slaves." Speech on the Reception of Abolition Petitions, February 6, 1837.

Despite opposition, reformers in the Reconstruction Era followed new statutory law with constitutional provisions that elevated the status of colored people. Most pertinent to our concerns, the Fourteenth Amendment directed the states to provide to all persons "the equal protection of the law." A proposed version of the amendment directed public authorities to disregard altogether the race of individuals. Authored by the great slavery abolitionist Wendell Phillips, this version declared, "No State shall make any distinction in civil rights and privileges . . . on account of race, color or descent."[7] But the framers of the Fourteenth Amendment eschewed that rule in favor of the open-textured standard that won ratification.

Andrew Johnson opposed the Fourteenth Amendment, claiming that it, like the Civil Rights Act, was part of a series of steps being taken on behalf of the Negro that had never been taken on behalf of any other group. Johnson's description was partially correct. After all, as Professor Arval Morris notes, the Fourteenth Amendment can rightly be considered "a type of affirmative action by the nation."[8] Moreover, additional legislation enacted by framers of the Fourteenth Amendment expressly singled out blacks for benefits. In July 1866, the same Congress that sent the Fourteenth Amendment to the states for ratification enacted legislation appropriating funds for "the relief of destitute colored women and children," confirmed land sales limited to "heads of families of the African race," and donated property in Washington, D.C., for schools "for colored children." The next year, the Congress appropriated money for the relief of destitute "colored" persons in Washington, D.C. On other occasions during this period, Congress made special awards to the "colored" soldiers and sailors of the Union army and navy.[9]

This history poses a problem for constitutional "originalists" who also champion the idea of the color-blind Constitution. Overwhelming evidence indicates that the framers of the Fourteenth Amendment did *not* intend to create a color-blind Constitution. I am not saying that an answer to the historical inquiry should determine the matter. Nor am I saying that the results of historical analysis are altogether clear; the laws noted above applied to the federal government, while the pertinent provision of the Fourteenth Amendment applies expressly only to the states.[10] I am not an originalist. I do not believe that the views, including the woeful prejudices, of eighteenth- and nineteenth-century statesmen should shackle us today. Just as there is evidence that the framers and ratifiers of the Fourteenth Amendment saw it as no bar to legislation that offered benefits on the basis of racial identities, so, too, is there evidence that many of the framers and ratifiers of the Fourteenth Amendment saw it as no bar to segregation, particularly antimiscegenation statutes.*[11] My point is simply that the issue of positive and negative racial selectivity did arise during the time of the framing of the Fourteenth Amendment and that the response of many of its framers is at variance with the color-blindness mantra of certain so-called originalists.

---

* "So bizarre would discrimination against whites in admission to institutions of higher learning have seemed to the framers of the Fourteenth Amendment that we can be confident that they did not consciously seek to erect a constitutional barrier against such discrimination." Richard Posner, "The *DeFunis* Case and the Constitutionality of Preferential Treatment of Racial Minorities," *Supreme Court Review* (1974): 1, 21–22. "The notion . . . that '[t]he clear and central purpose of the Fourteenth Amendment was to eliminate all official state sources of invidious racial discrimination in the States' is simply an anachronism—an attribution to the framers of the amendment of views that did not achieve currency until much later." Terrence Sandalow, "Racial Preferences in Higher Education: Political Responsibility and the Judicial Role," *University of Chicago Law Review* 42 (1974): 653, 664.

ANTIDISCRIMINATION LAW AS RACIAL FAVORITISM: THE 1940S

A second important phase in the historical groundwork of affirmative action arose in the 1940s with the emergence of debates over whether and how government, at either the state or federal level, should prohibit racial discrimination in employment. In 1941, President Franklin D. Roosevelt promulgated Executive Order 8802, which prohibited racial discrimination in the employment of workers in defense industries, and he established the Fair Employment Practices Commission (FEPC) to implement the order. In 1945, with the Ives-Quinn Act, New York passed the first state law banning racial discrimination in employment. These reforms and kindred proposals were repeatedly opposed on the grounds that they would lead to "quota hiring" of Negroes. Assailing the FEPC, segregationist representative Jamie L. Whitten, a Mississippi Democrat, complained in 1944 that the aim of the committee was not to "prevent unfair discrimination against Negroes" but "to discriminate in favor of the Negro."[12]

This line of attack was by no means limited to Southern white supremacists. White racial conservatives up north put it to use as well. Inveighing against the Ives-Quinn legislation, New York City administrator Robert Moses spoke as if the proposed law portended more danger than the existing reality of racial exclusion:

> The most vicious feature of this proposal is that it will inevitably lead to the establishment of what in European universities and institutions . . . was known as the "numerous clauses," that is, the quota system under which Jews and other minorities were permit-

ted only up to a fixed number proportionate to their percentage of the total population. . . . It means the end of honest competition, and the death knell of selection and advancement on the basis of talent.[13]

Amplifying Moses's charge, the conservative columnist Westbrook Pegler complained that the Ives-Quinn bill "would emphasize origin, creed, color and race and result in the Hitlerian rule of quotas."[14] It is no wonder that in congressional testimony in 1945 on behalf of the NAACP, William Hastie* referred to "quotas" as "Specter No. 1" in the parade of horribles evoked by opponents of antidiscrimination legislation.[15]

Hastie and many other supporters of antidiscrimination measures carefully eschewed demands and rhetoric that might give ammunition to adversaries.[16]

Others insisted, however, that the only way of ensuring relief from discrimination was to demand tangible results—to require employers to hire Negroes in numbers proportionate to the black clientele of the business, or proportionate to the black population of the neighborhood in which the business was located, or proportionate to the population of available qualified Negro workers.[17] Those in this camp also contended, after World War II, that when demobilization hit industries that had begun only belatedly to hire blacks, there should be racial exceptions to seniority rules to avoid a situation in which most or all of the new black hires, as junior employees, would face dismissal.[18]

The most significant of the court cases prompted by "racial

* William Hastie was an attorney, law professor, civil rights advocate, and dean of the Howard University School of Law. In 1937, President Franklin Roosevelt put Hastie on the United States District Court of the Virgin Islands—a black first. In 1949, President Harry Truman put him on the United States Court of Appeals for the Third Circuit—another black first. See Gilbert Ware, *William Hastie: Grace Under Pressure* (1985).

proportionalism"[19] was *Hughes v. Superior Court.*[20] In 1947, a group of black and white protesters in a predominantly African American neighborhood in Richmond, California, picketed a Lucky grocery store. They carried signs reading "Lucky Won't Hire Negro Clerks in Proportion to Negro Trade—Don't Patronize" and insisted that managers hire Negro clerks until their proportion of the workforce approximated the proportion of black patronage—about 50 percent. Lucky obtained an injunction against the picketing from a state court, but the picketing continued. The picketers were then held in contempt of court. The picketers maintained that their conduct was "speech" protected by the First Amendment. The resolution of the dispute turned on whether the purpose of the picketing was lawful. The California Supreme Court held that the purpose of the picketing was illegitimate, because the policy the protesters sought to institute would violate the state's common law. According to the court, "If Lucky had yielded to the demands of [the picketers], its resultant hiring policy would have constituted, as to a proportion of its employees, the equivalent of both a closed shop and a closed union in favor of the Negro race." If the picketers had been upheld in their demand, the court wrote with alarm, "then other races, white, yellow, brown and red, would have equal rights to demand discriminatory hiring on a racial basis."[21]

The United States Supreme Court affirmed the judgment of the California courts in an opinion by Justice Felix Frankfurter, which observed,

> To deny California the right to ban picketing [here] . . . would mean that there could be no prohibition on the pressure of picketing to secure proportional employment on ancestral grounds of Hungarians in Cleveland, of Germans in Milwaukee, of Portuguese in New Bedford, of Mexicans in San Antonio, of the numer-

ous minority groups in New York, and so on through the whole gamut of racial and religious concentrations in various cities.[22]

Professor Mark Tushnet observes that the arguments in *Hughes* "track virtually all of the arguments that have more recently been made in affirmative action cases."[23] Just as affirmative action has divided the ranks of anti-racists over the past forty years, so, too, did the picketing at issue in *Hughes* divide the NAACP. A local branch of the NAACP was one of the sponsors of the picketing. But members of the national organization internally expressed disquiet. One was "very disturbed," because the picketing "appear[ed] to condone a quota system" that would backfire on blacks seeking employment opportunities outside of communities with large numbers of Negroes. Another saw the demand for proportional hiring as "unsound." The NAACP, this member contended,

> should base its demands on "the democratic principle that [everyone is] entitled to equal opportunity based upon merit and ability to compete in the labor market without being pre-judged on account of race or color. . . . But proportional picketing is at variance with this great sustaining principle and in place of the criterion of equality and merit substitutes artificial criteria measured by the amount of business the particular employer may derive in the particular community."[24]

The Supreme Court decided *Hughes* at a time when, as a matter of federal constitutional law, racial segregation was deemed to be consistent with the Equal Protection Clause so long as racially separate facilities were equal. This was also a period during which there existed no federal statutes prohibiting private employers from engaging in racial discrimination and in which state or local antidiscrimination laws were notoriously underenforced. In other words, *Hughes* was decided when open, racist discrimination in employment (and many other activities) was pervasive and largely beyond legal redress. Yet even then, the prospect of "quotas" proved more unsettling to a wide range of observers than the plight of those who sought to use picketing and proportionalism to gain what Justice Roger B. Traynor called, sympathetically, "a foothold in the struggle for economic equality."[25]

CIVIL RIGHTS AS "SPECIAL BENEFITS" FOR BLACKS: THE 1950s AND 1960s

A third development prior to the emergence of widespread institutionalized affirmative action was the Civil Rights Revolution—the eruption of protest and reform between the mid-1950s and mid-1960s that prompted invalidation of government-sponsored racial segregation (*Brown v. Board of Education*), prohibitions against racial discrimination in private business enterprises (Civil Rights Act of 1964), action against racial disenfranchisement (Voting Rights Act of 1965), the removal of racial criteria from immigration and naturalization requirements, and a decisive turn in public opinion against the proposition that, in principle, whites ought to be privileged over nonwhites. Open, obdurate, unapologetic, nationwide discrimination against racial minorities was such a massive obstacle that removing it took up virtually all of the energy and attention of anti-racist activists. Many could think of nothing beyond prohibiting explicit racial exclusion. Some thought that the cessation of invidious racial discrimination would constitute the end of the race problem and that a legal system in which race was banished as an acceptable signal or marker for any purpose would allow the flowering of a racially egalitarian promised land.

As the walls of Jim Crow segregation and open exclusion collapsed, however, increasing numbers of observers began to perceive that the mere cessation of invidious discrimination, though critical, would leave unaddressed destructive vestiges of past oppression, such as education deficits caused by many decades of inferior schooling. It dawned on these onlookers that the consequences of past wrongdoing would, without intervention, continue to hobble blacks. Dissidents began to argue in favor of programs that would discriminate racially in favor of blacks to compensate (at least partially) for the losses caused by anti-black discrimination. In 1962, for example, a chapter of the Congress of Racial Equality (CORE) negotiated an agreement in which a firm promised to give Negroes and Puerto Ricans "exclusive exposure" for at least a week when it hired its next fifty employees. Theretofore, a CORE official explained, "we used to talk simply of merit employment, i.e., hiring the best qualified person . . . regardless of race." But now, he continued, "CORE is talking in terms of 'compensatory' hiring. We are approaching employers with the proposition that they have effectively excluded Negroes from their work force for a long time and that they now have a responsibility and obligation to make up for past sins."[26]

The upward mobility of such views was strikingly reflected by their arrival in the speeches and writings of Whitney M. Young, Jr., head of the moderate, buttoned-down, business-oriented National Urban League. Young began calling for "a decade of discrimination in favor of Negro youth." Racial impartiality, he insisted, was "unrealistic at this moment in history." Instead, this moment required placing a "higher value" on "human potential when it comes encased in a black skin." Employers who had "never considered a Negro for top jobs in their institutions must now recruit qualified Negro employees and give preference to their employment."[27] Elaborating, Young remarked,

> For more than 300 years the white American has received special consideration, or "preferential treatment," if you will, over the Negro. What we now ask is that for a brief period there be a deliberate and massive effort to include the Negro citizen in the mainstream of American life.*[28]

Martin Luther King, Jr., also propounded ideas we associate with affirmative action. "Our society has been doing something special *against* the Negro for hundreds of years," King observed in 1963. "How then can he be absorbed into the mainstream of American life if we do not do something special *for* him now, in order to balance the equation and equip him to compete on a just and equal basis?"†[29] King went on to declare,

> Few people consider the fact that, in addition to being enslaved for two centuries, the Negro was, during all those years, robbed of the

* Addressing the issue again, Young declared in words pertinent today, "The basic issue here is one of simply logic and fairness. The scales of justice have been heavily weighted against the Negro for over three hundred years and will not suddenly in 1964 balance themselves by applying equal weights. In this sense, the Negro is educationally and economically malnourished and anemic. It is not 'preferential treatment' but simple decency to provide him for a brief period with special vitamins, additional food, and blood transfusions." *To Be Equal* (1964), 25.

† It is particularly important to quote King on this point since he is constantly cited by opponents of racial affirmative action as if he would have unequivocally backed their position in the debate. During the campaign to pass Proposition 209, the state constitutional initiative that largely prohibits affirmative action in California, supporters broadcast advertisements suggesting that the civil rights icon would have embraced the measure. Those ads were quickly rescinded in the face of furious opposition from Coretta Scott King and other activists. See Edward W. Lempinen and Robert B. Gunnison, "King Ad for Prop 209 on Hold / State GOP Halts TV Campaign after Protest Erupts," *San Francisco Chronicle*, October 24, 1996.

wages of his toil. No amount of gold could provide an adequate compensation for the exploitation and humiliation of the Negro in America down through the centuries. Not all the wealth of this affluent society could meet the bill. Yet a price can be placed on unpaid wages. The ancient common law has always provided a remedy for the appropriation of the labor of one human being by another. This law should be in the form of a massive program by the government in special, compensatory measures which could be regarded as a settlement in accordance with the accepted practice of common law.*[30]

The idea that merely ending invidious discrimination would be inadequate for the purpose of attaining a satisfactory sort of racial equality was held not only by dissident outsiders; it was voiced as well by the ultimate American insider. In June 1964, at a commencement address at Howard University, President Lyndon B. Johnson declared:

> Freedom is not enough. . . . You do not take a person, who, for years, has been hobbled by chains and liberate him, bring him up to the starting line of a race and then say "you are free to compete with all the others," and still justly believe that you have been completely fair. Thus it is not enough just to open the gates of opportunity.[31]

Talk of special benefits for blacks, however, provoked strong negative reactions across much of the political spectrum. Reactionary defenders of segregation abhorred the notion of positive discrimination benefiting blacks. Opposed to granting Negroes

---

* "Whenever the issue of compensatory or preferential treatment for the Negro is raised, some of our friends recoil in horror. The Negro should be granted equality, they agree; but he should ask for nothing more. On the surface this appears reasonable, but it is not realistic. For it is obvious that if a man is entering the starting line in a race three hundred years after another man, the first would have to perform some impossible feat in order to catch up with his fellow runner." Martin Luther King, Jr., *Why We Can't Wait* (1964), 134.

even mere formal equality, they bitterly objected to preferring blacks in any fashion. Important, too, was opposition from non-Southern working-class whites and their representatives. These people did not embrace de jure segregation. But they did insist upon excluding blacks from "their" neighborhoods, schools, social networks, and work sites. Drawn to the economic liberalism, especially the pro-unionism, of the New Deal, they fiercely resisted efforts to reform the racist hierarchies outside the South that governed urban and suburban communities. When civil rights activists confronted these working-class whites in Philadelphia, Chicago, Detroit, Newark, and other locales, seeking to open opportunities long closed to racial minorities, they encountered sentiments, rhetoric, and strategies that surface repeatedly today in the ranks of affirmative action's enemies. Among these familiar refrains are assertions of white racial innocence, objections to "reverse discrimination," and protests against the supposed intrusiveness of "big government."[32]

Some on the anti-racist Left also objected to especially favoring blacks. Bayard Rustin,* for example, saw that strategy as arising from a misdiagnosis that wrongly elevated racial conflict over the centrality of class conflict and a misprescription that would further weaken the prospects for progressive working-class unity by exacerbating racial resentments.†

Perhaps the most politically potent opposition in the 1960s

---

* Bayard Rustin, a lifelong socialist and pacifist, was also a civil rights activist who organized the landmark March on Washington for Jobs and Freedom, in August 1963. See John D'Emilio, *Lost Prophet: The Life and Times of Bayard Rustin* (2004).

† Rustin, for instance, maintained that "any preferential approach postulated on racial, ethnic, religious or sexual lines will only disrupt a multicultural society and lead to a backlash." According to him, "special treatment" can suitably be provided only to those who have been exploited or denied opportunities if solutions are predicated on class lines, precisely because all religious, ethnic, and racial groups have a depressed class who would benefit." Quoted in Richard Kahlenberg, *The Remedy: Class, Race, and Affirmative Action* 15 (1997).

to what we now refer to as affirmative action arose from highly placed liberals who saw calls for discrimination in favor of racial minorities as inconsistent with the individualistic, meritocratic, race-blind sentiments they championed against white supremacists. Asked his impression of demands of the sort voiced by the CORE official cited above, President John F. Kennedy remarked:

> I don't think we can undo the past. . . . We have to do the best we can do now. . . . I don't think quotas are a good idea. I think it is a mistake to begin to assign quotas on the basis of religion, or race, or color, or nationality. I think we'd get into a good deal of trouble.*[33]

Many white liberals in the early 1960s agreed. Answering the question "Should there be 'compensation' for Negroes?" a writer in the *New York Times Magazine* responded in the negative, stating that doing so would "penalize the living in a futile attempt to collect a debt owed by the dead." He also feared that attempting to compensate blacks would deepen racial division, redound unfairly to the detriment of other mistreated racial minorities, and work a new injustice on innocent whites.[34] "Demand for a discrimination in reverse . . . to the advantage of the Negroes, is misdirected," asserted the liberal icon Gunnar Myrdal. It would, he warned, "create hatred for Negroes."[35] Reviewing the debate as it existed in the early to mid-1960s, Professor Hugh Davis Graham notes that proposals for compensatory discrimination

---

* President Kennedy's remark that it would be a mistake "to begin" to assign quotas is noteworthy. It reflects a common misimpression that racial politics "begin" only when those who have been marginalized make demands for equitable treatment. When Kennedy spoke, quotas had long existed that permitted white men to monopolize almost entirely the upper ranks of government, business, academia, the Fourth Estate, and other key domains. When Kennedy spoke, the white male quota for cabinet officials and Supreme Court justices was complete and unbroken. Yet it was only when facing protests against this form of monopolization that Kennedy was moved to deplore quotas in general.

in favor of blacks "elicited a virtually unanimous public condemnation. . . . The traditional liberalism shared by most of the civil rights establishment was philosophically offended by the notion of racial preference."[36]

The opposition to, and absence of support for, positive discrimination in Congress was evidenced in the debate over Title VII of the 1964 Civil Rights Act, the provision that prohibits racial discrimination across large areas of employment. Opponents repeatedly charged that Title VII would compel employers to avoid racial imbalance by hiring or promoting blacks regardless of their qualifications for employment. In response, proponents insisted that Title VII's mission was antidiscrimination, *not* rectification, that it aimed to prohibit racial selectivity going forward, *not* compensation for past wrongs, that it sought the removal of racial considerations from personnel decision making, *not* the institutionalization of racial balance. As Senator Hubert Humphrey declared,

> Contrary to the allegations of some opponents of this title, there is nothing in it that will give any power [to any agency or court] to require hiring, firing, or promotion of employees in order to meet a racial "quota" or to achieve a certain racial balance.
>
> That bugaboo has been brought up a dozen times; but it is nonexistent. In fact, the very opposite is true. Title VII prohibits discrimination. In effect, it says that race, religion and national origin are not to be used as the basis for hiring and firing. Title VII is designed to encourage hiring on the basis of ability and qualifications, not race or religion.[37]

On another occasion, Humphrey averred,

> [Title VII] does not provide that any preferential treatment in employment shall be given to Negroes or to any other persons or

groups. . . . In fact [the legislation] would prohibit preferential treatment for any particular group.[38]

Senatorial allies echoed Humphrey. Under Title VII, Senator Thomas Henry Kuchel insisted, "employers and labor organizations could not discriminate in favor or against a person because of his race, his religion, or his national origin. In such matters . . . the bill now before us . . . is color blind." Similarly, according to Senators Joseph S. Clark and Clifford P. Case, the reach of Title VII

is prospective not retrospective. Thus, for example, if a business has been discriminating in the past and as a result has an all-white working force, when [Title VII] comes into effect the employer's obligation would be simply to fill future vacancies on a non-discriminatory basis. He would not be obligated—or indeed permitted—to fire whites in order to hire Negroes, or prefer Negroes for future vacancies, or, once Negroes are hired, to give them special seniority rights at the expense of the white workers hired earlier.[39]

In reading the legislative history of the 1964 Civil Rights Act, one must, of course, be attentive to the circumstances in which members of Congress were speaking. The principal purpose of those supporters of Title VII cited above was not to offer a considered view on the merits of affirmative action; it was to negate the efforts of white supremacists who opposed *any* intervention that might emancipate blacks from the strictures of Jim Crow subordination. Just as opponents of the first Reconstruction used the specter of "miscegenation" to embarrass the proponents of federal civil rights legislation in the 1860s, so, too, did opponents of the second Reconstruction use the specter of "preferential treatment" to embarrass the proponents of civil rights legislation in the 1960s. To some extent, therefore, the words of Senator Humphrey and his allies forswearing affirmative action should be understood as mere strategic feints. To some extent, though, their disavowal of preferential treatment was an authentic representation of early-1960s white racial liberalism of a certain sort—a perspective commendably opposed to invidious discrimination, but a perspective that, regrettably, underestimated the barriers that would continue to ensnare racial minorities even after the passage of Title VII and other antidiscrimination legislation.[40]

LYNDON JOHNSON, RICHARD NIXON, BLACK MILITANCY, AND THE NEW AFFIRMATIVE ACTION OF THE 1970S

It was not until the late 1960s and early 1970s that there arose another affirmative action regime, the one that remains controversial today: widespread public- and private-sector programs that channel benefits on an expressly racial basis to groups that are deemed in need of special assistance. The new affirmative action emerged fitfully, on an ad hoc basis, often in settings cloaked by low visibility at the behest of influential but obscure bureaucrats. There was no grand, national, centralized, openly deliberated decision. There was, instead, an accretion of local decisions reflecting a wide range of motivations, aims, strategies, and justifications. These decisions generated special recruitment efforts, racially exclusive scholarships, set-asides for minority-owned businesses, advantageous "breaks" to racial-minority candidates for coveted educational and employment opportunities, and efforts to lure, retain, and promote minority workers to industries or occupations from which they had previously been barred or where, for some other reason, they were scarce or absent.*

A confluence of events, personalities, and sentiments led to the affirmative action breakthrough. By the mid-1960s even moderate civil rights leaders were demanding "Freedom Now," "Equality Now," and "Desegregation Now."† Radicals pushed the point further. In May 1969, James Forman, a former leader of the Student Non-Violent Coordinating Committee (SNCC) and the Black Panther Party, interrupted services at the Riverside Church, in New York City, to unveil his Black Manifesto, in which he demanded $500,000 in reparations for the mistreatment of black Americans. Forman did not obtain much concretely in the short run. He and like-minded actors, however, gave new vitality and prominence to the call for reparations, a demand much derided, but one that has subsequently remained an important concept in American political culture.

* As early as 1964, an investigation by the Association of American Law Schools (AALS) was reporting, "Several institutions have either made efforts to recruit well qualified Negro students or have given consideration to the possibility of adjusting admission standards to accommodate the few Negro applicants whose records approach acceptability." (Benjamin F. Boyer, et al., "Report of the Committee on Racial Discrimination: Problems of Negro Applicants," 1964 Association of American Law Schools Proc. Part One 195, 160–161.) In 1965, the Emory University School of Law offered a summer program for black students under which any participant completing the program won a seat in the first-year class. (Richard A. Sanders, "A Systematic Analysis of Affirmative Action in American Law Schools," *Stanford Law Review* 57 [2004]: 367, 378 n. 29). These episodes, however, were mere straws in the wind, precursors of an affirmative action regime that had yet to emerge.
† "We have waited for more than 340 years for our constitutional and God given rights. The nations of Asia and Africa are moving with jetlike speed toward gaining political independence, but we still creep at horse and buggy pace toward gaining a cup of coffee at a lunch counter. Perhaps it is easy for those who have never felt the stinging darts of segregation to say, 'Wait.' But when you have seen vicious mobs lynch your mothers and fathers at will and drown your sisters and brothers at whim; when you have seen hate filled policemen curse, kick and even kill your black brothers and sisters; when you see the vast majority of your twenty million Negro brothers smothering in an airtight cage of poverty in the midst of an affluent society . . . when you are forever fighting a degenerating sense of 'nobodiness'—then you will understand why we find it difficult to wait." Martin Luther King, Jr., "Letter from a Birmingham Jail" (1963).

Dissatisfaction with the pace of change spread from protesters to government officials, including federal judges. Consider public school desegregation. In 1954, the Supreme Court of the United States ruled in *Brown v. Board of Education* and *Bolling v. Sharpe* that it was a violation of the federal Constitution for governments to segregate students in public schools on a racial basis. In spelling out the terms for complying with these rulings, the Court was permissive, requiring only a good-faith start toward desegregation and an understanding that the process might be able to unfold only with "all deliberate speed." For more than a decade the Court permitted local authorities to delay to the point of open obstruction. But by the tenth anniversary of *Brown,* the demographics of public schooling in the South had changed hardly at all. In 1964, the vast majority of Negro students attended the same schools that they would have attended had *Brown* never been decided. Some local authorities refused to change anything in the absence of court orders. Others put the burden of desegregation squarely on the backs of blacks, many of whom refrained from leaving "their" schools out of realistic fears of retaliation. By 1968, the Court's patience was exhausted. It finally declared that the time for "all deliberate speed" had passed and that a new day had arrived—the day of desegregation *now*. In *Green v. County School Board*,[41] the Court confronted a jurisdiction in which authorities had removed the official color bar separating white and black students. Whites were free to attend the historically black school, while blacks were free to attend the historically white school. Yet, with a few exceptions (all of whom were African Americans), students under "freedom of choice" attended the same schools they would have attended under segregation. The Supreme Court concluded that freedom of choice that yielded the same racial patterns as those that existed under de jure segregation was an insufficient response to *Brown*. It demanded an actual change in the racial demographics of schools so that there would be no more white schools or black schools but "just schools." The Court, in other words, demanded that authorities engage in race-conscious policymaking for the purpose of effecting actual, as opposed to merely nominal, desegregation. Three years after *Green,* in *Swann v. Charlotte-Mecklenburg Board of Education,*[42] the Supreme Court upheld judicially mandated busing with racial balancing requirements, ruling that, at least in jurisdictions that were once governed by segregation, courts could properly demand integration *now* through racially selective means.

President Lyndon Baines Johnson also helped prepare the way for affirmative action. In addition to guiding the enactment of the Civil Rights Act of 1964 and the Voting Rights Act of 1965, he voiced the urgent dissatisfaction that gripped Americans who were energized by the Civil Rights Revolution but flustered by its seeming inability to improve the material circumstances in which many Negroes, particularly poor blacks, found themselves. An example is the speech LBJ delivered at Howard University on June 4, 1965.[43] Two features of this speech are pertinent here. One is its searing critique of the mistreatment of blacks. "In far too many ways," President Johnson averred, "American Negroes have been another nation: deprived of freedom, crippled by hate, the doors of opportunity closed to hope." Johnson acknowledged elements of positive change, noting, for instance, that the number of blacks in schools of higher learning had almost doubled in the previous fifteen years. The story of the growing black middle class, he observed, was an impressive achievement. "But for the great majority of Negro Americans—

the poor, the unemployed, the uprooted, and the dispossessed—there is a much grimmer story. They still . . . are another nation. Despite the court orders and the laws . . . for them the wells are rising and the gulf is widening. . . . In the battle for equality too many—far too many—are losing ground every day."

The other pertinent feature is LBJ's declaration that while freedom and equal opportunity are essential, even combined they are insufficient to overcome the obstacles erected by racial oppression in the past. According to Johnson: "You do not take a person, who, for years, has been hobbled by chains and liberate him, bring him up to the starting line of a race and then say 'you are free to compete with others,' and still justly believe that you have been completely fair." Although he did not elaborate upon the "hobbled by chains" metaphor, one implication is that ending invidious discrimination without attending to its destructive vestiges would be unjust. "It is not enough," Johnson asserted, "just to open the gates of opportunity. All our citizens must have the ability to walk through those gates." According to LBJ, "we seek not just legal equity but human ability, not just equality as a right but equality as a fact and equality as a result." While there was little programmatic follow-up to the speech, that a president articulated such a sweeping criticism and far-reaching (albeit vague) prescription helps to explain how affirmative action emerged despite the powerful forces arrayed against it.

Distrust was another emotion that helped to prompt the emergence of affirmative action. In many settings, the mere assertion that authorities had engaged in a nondiscriminatory process no longer sufficed—especially if an ostensibly fair process generated results similar to those that could reflect a process infected by prejudice. Observers wanted clear proof of nondiscrimination, with the best evidence being the actual presence of African

Americans and others who had long been purposefully excluded for reasons of race. Commenting on unprecedented actions taken by his company to hire and retain black workers, an executive stated that they constituted "discrimination in reverse" but defended them anyway. "Such steps are required," he observed, "to convince the Negroes that we are serious and want them to apply for work with us."[44] Coleman Young, Detroit's first black mayor, would have agreed. Recalling his support for hard-edged affirmative action in his city's police department, Young candidly explained, "If quotas are the only way to keep white folks honest, let there be quotas."[45]

A belated but decent shame seeped into important precincts of American life as revelations of long-ignored facts and revisions of well-known narratives emerged, underscoring the egregious ways in which racism had been deployed to subordinate people of color.[46] Disturbed by this unflattering portrayal of the American past and present, some onlookers began lending their support not only to antidiscrimination but also to rectification and reconciliation. An example is the *Report of the National Advisory Commission on Civil Disorders*. Lyndon Johnson created the commission on July 28, 1967, in the aftermath of rioting in Newark, Detroit, and other cities. The commission was charged with investigating the causes of the rioting and recommending responses. The most striking feature of the report was its allocation of blame: "What white Americans have never fully understood—but what the Negro can never forget—is that white society is deeply implicated in the ghetto. White institutions created it, white institutions maintain it, and white society condones it." Even though the commission was acting soon after the high tide of the civil rights movement, it nonetheless declared (echoing the president's speech at Howard),

"Our nation is moving toward two societies, one black, one white—separate and unequal."

Having offered an ominous portrayal of American race relations, the commission posited that "this deepening racial division is not inevitable. The movement apart can be reversed." But turning things around, the commission declared, would "require a commitment to national action—compassionate, massive, and sustained, backed by the resources of the most powerful and richest nation on earth. From every American it will require new attitudes, new understanding, and, above all, new will." Exhorting Americans to address racial conflict in a way that is now difficult to recall or imagine, the commission insisted,

> It is time now to turn with all the purpose at our command to the major unfinished business of this nation. It is time to adopt strategies for action that will produce quick and visible progress. It is time to make good the promises of American democracy to all citizens.*

As with Johnson's Howard University speech, there was little follow-up to the commission report. It did, however, facilitate the intellectual and emotional environment in which affirmative action would, on a wide scale, blossom and take root.

Supplementing white guilt as an ingredient in that environment was black anger. Previously, African Americans had typically kept their anger under wraps, aware that public display would likely trigger severe reprisals. In the latter half of the

---

* At another point in its report, the commission declared, "The vital needs of the nation must be met; hard choices must be made, and, if necessary, new taxes enacted." For programs of reconstruction "will require unprecedented levels of funding and performance. . . . There can be no higher priority for national action and no higher claim on the nation's conscience."

1960s, however, substantial numbers of blacks vented their fury openly, even ostentatiously. "Black Power" became a popular slogan. *Black Rage* became a publishing sensation. The Black Panther Party captured the imagination of radicalized youth. And for several summers, riots erupted in the black ghettos of cities across the United States, eventually causing hundreds of deaths, countless injuries, and the destruction of property worth many millions of dollars. These "long, hot summers" underlined the extent to which the cessation of Jim Crow segregation, albeit important, left untouched economic, cultural, and political dynamics that continued to pin the colored masses to the bottom of the American social pyramid.

A rising arc of civil unrest, culminating in the massive riots that shook the United States in the aftermath of the assassination of Martin Luther King, Jr., frightened decision makers, upended old assumptions, and encouraged the popularization of ideas that had theretofore been marginalized. Although some leading arbiters of opinion insisted that perpetrators of violence should receive only punishment, others maintained that violent dissent should also be addressed by nurturing faith in upward mobility. "Negroes, and more specifically lower-class Negroes, are social dynamite," remarked Stanford law professor John Kaplan. "Our only hope to avoid the most explosive and dangerous type of conflict is to grease the axle where it is squeaking and grant them special treatment."[47] "You can put these people to work," President Johnson stated to a group of business executives, "and you won't have a revolution because they've been left behind. If they're working, they won't be throwing bombs in your homes and plants. Keep them busy and they won't have time to burn your cars."[48] Johnson's successor, Richard Nixon, expressed a similar view, contending that "we sooner or later must bring those who threaten [domestic peace] back within the system."*[49]

Nixon ascended to the presidency in 1969 in part due to whites' unease with social disruption, including the loud protests of militant blacks who were widely viewed as pushing for too much, too hard, too fast. During his campaign against the classic racial liberal Hubert Humphrey, Nixon vowed that if elected he would honor "states' rights," restore "law and order," and appoint to the federal bench "strict constructionists"—all of which connoted a more conservative racial politics. In office, however, Nixon went further than any previous president toward advancing policies that reached beyond mere antidiscrimination norms.[50] Nixon supported race-targeted programs aimed at benefiting blacks and other racial minorities that would have been verboten in previous eras—and would probably be forbidden today. Nixon promulgated an executive order to create the Office of Minority Business Enterprise. He championed public-private ownerships aimed at seeding and promoting "black capitalism." Most important, he used the leverage of the federal government's role as a consumer to require businesses to try to reach certain goals in terms of hiring racial-minority workers.

The Nixon administration did not invent contracting as a technique for seeking to assure the employment of minority workers. In the waning months of the Johnson administration,

* "The Realpolitik argument is that preferential treatment of blacks and other militant minorities is the price the white majority must pay for avoiding the sort of unrest and violence of which the race riots of the 1960s were arguably just the portents. . . . Although university administrators publicly justify their preferential admissions policies in terms of increasing diversity, rectifying historical injustice and the like, in private they often will admit that appeasing student militancy was the dominant factor in the adoption of the policies." Richard Posner, "The *DeFunis* Case and the Constitutionality of Preferential Treatment of Racial Minorities," *Supreme Court Review* (1974): 1, 21.

Labor Department officials involved with construction projects sought to prod local governments, private contractors, and unions into hiring black workers, particularly in the craft trades. In Philadelphia in 1967, the Sheet Metal Workers Local 19 had 1,300 to 1,400 members but no blacks. Similarly, Elevator Constructors Local 5 had nearly 650 members and helpers but not a black among them. The locals claimed, of course, that they did not discriminate, that the absence of blacks was due to a lack of training, experience, or references. This was true to some extent. Even truer, though, was that the union locals established or retained their procedures at least in part to "protect" the racial homogeneity of their guilds.

To disrupt this pattern of exclusion, Labor Department officials threatened to cut off federal funding unless contractors promised that they would affirmatively act in accord with antidiscrimination mandates and show good faith toward hiring racial-minority workers. This Labor Department intervention became known as the Philadelphia Plan. In its initial incarnation, near the end of the Johnson administration, it lasted only briefly. When the United States comptroller general declared that the plan was procedurally invalid, the Johnson administration quickly and quietly abandoned it.

But then came a surprising turn of events: the incoming administration of Richard Nixon revived, strengthened, and enlarged the Philadelphia Plan.[51] The revised plan modified the procedure to which the comptroller general had objected. In the initial plan, the Office of Federal Contract Compliance Programs (OFCCP) declined to state definite minimum standards for bidders, in order to avoid the charge that it was imposing "quotas." If the OFCCP was dissatisfied with the hiring goals set forth by the lowest bidder, it would seek to negotiate a higher goal or even reopen the bidding. The comptroller general ruled that the indefiniteness of this arrangement was unfair and unlawful.

The Nixon administration's revised Philadelphia Plan set forth, by trade, a range of minority hiring goals that the OFCCP expected to see reflected in bids. The underlying metric on which the ranges were based was representational: employers were expected to hire percentages of minority workers that roughly mirrored the percentage of qualified minority workers in the relevant locale. Failures to reach that standard triggered concerns that the employer was underutilizing available minority labor. The goals were flexible. Employers were given the opportunity to explain any apparent underutilization. Moreover, the bureaucrats administering the plan were loath to shut off federal funding; time and again, they displayed that their bark was far more menacing than their bite. Still, the threat of shutoff appears to have focused the attention of all of the relevant stakeholders.

The principal actors behind this initiative were Nixon's labor secretary, George P. Shultz, and his subordinates, several of whom were African American, including, most notably, Arthur A. Fletcher. A former dean of the University of Chicago Graduate School of Business, Shultz displayed an attentiveness to the plight of working-class and poor blacks that was unusual in the conservative, business-oriented circles in which he traveled. In his presidential address to the annual meeting of the Industrial Relations Research Association on December 8, 1968, Secretary-designate Shultz declared that the most important issue of political economy facing the nation was the "appalling unemployment experience of black teenagers." He called for "special measures" to address this problem, though he neglected to describe any with specificity. What he lacked in specifics, however, he made up for with emphasis, asserting that in the "explosive" racial environment obtaining, employers would simply be unable to conduct business as usual.[52]

The Philadelphia Plan and fifty-six similar programs established in cities across the country generated unusual coalitions of allies and adversaries.[53] Conservative Republicans and Democrats staunchly opposed them. But so, too, did some liberal Democrats, because of their close ties to organized labor, which generally despised these plans. Reasons for opposition varied. Detractors argued that the plans involved a wasteful regulation of private enterprise, that they encroached upon the prerogatives of organized labor, that they represented the entering wedge of racial quotas, and that they violated a provision of Title VII of the 1964 Civil Rights Act that expressly prohibits the government from requiring any employer to hire anyone on a racial basis.

More interesting is speculation as to why Nixon supported the plans. Many of their backers were not only outside of Nixon's electoral coalition but un-amenable to being won over by him. At the same time, many of the plans' enemies were people essential to the Nixon coalition. The formidable Senate minority leader, Everett M. Dirksen, angrily denounced the Philadelphia Plan, remarking privately that to Senate Republicans it was "about as popular as a crab in a whorehouse."[54] Thus, in terms of electoral advantage, Nixon's backing of the Philadelphia Plan and its analogues made little sense, at least in the short run.

Recognizing this, Nixon nonetheless invested political capital in supporting the Philadelphia Plan. Why? Theories abound. One is that the Machiavellian Nixon calculated that he could reap political advantage by dividing racial liberals and labor Democrats, two camps that usually coalesced against him. "Not lost on Nixon," Professor Hugh Davis Graham writes, "was the delicious prospect of setting organized labor and the civil rights establishment at each other's Democratic throats."[55]

Another theory is that Nixon was acting out of a sincere desire to assist blacks, notwithstanding his racism and their general aversion to him. Throughout his political career, Nixon exhibited strong mood swings on the race question, sometimes showing outright bigotry, sometimes displaying a surprising solicitude for racial minorities. On the eve of launching the presidential campaign that took him to the White House, Nixon told reporters that "people in the ghetto have to have more than an equal chance. They should be given a dividend."[56] Later he promised to give "those who haven't had their chance . . . that little extra start that they need."[57] Nixon may well have seen the Philadelphia Plan as one of those "little extra start[s]" for which he sometimes evinced pride. Comparing his adoption of the Philadelphia Plan to the Johnson White House abandonment of it, Nixon gibed, "Dem[ocrat]s are token-oriented. We are job-oriented."[58]

Another theory is that support for the Philadelphia Plan had to do with the Nixon administration's determination to lower construction costs. By keeping barriers to entry high for labor, unions were able, so the Nixonians believed, to inflate costs for construction. Shultz and others believed that exorbitant costs could be lowered by removing impediments to market forces, including the obstacle of union-supported racial exclusion.

The Nixon administration invested a substantial amount of effort protecting the Philadelphia Plan. It quashed a congressional attempt to defund the plan and fended off charges that the plan violated the Civil Rights Act. One of the most impressive of the administration's spokesmen turned out to be Assistant Secretary of Labor Fletcher. "We must set goals, targets and timetables," he told reporters in August 1969. "The way we put a man on the moon in less than ten years was with goals, targets and timetables."[59]

The Nixon administration's surprising support did not last long. By mid-1971 White House operatives had succeeded in transferring Fletcher from his post in the Labor Department to the United Nations, where he could conveniently be ignored. During the reelection campaign of 1972, Nixon was no longer speaking of "little extra starts" for racial minorities but was instead condemning "quotas." When Nixon won reelection, his new Labor Department secretary was Peter J. Brennan, a former president of the New York Building Trades Council and an outspoken opponent of the sentiments that had generated the Philadelphia Plan.

The Philadelphia and associated plans constitute important landmarks in the history of affirmative action. They did not succeed in quickly opening up employment opportunities for substantial numbers of blacks, and several of the most recalcitrant unions maintained their virtually lily-white memberships.[60] Nevertheless, the plans made three important contributions. First, they disseminated the affirmative action ethos and endowed it with new prestige. Second, they prompted the Labor Department to extend its policy of goal-setting to all entities doing sizable business with the federal government, including colleges and universities. Third, they served as precedents for subsequent affirmative action initiatives.

Across the country in the early 1970s, in all sorts of forums, public and private, authorities adopted procedures designed to ensure an enlarged colored presence. Explaining his institution's practice of assessing minority applicants according to a somewhat different metric than that applied to white candidates, the president of the University of Washington observed,

> More and more it became evident to us that just an open door,
> as it were, at the point of entry to the University, somehow or
> other seemed insufficient to deal with what was emerging as the
> greatest internal problem of the United States of America. . . .
> [J]ust an open door . . . in view of the cultural circumstances that
> produced something other than equality was not enough . . . some
> more positive contribution had to be made . . .[61]

Other institutions also concluded that an "open door," albeit
preferable to a closed door, would be an insufficient basis for
substantial change given prevailing circumstances. Hence, after
several years during which a new medical school at the University of California–Davis had had virtually no students of color,
it devised a special admissions program under which "disadvantaged" black, Chicano, Asian, and Native American applicants
received preferential attention. In 1973, no blacks or Chicanos
gained admission via the regular program, but six blacks and
eight Chicanos gained admission via the special program. In
1974, no blacks but four Chicanos gained admission via the
regular program, while six blacks and seven Chicanos gained
admission via the special program.[62]

Another example of early-1970s affirmative action was a collective bargaining agreement between the United Steelworkers
of America and the Kaiser Aluminum & Chemical Corporation. Pursuant to this arrangement, the Steelworkers and Kaiser
reserved for black employees 50 percent of the openings in craft
training programs. Prior to this plan, blacks had long been categorically excluded from craftwork. To remedy the continuing
effects of past discrimination, the collectively bargained affirmative action program offered craft training to blacks even when
they had less seniority than whites who sought craft training.[63]

The growing influence of the nascent affirmative action
regime generated yet another round of opposition. After hav-

ing assisted with the institutionalization of affirmative action, President Nixon turned against it. By 1972 he was warning of the specter of a "quota democracy" and, invoking the trope of reverse discrimination, insisting that "you do not correct an ancient injustice by committing a new one."[64] Unreconstructed white supremacists, of course, continued to oppose affirmative action. But so, too, did some former racial liberals, including an influential cadre that developed a distinctive critique. Dubbed "neoconservatives," this formidable network of academics, journalists, politicians, and policy analysts made rolling back affirmative action one of its principal missions. Disturbed by Black Power sloganeering, offended by assertions of Third Worldism that included denunciations of Israel, alienated by "positive" racial distinctions, which seemed to eschew an earlier commitment to "color blindness," and fearful of a proportionalism that they perceived as threatening to small ethnic groups (most notably Jews) that achieved a presence in elite institutions and occupations disproportionate to their numbers, neoconservatives emerged as persistent critics of affirmative action.

The Affirmative Action Stalemate: From Carter to Obama

Since the mid- to late 1970s, affirmative action has been mired in a stalemate. On the one hand, special efforts to ensure the presence of racial minorities in key institutions have become a widespread feature of social life. Every president since Lyndon Johnson has had at least one black in his cabinet, the consequence of an implicit quota (just as there was a period when there existed an implicit quota of one Jewish seat on the Supreme Court). Even presidents on record as opposing affirmative action—Ronald Reagan and the two Bushes—have felt compelled to select at least one Negro to lead an executive branch department. A similar dynamic is observable in virtually every prominent setting imaginable—the allocation of awards (e.g., honorary degrees), the composition of orchestras, the selection of workers, the admission of students, the distribution of governmental largesse.

To some extent, these practices have received validation from presidents and courts. In 1978, in *Regents of the University of California v. Bakke,* the Supreme Court held that universities could take race into account in certain ways in selecting students, for purposes of "diversity." In 1979, in *United Steelworkers v. Weber,* the Court held that Title VII of the 1964 Civil Rights Act did not prohibit private employers from voluntarily preferring racial-minority applicants to redress past racial discrimination in traditionally segregated jobs. In 1980, in *Fullilove v. Klutznick,* the Court upheld legislation that provided that recipients of federal funds for public works projects must, absent a waiver, use a certain percentage of those funds to purchase goods and services from minority contractors.

President Jimmy Carter made a concerted effort to elevate blacks to high positions. He placed thirty-seven blacks on the federal bench—more than all of the previous presidents combined—and selected the first black woman, Patricia Harris, for a post in the cabinet.[65] The Carter administration, moreover, defended affirmative action in litigation.

Although Ronald Reagan as a candidate and president was largely hostile to affirmative action, during his 1980 campaign he, too, reflected and reinforced affirmative action consciousness by pledging that, if elected, "one of the first Supreme Court vacancies in [his] administration [would] be filled by the most qualified woman [he could] find"[66]—a promise he kept by nominating Sandra Day O'Connor. Reagan also took care to have at least one black in his cabinet and to appoint conservative blacks to important posts, actions also taken by his successor, George H. W. Bush.

President Bill Clinton was conspicuously friendly to affirmative action, insisting upon a cabinet that "looked like America." He was the first president to devote an entire speech to justifying affirmative action. Addressing the subject in 1995, he maintained that "affirmative action remains a useful tool for widening economic and educational opportunity." Clinton assured the public that he would not abide "unjustified preference," "numerical quotas," or selections "solely on the basis of race or gender regardless of merit." But he declared that he supported affirmative action that is flexible, fair, efficient, and transitional. "Affirmative action should not go on forever," he said, but "the job of ending discrimination in this country is not over. . . . We should reaffirm the principle of affirmative action and fix the practice. We should have a simple slogan: Mend it, but don't end it."[67]

Despite considerable support for affirmative action, opposition has curtailed it, driven it underground, limited the justifications on which its opponents can openly rely, and put it on the defensive politically, legally, psychologically, and morally. Since 1976 the Republican Party has expressly condemned "quotas" and "preferential treatment" in its party platforms.* In his first

* In 1976, the Republican Party platform stated that while "there must be vigorous enforcement of laws to assure equal treatment . . . the way to end discrimination . . . is not by resurrecting the much discredited quota system and attempting to cloak it in an aura of new respectability." (By contrast, the Democratic Party platform reaffirmed a "commitment to . . . affirmative action.") In 1996, the Republican platform announced its endorsement of the Dole-Canady Equal Opportunity Act, "to

press conference as president, Ronald Reagan complained that "some affirmative action programs [are] becoming quota systems."[68] He chose a fervent opponent of affirmative action, William Bradford Reynolds, to head the Civil Rights Division of the Department of Justice. He chose another foe, Clarence Thomas, to head the Equal Employment Opportunity Commission. He elevated yet another committed adversary, Antonin Scalia, to the Supreme Court, the branch of the federal government that has become the main brake to affirmative action's momentum.

Prior to Reagan's ascension, the Supreme Court had evinced a grudging toleration for affirmative action. After the appointment of the Reagan, Bush I, and Bush II justices, however, the Court became increasingly hostile. Illustrative are three rulings: *Wygant v. Jackson [Michigan] Board of Education* (1986), *City of Richmond v. J. A. Croson Co.* (1989), and *Adarand Constructors v. Peña* (1995).

Wygant involved a challenge to a collective bargaining agreement forged in 1972 by the Board of Education of Jackson, Michigan, and a local teachers' union that provided special protection against layoffs to teachers "who are Black, American Indian, Oriental, or of Spanish descendency."[69] The provision in question stated:

---

end discrimination [i.e., affirmative action] by the federal government," and Proposition 209, the California Civil Rights Initiative, "to restore to law the original meaning of civil rights." (The Democratic platform, on the other hand, asserted that "when it comes to affirmative action, we should mend it, not end it.") In 2008, the Republican platform declared that "precisely because we oppose discrimination, we reject preferences, quotas, and set-asides." (By contrast, the Democratic platform stated: "We support affirmative action . . . to make sure that those locked out of the doors of opportunity will be able to walk through those doors in the future.") In its 2012 platform, the Republican Party stated: "We reject preferences, quotas, and set-asides as the best or sole methods through which fairness can be achieved." (By contrast, the Democratic platform declared: "We support affirmative action to redress discrimination and to achieve the diversity from which all Americans benefit.")

> In the event that it becomes necessary to reduce the number of
> teachers through layoff from employment by the Board, teach-
> ers with the most seniority in the district shall be retained, except
> that at no time will there be a greater percentage of minority per-
> sonnel laid off than the current percentage of minority personnel
> employed at the time of the layoff.[70]

Concern with the consequences of allowing conventional
"last hired, first fired" seniority rules to proceed uninhibitedly
stemmed from a history of racial tension in Jackson. Authorities
there did not hire a black teacher until 1954. Fifteen years later, a
local branch of the NAACP filed a complaint with the Michigan
Civil Rights Commission alleging racial discrimination against
black applicants for teaching positions. The commission concluded that evidence substantiated the allegations. A result was
a settlement under which the Board of Education promised to
take "affirmative steps to recruit, hire, and promote minority
teachers." It was because of the recent vintage of minority hires
that the specter of contraction loomed large, since layoffs would
foreseeably exact a disproportionate racial burden when the next
economic downturn hit. The special layoff provision was crafted
with that prospect in mind.

When layoffs became necessary in 1974, the board reneged;
it was simply unwilling to lay off senior tenured nonminority
teachers while retaining junior probationary minority teachers.
The union and two minority teachers sued. Subsequently, after
litigation in federal and state courts, the board decided to adhere
to the collectively bargained layoff provision. During the 1976–77
and 1981–82 school years, nonminority teachers were laid off
while minority teachers with less seniority were retained. This
time, several laid-off nonminority teachers sued, charging that
they were the victims of unconstitutional racial discrimination.
Lower courts ruled against them, determining that minority

teachers were substantially and chronically underrepresented in the school district and that the layoff provision met a "reasonableness" standard for addressing the school board's interests in uprooting entrenched exclusion, promoting racial harmony, and providing role models for minority students.

The Supreme Court reversed, in an opinion written by Justice Lewis F. Powell that stressed the insufficiency of general claims of societal discrimination as a justification for remedial racial selectivity and the requirement that any governmental racial classification be subjected to "strict scrutiny." Powell also advanced two arguments new to the Court's affirmative action jurisprudence, one having to do with "role models" and another having to do with the status of layoffs. A justification for the preferential-layoff provision embraced by the lower courts was that something had to be done to protect at least a minimum number of minority teachers against layoffs to preserve minority role models in the schools. Powell scoffed at that claim, remarking that, "carried to its logical extreme, the idea that black students are better off with black teachers could lead to the very system the Court rejected in *Brown v. Board of Education*."*[71]

---

* Powell's description of the role model theory is tendentious. The theory's champions were not saying that black pupils "are better off with black teachers." Rather, they were saying that black pupils are better off in schools in which there are at least a nontrivial number of black teachers. Furthermore, there was no good reason to limit the discussion of the pedagogical usefulness of minority teachers only to minority students; many people sensibly contend that nonminority students also benefit from minority teachers as role models. "In the context of public education," Justice Stevens observed, "it is quite obvious that a school board may reasonably conclude that an integrated faculty will be able to provide benefits to the student body that could not be provided by an all-white, or nearly all-white, faculty. For one of the most important lessons that the American public schools teach is that the diverse ethnic, cultural, and national backgrounds that have been brought together in our famous 'melting pot' do not identify essentially differences among the human beings that inhabit our land. It is one thing for a white child to be taught by a white teacher that color, like beauty, is only 'skin deep'; it is far more convincing to experience that truth on a day-to-day basis during the routine, ongoing learning process." *Wygant v. Jackson Board of Education,* 476 U.S. 267, 315 (1986) (Stevens, J., dissenting).

Second, Powell maintained, on behalf of a majority of the justices, that the particular type of racial selectivity at issue in *Wygant*—racially selective layoffs—was too burdensome to permit. "Layoffs disrupt . . . settled expectations," he wrote, "in a way that general hiring goals do not. Layoffs impose the entire burden of achieving racial equality on particular individuals, often resulting in serious disruptions of their lives. That burden is too intrusive."[72]

In *City of Richmond v. J. A. Croson,* the Court faced a controversy drenched in ironic historical symbolism. It involved the constitutionality of a program enacted in 1983 in Richmond, Virginia, the former capital of the Confederacy. The Richmond City Council established a Minority Business Utilization Plan under which nonminority prime contractors awarded construction contracts with the city were required, in the absence of a waiver, to subcontract at least 30 percent of the dollar amount of the contracts to minority business enterprises (MBE). The plan described itself as "remedial" and enacted "for the purpose of promoting wider participation by minority business enterprise in the construction of public projects."[73] Proponents of the plan relied upon a study that indicated that while the general population of Richmond was about 50 percent black, only 0.67 percent of the city's prime construction contracts between 1978 and 1983 had been awarded to minority businesses. In the hearings and deliberations preceding enactment of the plan, observers differed on the reasons behind the paucity of black business participation. City Councilman Henry Marsh declared:

> I have been practicing law in this community since 1961, and I am familiar with the practices in the construction industry in this area, the State, and around the nation. And I can say without equivoca-

tion, that the general conduct of the construction industry . . . is one in which race discrimination and exclusion on the basis of race is widespread.[74]

Others perceived the situation differently, with one councilman observing that, in his view, the witnesses had "indicated that the minority contractors were just not available. There wasn't a one that gave any indication that a minority contractor would not have had an opportunity, if he were available."*[75]

J. A. Croson had bid on a project to provide and install toilets at the city jail. He won the bid—he was the only participant—but lost the business when he ran afoul of the plan's MBE set-aside. Croson sought an MBE subcontractor but failed to find one he considered to be suitable. He then sought a waiver from the plan's MBE requirement. Croson's petition was rejected. The city then decided to rebid the project. At that point Croson sued.

A United States district court upheld the plan and was initially affirmed by the United States Court of Appeals for the Fourth Circuit. When the Supreme Court instructed the Court of Appeals to reconsider its judgment in light of *Wygant,* however, the Court of Appeals changed its mind, striking down the Richmond plan. The Supreme Court reviewed that judgment, agreed with it, and issued an opinion written by Justice O'Connor. The majority constituted what could be called the Reagan Court.

* These statements, of course, are potentially reconcilable, depending on what one means by "discrimination." They conflict if "racial discrimination" is taken to mean a situation in which a decision maker, for racial reasons, selects one competitor over another. The statements are consistent, however, if "discrimination" is defined more broadly to embrace the circumstances that facilitate or stunt the growth of competitors. Councilman Marsh could have been saying that racial discrimination in Richmond and elsewhere had been so pervasive and effective that it had thwarted the rise of black construction entrepreneurs, making them unavailable. They had been so marginalized that they did not even make it to the bidding.

It included four Reagan appointees: Justices Rehnquist, Scalia, Kennedy, and O'Connor.*

The Court majority asserted three points. First, the Court held that, pursuant to Section 5 of the Fourteenth Amendment, the federal government has more leeway than states and municipalities to redress the effects of racial discrimination.† Second, the Court expressly declared that all governmental racial selectivity should be subjected to judicial "strict scrutiny." The standard of review under the Equal Protection Clause, Justice O'Connor declared, "is not to be dependent on the race of those burdened or benefited by a particular classification."[76] Third, the Court found fault with the factual predicate relied upon to justify the affirmative action plan. O'Connor complained that Richmond's allegations of past discrimination were too conclusory and general. She objected to Richmond's inference of discrimination from the disparity between the number of prime contracts awarded to minority firms and the minority population of the city. This comparison, she said, was erroneous. The proper comparison, she maintained, was between the number of prime contracts awarded to minority firms and the number of qualified minority firms in the Richmond area.

O'Connor also disapproved of Richmond's reliance on congressional findings of nationwide discrimination. That evidence, she believed, has "extremely limited" probative value about the situation in Richmond. Noting that the Richmond program included as beneficiaries a list of groups other than African Americans, she remarked that "there is *absolutely no evidence* of past discrimination against Spanish speaking, Oriental, Indian, Eskimo,

---

* The justices appointed by Reagan were joined by Justices Byron White (nominated by President John F. Kennedy) and John Paul Stevens (nominated by President Gerald R. Ford.)

† Later, in *Advanced Constructors v. Pena*, 515 U.S. 200 (1995), the Supreme Court abandoned this dual standard, implicitly eschewing *Fullilove*.

or Aleut persons in any aspect of the Richmond construction industry. . . . It may well be that Richmond has never had an Aleut or Eskimo citizen."[77] In the Court's view, because "none of the evidence presented by the city point[ed] to any identifiable discrimination in the Richmond construction industry," the city had failed "to demonstrate a compelling interest in apportioning public contracting opportunities on the basis of race."[78]

Reaching a crescendo of alarm and disapproval, O'Connor declared that for the Court "to accept Richmond's claim that past societal discrimination alone can serve as a basis for rigid racial preferences would be to open the door to competing claims for 'remedial relief' for every disadvantaged group." If that were to happen, she remarked, "the dream of a nation of equal citizens in a society where race is irrelevant to personal opportunity and achievement would be lost in a mosaic of shifting preferences based on inherently unmeasurable claims of past wrongs."[79]

Justices Marshall, Brennan, and Blackmun dissented. Far from condemning the Richmond Plan, they lauded it as "a welcome symbol of racial progress."[80] "I never thought I would live to see the day," Blackmun wrote, when "the cradle of the Old Confederacy, sought on its own . . . to lessen the stark impact of persistent discrimination. But Richmond, to its great credit, acted."[81] The dissenters believed that the notoriety of racial discrimination in Richmond, the congressional findings supporting federal set-asides, the stated experience of municipal officials, and the paucity of minority contracting—no matter how that paucity was calculated—provided a suitable basis for the plan. According to Justice Marshall, the Court's ruling sounded "a full-scale retreat" from the Court's previous solicitude for "race-conscious remedial efforts directed toward deliverance of the century-old promise of equality of economic opportunity."[82]

The "full-scale retreat" to which Marshall alluded was by

no means uniform. A year after *Croson,* in *Metro Broadcasting, Inc. v. Federal Communications Commission,* the Court upheld minority preferences in awarding radio and television broadcast licenses primarily for the purpose of promoting programming diversity. Citing deference to Congress, the Court stated that it did not need to apply strict scrutiny to the racially selective program at issue. It decided that benign race-conscious measures mandated by Congress are constitutionally permissible to the extent that they serve "important" (as opposed to "compelling") governmental objectives and are substantially related to the achievement of those objectives.

Metro Broadcasting was decided only 5–4, however, and featured impassioned dissents by O'Connor and Kennedy. In light of subsequent events, it is noteworthy that O'Connor maintained that the government's interest in increasing the diversity of broadcast viewpoints "is clearly not a compelling interest. It is simply too amorphous, too insubstantial, and too unrelated to any legitimate basis for employing racial classifications."[83] According to O'Connor, "the interest in diversity of viewpoints provides no legitimate, much less important, reason to employ racial classifications apart from generalizations impermissibly equating race with thoughts and behavior."[84]

Justice Kennedy was similarly upset with the Court's toleration for what seemed to him an unjustified resort to racial selectivity. Pointing to segregation in the Jim Crow South and apartheid in South Africa, Kennedy expressed doubt regarding the Court's capacity to distinguish suitably between malign and benign racial discrimination. This very case displayed the difficulty, Kennedy maintained, since the preference in question stemmed from what he saw as the stereotypical assumptions that the race of broadcast owners is linked to broadcast content—

assumptions that, he said, the government should be forbidden to make.

Metro Broadcasting raised a variety of issues that would recur in the ongoing struggle over affirmative action, particularly the relationship between racial status and individuals' perspectives—i.e., "diversity." But for the purposes of understanding the evolution of the Supreme Court's affirmative action jurisprudence, the most important thing to know about *Metro Broadcasting* is that the Court soon rejected much of its reasoning. After five years the Court effectively buried *Metro Broadcasting* with a new ruling, *Adarand Constructors v. Peña*.[85]

Adarand involved a challenge to legislation that used racially selective presumptions to identify "socially and economically disadvantaged individuals" that firms were nudged to hire by financial incentives authorized by Congress. Lower courts upheld this program, in reliance on *Fullilove* and *Metro Broadcasting*. In an opinion written by Justice O'Connor, however, a majority of the justices largely repudiated those precedents on two grounds. First, the Court ruled that, contrary to prior pronouncements, Congress ought to be held to the same standards as the states in terms of justifying racial selectivity. Second, the Court determined that *all* governmental racial distinctions, federal as well as state, must be subjected to strict scrutiny.* Given its change in course in terms of evaluating racial affirmative action, the Court remanded the dispute to the Court of Appeals to allow the lower court a chance to reassess the dispute in light of the Court's new doctrine.

---

* "We hold today that all racial classifications, imposed by whatever federal, state, or local governmental actor, must be analyzed by a reviewing court under strict scrutiny. In other words, such classifications are constitutional only if they are narrowly tailored measures that further compelling governmental interests." *Adarand Constructors v. Peña*, 515 U.S. 200, 227 (1995).

A significant feature of *Adarand* was a concurring opinion authored by the lone black on the Supreme Court, Thurgood Marshall's successor, Justice Clarence Thomas. Whereas Marshall had been a defender of affirmative action, Thomas was (and remains) an enemy.

That racial affirmative action programs "may have been motivated, in part, by good intentions," Thomas declared, "cannot provide refuge from the principle that under our Constitution, the government may not make distinctions on the basis of race."[86] According to him, "it is irrelevant whether a government's racial classifications are drawn by those who wish to oppress a race or by those who have a sincere desire to help those thought to be disadvantaged." Eager to confront those who accused him of drawing an equivalence between negative and positive discrimination, Thomas asserted unapologetically that, yes, he did "believe that there is a 'moral [and] constitutional equivalence' . . . between laws designed to subjugate a race and those that distribute benefits on the basis of race in order to foster some current notion of equality." To him, "government-sponsored racial discrimination based on benign prejudice is just as noxious as discrimination inspired by malicious prejudice. In each instance, it is racial discrimination, plain and simple."

Despite wide-ranging attacks against affirmative action, it has, remarkably, continued to survive. One might have thought during the Reagan administration that its days were few, given the commitment of highly placed opponents. Key officials, most notably Attorney General Edwin Meese, urged President Reagan to rescind or revise the executive orders stemming from the Nixon era that require businesses under contract with the federal government to make good-faith efforts to utilize minorities in proportions consistent with their percentage of relevant workforces. Under these protocols, if a company does not make a good-faith effort, it could lose its federal business (though this threat has been carried out only sparsely).* Opponents of affirmative action denounce these arrangements as a threat that wrongly prods businesses to engage in "quota hiring" to avoid expensive wrangling with the government. Meese drafted an executive order for President Reagan that would have prohibited the Office of Federal Contract Compliance Programs (OFCC) from continuing its use of statistical underutilization formulae to police businesses. But Reagan, to the sharp disappointment of some conservatives, decided to forgo taking that step. He calculated that siding with Meese would be too politically costly. The liberal civil rights establishment vigorously resisted the threatened revision. But its opposition was not the key factor that dissuaded Reagan; after all, the people in that camp were going to be political foes regardless of what he did on this issue. Rather, he wanted to avoid alienating moderate Republicans who supported various soft forms of affirmative action and simultaneously played important roles in the Reagan coalition. This camp included such important politicians as William Brock, Reagan's secretary of labor, and Bob Dole, then the leader of the Republicans in the Senate. Ultimately, it was out of deference to their sensibilities that Reagan declined to authorize the action for which Meese had forcefully lobbied. To avoid exacerbating a painful division among Republicans, Reagan stayed his hand.[87]

Also disappointing to anti–affirmative action conservatives was the survival of the disparate-impact theory of racial dis-

---

* According to one account, between 1977 and 1985, only fifteen employers lost federal contracts on account of violating Executive Order 11246. See Raymond Wolters, *Right Turn: William Bradford Reynolds, the Reagan Administration, and Black Civil Rights* (1996), 269.

crimination which stemmed from the landmark Supreme Court ruling in *Griggs v. Duke Power Co.*[88] This theory prohibits a screening device (for instance, a standardized test) that disproportionately excludes members of a given racial group, regardless of the intent of the employer, if a judge is unconvinced that the business needs of the employer justifies the screening device in question. Detractors attack this theory on two grounds. First, it is race conscious. It demands that employers take affirmative steps to avoid what a judge deems to be avoidable negative collateral damage that disproportionately falls upon racial minorities. With its group-based, statistical inquiry, which disavows reliance on a finding of racial intent, the disparate-impact model of discrimination implicitly validates demographic proportionality as an acceptable presumptive baseline against which to determine the legitimacy of employer selections. A second objection is that the disparate-impact theory puts pressure on employers to avoid any substantial disproportionality in hiring (even if that means choosing suboptimal candidates) to avoid having to justify screening devices to federal judges (who might be insufficiently attentive to the imperatives that burden entrepreneurs).[89]

In 1989, the Supreme Court substantially contracted the *Griggs* disparate-impact doctrine.[90] It required more specificity on the part of plaintiffs in terms of identifying precisely offending selection devices. It reallocated the burden of proving that challenged selection devices are "necessary." And it diluted the requirements of the business necessity defense. The aggressiveness of the Court's push-back against its own previous disparate-impact jurisprudence generated internal opposition that was unusually pointed. Dissenting, Justice Blackmun (joined by Justices Brennan and Marshall) wrote that observers should well wonder whether the Court "still believes that race discrimination—or, more accurately, race discrimination against non-whites—is a problem in our society, or even remembers that it ever was."[91] The Court's turnabout also generated a legislative response. Congress passed a law that negated each of the Court's revisions. President George H. W. Bush vetoed it, however, complaining that it created "powerful incentives for employers to adopt hiring and promotion quotas."* Enemies of affirmative action cheered, sensing an opening for a dramatic rollback of doctrines facilitating or even permitting minority-friendly racial selectivity. Once again, however, they encountered frustration as President Bush subsequently acceded to a legislative compromise.[92] The deal did dilute the *Griggs* doctrine. But it also gave that doctrine a congressional imprimatur that it had never had before.[93]

THE ANTI–AFFIRMATIVE ACTION BALLOT INITIATIVE

During the first quarter century of the struggle over affirmative action, the fighting took place almost exclusively among insiders in academic offices, judges' chambers, and government bureaucracies. These actors were influenced by their perceptions of public opinion. But public opinion did not make itself known through its paradigmatic act—voting. That changed in the early 1990s when opponents of affirmative action attacked it in California by revising the state constitution through a ballot initiative. Under California law, the state constitution can be changed by securing a sufficient number of signatures within a given period to place a proposition before the voters and obtaining

---

* See Veto S. 2104: Message from the President of the United States, S. Doc. No. 35, 101st Cong., 2d Sess. 2 (1990). The Senate failed by one vote to override the veto. See 136 Cong. Rec. S16, 589 (daily ed. October 24, 1990).

a sufficient number of votes to add the proposition to the state constitution. The organizers of the anti–affirmative action ballot initiative garnered enough signatures in 1996 to put their initiative on the ballot. The California Civil Rights Initiative (CCRI), also known as Proposition 209, declares in pertinent part: "The State shall not discriminate against, or grant preferential treatment to, any individual or group on the basis of race, sex, color, ethnicity, or national origin in the operation of public employment, public education, or public contracting."[94]

The anti–affirmative action forces had already won a big victory the previous year when the Regents of the University of California passed a resolution barring race as a factor in selecting students for admission to the university. Proposition 209, however, promised to sweep far more broadly and permanently.[95] Not only would it bar racial considerations from public-education admissions decisions as a matter of state constitutional law (as opposed to an administrative decree that could be rescinded with relative ease), but Proposition 209 also portended the end of racially targeted recruitment and financial aid. Furthermore, Proposition 209 extended beyond education to bar any form of race-targeted assistance in public employment or contracting.

On November 4, 1996, 54.6 percent of the California electorate voted in favor of Proposition 209. Among whites that approval was 63 percent, among Asian Americans, 39 percent; among Latinos, 24 percent; and among African Americans, 26 percent.[96]

Two features of the campaign for Proposition 209 are especially pertinent.[97] First, it came to the fore in California and national politics at a propitious moment for affirmative action's enemies. In the midterm elections of 1994, Republicans had made large gains, winning majority status in the United States House of Representatives for the first time in nearly three decades. In the aftermath of this landscape-changing electoral eruption, politicians of all stripes sought to tap into the volatile sources of the Republican landslide, including anxieties and grievances common among white men, many of whom viewed affirmative action as threatening and unfair. Among those most interested in harnessing this discontent was the Republican governor of California, Pete Wilson. As a state legislator, mayor of San Diego, and United States senator, Wilson had long been content to let affirmative action alone. But in 1996 when Wilson set his sights on the White House, he tried to use opposition to affirmative action as a launching pad. Endorsing Proposition 209, he asked Californians "to once again send East . . . a message about fairness. . . . I ask you to join me in changing the law to restore fairness, to make real again that American dream."[98]

Bob Dole of Kansas, leader of the Republicans in the Senate and the eventual Republican presidential nominee that year, had also been content to leave affirmative action alone. Indeed, he had been one of those who, in the 1980s, had blocked the Meese faction of Reagan Republicans from removing racial proportionality goals from the Federal Contracts Compliance regime. Subsequently, however, Dole's priorities shifted: instead of defending race-conscious efforts to remedy the effects of past racial injustices, he became intent on attacking them, proposing legislation (never enacted) that would have done at the federal level what Proposition 209 did at the state level. On the Senate floor, he insisted that "race-preferential policies, no matter how well-intentioned, demean individual accomplishment. They ignore individual character. And they are absolutely poisonous to race relations in our great country."[99]

President Bill Clinton felt torn while running for reelection in 1996. On one hand, an essential element of his electoral coalition—African Americans—overwhelmingly supported affirmative action. He certainly wanted to avoid angering this sector of his base. It seems, moreover, that Clinton personally supported affirmative action with authentic enthusiasm, a sentiment that many blacks appreciated. On the other hand, Clinton was also determined to avoid electoral punishment from voters favoring the initiative. He resolved this dilemma by distancing himself from the fight. Although he opposed Proposition 209, he expended little energy actively resisting it, anxious to prevent the dispute from threatening his hold on California's large cache of Electoral College votes.

A second notable feature of Proposition 209 has to do with its leadership. The single person most responsible for its success in California and its dissemination to other states is a black man, Ward Connerly.[100] What Clarence Thomas is to affirmative action in the federal courts, Ward Connerly is to affirmative action in state ballot initiatives. Connerly did not write Proposition 209; that distinction belongs to two white academics, Thomas Wood and Glynn Custred. But when Connerly accepted their invitation to take over the leadership of the initiative, he brought to it impressive skills as a speaker and organizer, a formidable network of allies (particularly Governor Pete Wilson, with whom he had a close friendship), and, very importantly, his status as a black.* Although Connerly champions color blindness, his colleagues in the Proposition 209 campaign were any-

* Governor Pete Wilson named Ward Connerly to the University of California Board of Regents in 1993. It was from that platform that Connerly began his crusade against affirmative action. Wilson likely named Connerly for several reasons. They were friends. Wilson liked Connerly's political views, especially his detestation of affirmative action. Appointing Connerly also enabled Wilson, ironically, to blunt the criticisms of those who complained that the board lacked diversity. A 1974 revision of the state constitution required the Board of Regents to reflect the state's "economic, cultural, and societal diversity . . . including minorities and women." See Andrea Guerrero, *Silence at Boalt Hall: The Dismantling of Affirmative Action* (2002), 70.

thing but color blind in making him its spokesman and public face. They saw his blackness as a distinct plus and proceeded to use it to their advantage. His race provided a dramatic attraction to their cause; the anomaly of an African American fighting affirmative action attracted valuable publicity. Connerly's race, moreover, provided moral insulation for the campaign. With him championing Proposition 209, framing it as a movement of white resentment and retaliation became more difficult. Commenting on the recruitment of Connerly, one of the proposition's organizers observed: "To be blunt, the fact that he was black was very important. It's like using affirmative action to defeat affirmative action."[101]

After prevailing with Proposition 209, Connerly founded the American Civil Rights Institute (ACRI), an anti–affirmative action think tank and lobbying operation that has enabled him to publicize his message nationally and to try to achieve in other states what he succeeded in accomplishing in California. Initially, he won a string of victories. In 1998, voters in Washington State approved a statutory version of Proposition 209. Then voters approved initiatives in Michigan (2006), Nebraska (2008), Arizona (2010), and Oklahoma (2012). Over time, though, opponents became more adept at countering Connerly's campaigns. They challenged the veracity of signatures, the wording of initiatives, the propriety of out-of-state influences, and the substantive merits of the anti–affirmative action position. In the face of strong opposition, initiatives in Missouri (2008) and Oklahoma (2008) failed to garner a sufficient number of signatures to be placed on the ballot (though subsequently voters in Oklahoma did approve an initiative). In Colorado (2008), the initiative made it to the ballot but was rejected by the electorate.*[102]

---

* Yet another wrinkle involves the legal status of anti–affirmative action voter initiatives. The validity of some of these initiatives has been challenged under the federal

Throughout the 1990s and the first decade of the twenty-first century, the trench warfare over affirmative action continued unabated, with victories giving way to frustrations and disappointments on both sides. In 1995, in *Hopwood v. University of Texas Law School,* the federal Court of Appeals for the Fifth Circuit invalidated on broad grounds a challenged racial affirmative action program. The court essentially banned the use of race in admissions in public higher education in the states it covered. This constituted a direct repudiation of Justice Powell's landmark *Bakke* opinion. The Fifth Circuit acknowledged as much but justified its action by saying that Powell's opinion was not binding insofar as it represented the views of only one Justice. When the Supreme Court declined to review this decision, the Fifth Circuit's rejection of Powellian affirmative action became binding federal law in Texas, Mississippi, and Louisiana.

For a while, *Hopwood* seemed to augur a thoroughly bleak future for affirmative action, at least as practiced in higher education. But then came two surprises. First, the Texas legislature, disturbed by the prospect of a dramatic downturn in Latino and black students in the state's flagship university, enacted a measure under which the top 10 percent of graduating students at any high school gained automatic admission to the state's public university system, which includes the University of Texas (UT). This

---

Constitution. Opponents contend that they violate the Equal Protection Clause of the Fourteenth Amendment by changing the rules of governance in a fashion that places an unfair burden on the ability of minority groups to win beneficial legislation. The United States Court of Appeals for the Ninth Circuit rebuffed this objection to Proposition 209 in California. See *Coalition for Economic Equity v. Wilson,* 122 F.3d 692 (CA 9 1997). On the other hand, the United States Court of Appeals for the Sixth Circuit sided with opponents in striking down the anti–affirmative action amendment to the Michigan constitution. *See Coalition to Defend Affirmative Action, et al. v. Regents of the University of Michigan, et al.* (CA 6 2012). On March 13, 2013, the Supreme Court announced that it would review the Sixth Circuit's handling of this issue. See *Schuette v. Coalition to Defend Affirmative Action.*

measure is applicable to all students, regardless of race, and is thus often referred to as a "race neutral" program. This program, however, was not only foreseeably advantageous to Latino and black Texas high school students desiring entry into UT; its openly acknowledged central purpose was to assist this cadre of students. Rural poor whites are deliberately and substantially assisted by the Top Ten Percent Law as well. This coalition of beneficiaries cements a powerful, albeit unusual, political coalition in that the reform is backed by Democrats from minority urban districts and Republicans from white rural districts. The fact remains, however, that a "but-for" cause of the Top Ten Percent Law was its acknowledged benefit to racial-minority applicants.

The intended racial consequences of the Top Ten Percent Law stemmed mostly from two factors. It diminished substantially the exclusionary effect of standardized testing: if you are in the top 10 percent of your high school class, you obtain automatic admission to UT regardless of your test scores. Since the test scores of black and Latino students typically lag behind those of white peers, negating test scores strongly and purposefully assists the racial minorities. Second, the Top Ten Percent Plan implicitly but purposefully uses widespread racial separation in secondary schooling to create the functional equivalent of racially distinct pools of candidates.

Absent a program attentive to the vulnerabilities of blacks and Latinos, many white students would be even more fully advantaged insofar as applicants in the middle of the class at an academically strong (typically predominantly white) high school might possess more attractive profiles (under certain conventional standards) than applicants in the top 10 percent of the class at an academically weak (typically predominantly black or Latino) high school. The Top Ten Percent Plan is thus a potent equalizer. It offers the same wonderful benefit—automatic admission to the University of Texas—to the best students at all high schools, notwithstanding variations in the quality of those schools.

The Supreme Court delivered a second big surprise after *Hopwood*. Proponents of color-blind constitutionalism had long anticipated burying Powell's *Bakke* opinion and thought that the moment for doing so had arrived when the Court decided to consider challenges to affirmative action at the University of Michigan.* In *Grutter v. Bollinger,* however, the Court embraced (and indeed enlarged upon) Powell's opinion. The Court did so, moreover, in an opinion written by one of its conservative members, Sandra Day O'Connor, who had previously displayed a deep distaste for racial affirmative action.

THE CURRENT STATUS OF AFFIRMATIVE ACTION: AMBIVALENCE TRIUMPHANT

The status of affirmative action remains unsettled, with antagonists trading victories and defeats. After the Supreme Court upheld racial affirmative action at the University of Michigan, voters in Michigan did away with it through a Ward Connerly–inspired ballot initiative. At the same time, authorities at the University of Texas reinstated race-plus affirmative action, layering it on top of the Top Ten Percent Plan enacted after the *Hopwood* decision. That new affirmative action program was challenged in a lawsuit, *Fisher v. University of Texas*. Lower federal courts upheld the program. The Supreme Court, however, is likely to invalidate it. One line of attack is that racial affirma-

* For discussion of these cases—*Grutter v. Bollinger* and *Gratz v. Bollinger*—see pages 205–221.

tive action is gratuitous at institutions that are able to obtain a minimally sufficient amount of diversity through so-called race-neutral means. By layering an explicit racial affirmative action plan on top of the Top Ten Percent Plan, the argument runs, university authorities place an excessive, hence constitutionally impermissible, focus on race. Another line of attack is aimed at racial affirmative action in any context. This argument aims to overturn the Court's holding in *Grutter*. That decision, after all, was only 5–4 and was written by Justice O'Connor, who has retired and been replaced by someone (Justice Alito) with even more conservative views. A third line of attack targets explicit racial affirmative action *and* the Top Ten Percent Plan. This argument denies that the plan is "race neutral." It posits that insofar as a racial motive animates the plan, it is racially discriminatory notwithstanding the absence of any express facial reference to race.

The Supreme Court heard oral argument in *Fisher* on October 10, 2012, a few weeks before the presidential election. One might have thought that the affirmative action controversy would be discussed at least a bit in the final weeks of a campaign that would decide whether, for the first time, Americans would reelect a black president. As it turned out, however, the controversy never became an issue, at least not openly. In the presidential debates, neither Mitt Romney nor Barack Obama alluded to affirmative action at all.

2

The Affirmative Action Policy Debate

The Key Arguments Pro and Con

The case for racial affirmative action consists of a body of arguments in which the whole is greater than the sum of its parts. The most important of these arguments are that affirmative action is justified as a means of (1) seeking reparatory justice, (2) creating "diversity," (3) facilitating "integration," and (4) countering ongoing racial prejudice. In this chapter, I unpack these arguments, set forth the best criticisms of them, and offer responses to those objections. I then discuss additional arguments against affirmative action, most notably claims that it hurts its intended beneficiaries. I conclude that, on balance, racial affirmative action as typically designed and administered does indeed help racial minorities—those assisted directly and those benefited indirectly—and that it helps America as a whole with its ongoing struggle to redress long-standing injustices and to knit together a deeply divided society.

AFFIRMATIVE ACTION FOR REPARATIONS

Making amends for the cruel, debilitating, racially motivated wrongs imposed upon racial minorities, particularly blacks, over a long period is the single most compelling justification for racial affirmative action. This rationale is often obscured now for strategic reasons; the Supreme Court has responded to it with skepticism and hostility. But however labeled, and whether acknowledged or not, the quest for reparations was and remains an important aim of many who champion affirmative action.[1]

The predicate for affirmative action as reparations is a history of racial wrongdoing in which people of color have been singled out for mistreatment on a racial basis. The paradigmatic case is the mistreatment of blacks. Before the Civil War, the United States of America permitted its constituent states to legalize racial slavery, protected slave trading and slaveholding, allowed local governments to discriminate invidiously against people of color, and contributed to creating a thoroughgoing racial hierarchy in which whiteness was privileged and coloredness subordinated. After the Civil War—despite the statutory and constitutional enactments of Reconstruction—the United States continued to permit peoples of color to be routinely stigmatized, exploited, intimidated, disenfranchised, and terrorized by private parties and public authorities.

Why attempt to redress past wrongs? Justice demands such an effort. An essential element of justice is righting wrongs to the extent reasonable under the circumstances obtaining. More-over, as Professor Kim Forde-Mazrui declares, "failures to redress adequately conditions that predictably perpetuate, and often worsen, the effects of past racial injustices, are recurring wrongs that create new remedial obligations."[2]

The reparations theory of affirmative action is known by various labels, including rectification, restitution, remediation, correction, and compensation. Key to this theory is the idea of making amends for past wrongs that, so long as they are unad-dressed, become, sadly, refreshed wrongs. This theory goes beyond claiming that compensation is due for discrete acts of mis-treatment as determined by authoritative organs of state power.

Compensation for what courts call "identified discrimination" is relatively uncontroversial. By contrast, reparatory affirmative action for "societal discrimination"—the condition of racial subordination—is intensely controversial. Indeed, that justification for affirmative action has largely been rejected by courts.

Some proponents of affirmative action as reparations prefer it to other models because the reparations model is a claim to simple justice, an argument that beneficiaries are *entitled* to their recovery. They see this theory as morally superior, less amenable to compromise, and more focused on the fate of colored beneficiaries than competing models.[3]

Some participants in the struggle over affirmative action have made sharp distinctions between "forward-looking" and "backward-looking" affirmative action. According to Professor Bernard Boxill, "backward-looking arguments justify preferential treatment considered as compensation for past and present wrongs," while "forward-looking arguments justify preferential treatment considered as a means to future and present goods."[4] While there is a distinction to be made, there is also a considerable overlap between the categories. Although the aim to rectify past injustice is the key feature of a reparations model of affirmative action, that model need not be indifferent to the present and future status of claimants and payers. Rectifying (or at least attempting to rectify) a past wrong responds to a present need and helps to create the predicate for a just future.

The remedial justification has been central to the actual practice of affirmative action, whether or not it is openly acknowledged. It is the idea that most animated calls for special measures in the 1960s as it became evident that the mere cessation of racial exclusion would fail to redress satisfactorily the continuing effects of past wrongs. It is the justification that figures most prominently in the popular understanding of affirmative action. It is what gives the most weight and urgency to the case for affirmative action, and it explains why blacks are always among the beneficiary groups. The reparations justification does not preclude others—diversity, integration, countering invidious discrimination, social peace, legitimation, etc. But at least in terms of policies directed toward racial minorities, the aim to redress the lingering effects of racial mistreatment in the past is almost always in the background.

Affirmative action as reparations has encountered fierce criticism from a wide array of sources, some of whom eschew positive racial discrimination, whatever the asserted rationale, and some of whom support positive discrimination for certain causes but not for the sake of rectifying past wrongs. Opponents voice several objections. One is that, characteristically, beneficiaries of affirmative action are not themselves actual victims of the past racial wrongs invoked to justify positive racial discrimination. Opponents claim that currently, and increasingly in the future, typical beneficiaries of racial affirmative action are not people who have been enslaved or Jim Crowed. To the contrary, they are people who have reaped the benefits of largely successful efforts to abolish slavery and de jure segregation. They are people armed with antidiscrimination laws and, perhaps more important, an aroused public antipathy to racial prejudice. They are people who, in terms of status and opportunity, occupy a radically better position than their mothers and fathers, not to mention their grandmothers and grandfathers.[5]

A second objection is that beneficiaries are typically better off than fellow minorities lower down on the socioeconomic ladder who lack the wherewithal to access affirmative action. This is objectionable, so the argument runs, because presumably those lower down on the ladder continue to suffer more than affirmative action beneficiaries from the present effects of past racial oppression. Yet it is precisely those who are suffering less who are reaping the most benefit from affirmative action as reparations. Moreover, they are imposing an opportunity cost on their more disadvantaged peers by siphoning attention and energy that would otherwise be more available to struggles that would more directly benefit lower-class racial minorities.[6]

A corollary objection is that the whites burdened by affirmative action are not responsible for the wrongs that reparatory affirmative action seeks to rectify. Opponents of affirmative action thus charge that "innocent" whites are being subjected to "reverse discrimination." Some object, moreover, that there is an unfair tilt regarding the incidence of the white burden. The whites who often lose out, it is claimed, are those on the margin, who hail from poorer, more vulnerable families than their wealthier, more secure white peers.[7]

What Is to Be Said in the Face of Objections?

Begin with recognizing that messy realities often confound the boundaries of received moral and legal doctrine. When that happens—and when there is simultaneously a felt need to address a perceived injustice—accommodations are made, imperfection is accepted, and reforms ensue. There was no legal mechanism in place to provide relief to victims of the horrific violence of the 9/11 attacks. Indeed, there were substantial arguments against providing relief. Why compensate these victims and not the victims of Timothy McVeigh? But because a desire to grant relief was sufficiently strong, reformers succeeded in establishing new laws, doctrines, and understandings to justify the compensatory intervention.[8]

Yes, the case for reparatory affirmative action would be stronger if all of its direct beneficiaries had themselves been *immediately* victimized by slavery or segregation, if all of its beneficiaries were the worst off among racial minorities, and if those disadvantaged by affirmative action had themselves perpetrated the wrongs whose remediation is sought. The absence of those precise conditions, however, should not be seen as dispositive. As Professor Kwame Anthony Appiah observes:

> The depressing truth is that almost every black person in the US has been the individual victim of racial wrongs.* But even if an exceptionally lucky black person should show up, what moral principle declares it wrong to adopt a policy that occasionally rewards the undeserving, if it normally awards the deserving? And, in any case, if you are worried about the tailoring of remedies to wrongs, why not draw attention to the black people who have suffered under-compensated wrongs? If the problem is the proper distribution of remedies, we should be as worried about under-compensating as about over-compensating.[9]

If one must choose between being overcompensatory as opposed to being undercompensatory, why not, as Appiah suggests, choose the former?

Furthermore, contrary to what is often suggested, a substantial number of affirmative action beneficiaries have been direct victims of massive racial wrongs. This includes any black person who attended segregated schools prior to *Brown v. Board of Education* or who attended schools that remained segregated in defi-

---

* Appiah was echoing Justice Thurgood Marshall, who had previously insisted that "it is necessary in twentieth-century America to have individual Negroes demonstrate that they have been victims of racial discrimination; the racism of our society has been so pervasive that none, regardless of wealth or position, has managed to escape its impact." *Regents of the University of California v. Bakke,* 438 U.S. 265, 400 (opinion of Marshall, J.)

ance of *Brown*. That category alone covers a sizable proportion of those who have benefited from affirmative action since the 1960s. Often in discussions about reparatory affirmative action, slavery is advanced as the all-important historic wrong. As Professor Boris Bittker noted years ago, however, there is good reason to put Jim Crow segregation at the center of the case.*[10] Slavery strikes many as an ancient wrong concerning which the victims and perpetrators are all long dead. By contrast, segregation is part of the lived experience of millions. It persisted full-blown in some locales into the 1960s, and its remnants are still highly visible today.

Then there is the matter of indirect victims. The children, grandchildren, and great-grandchildren of the immediate victims of segregation are indirect victims in that they have been demonstrably injured by the racial injustices visited upon their ancestors. They have lost out in terms of inherited financial wealth, access to education, and access to human capital (e.g., friends or relatives who can convey valuable information or offer useful occupational connections).[11]

An oft heard complaint against affirmative action is that it typically helps the most privileged among racial minorities, neglecting those most injured by the continuing effects of past discrimination.[12] The strength of this complaint depends on the design of the affirmative action program in question. Earlier in the history of affirmative action in higher education, officials

---

* The federal government and the states were *not* acting in blatant violation of the United States Constitution when they permitted, encouraged, and participated in Negro slavery. By contrast, the federal government and the states did act in blatant violation of the United States Constitution when, even after the Reconstruction Amendments, they joined with private parties in imposing upon blacks and other racial minorities a cruel and all-encompassing pigmentocracy in which colored skin became the target for humiliation, calumny, ostracism, insult, deprivation, and violence.

appear to have made more of an effort than evident currently to allocate assistance to poorer elements in minority communities.*
Recall that the affirmative action program at the University of California–Davis School of Medicine that was struck down by the Supreme Court in its *Bakke* decision of 1978 was open only to racial minorities who were "disadvantaged." But even "disadvantaged" racial-minority applicants to medical school are privileged in comparison with peers who fail to graduate from high school, let alone college.

To some extent, affirmative action's privileging of better-off racial minorities stems from an accommodation between, on the one hand, demands for reparatory justice and, on the other hand, the present functional needs of institutions. The former counsels making higher education available to underprepared racial minorities even at the high cost of remedial instruction. The latter counsels making higher education available only to racial minorities already prepared to take advantage of the opportunity. Affirmative action often represents a rough compromise between these two alternatives.†

While this compromise privileges the better-off among people of color, it also often redounds to the betterment of the group as a whole by facilitating the emergence of a vanguard that will

* In 1972, more than half of blacks entering elite colleges came from families in the bottom half of the socioeconomic distribution. By 1982 the proportion was down to a quarter. By 1992 the proportion was down to 8 percent. Two-thirds of the blacks at elite colleges in 1992 came from the top elite of the American socioeconomic distribution. Richard Sander and Stuart Taylor, Jr., *Mismatch* (2012), 248.

† In South Africa, legislation provides that the absence alone of certain qualifications is an insufficient reason for declining to hire a person eligible for affirmative action. The employer "may not unfairly discriminate against a person solely on the basis of that person's lack of relevant experience." The employer must determine the candidate's "capacity to acquire, within a reasonable time, the ability to do the job." See South African Employment Equity Act, No. 55 of 1998. See also Daniel Sabbagh, "Affirmative Action," in Michel Rosenfeld and Andras Sajo, eds., *The Oxford Handbook of Comparative Constitutional Law* (2012), 1131.

promote group uplift. This is a theory that has manifested itself repeatedly—from W. E. B. DuBois's "talented tenth" to Charles Hamilton Houston's "social engineers."[13] Under this theory, the enhanced opportunity that relatively privileged racial minorities receive redounds not only, and perhaps not principally, to their own personal benefit, but redounds to the benefit of their group and, more generally, to the benefit of society as a whole.[14] Given prevailing social dynamics, the power, wealth, connections, and prestige that accrue to the talented tenth will be shared with non-elite minorities. The success of affirmative action beneficiaries will inspire other people of color and erode damaging stereotypes. This is why it is important to be careful in selecting the beneficiaries of racial affirmative action. Poor performance on their part can be dispiriting and reinforce stereotypes. Thus, the fact that relatively privileged racial minorities frequently enjoy greater access than their racial peers to resources that nurture superior performance in selective institutions should not be seen as a reason for dispreferring them. If *racial* rectification is the aim, then it may well be that racial elites are the best agents for carrying out the mission. Regardless of their own aims, elite racial beneficiaries of affirmative action will unavoidably serve as closely scrutinized "firsts" or "seconds," widening the possibilities of a nascent and still vulnerable racial-minority vanguard that is expected to advance the fortunes of racial minorities in general.*

---

* "The most important purpose that can be served by ethnicity-based [positive discrimination] in admissions to [higher educational institutions] is not to redistribute educational opportunities from the rich to the poor. Instead it is to reduce identity-based differentials in access to the upper strata of a society, that is, to integrate the societal elite." Thomas E. Weisskopf, "Rethinking Affirmative Action in Admissions to Higher Educational Institutions" in Zoya Hasan and Martha C. Nussbaum, eds., *Equalizing Access: Affirmative Action in Higher Education in India, United States, and South Africa* (2012), 48.

The complaint that affirmative action wrongly benefits blacks who are already privileged tends to misportray the African American middle class, making it seem richer and more secure than it is. Arguing that affirmative action is no longer needed, its enemies refer constantly to black celebrities who are already among the society's winners. These lucky few, however, constitute an infinitesimal sliver of the black population. Much more characteristic are the people who constitute the great bulk of the black middle class—teachers, social workers, and postal agents on the low end and lawyers, engineers, and physicians on the high end. It is true that this group is better off than blacks further down the socioeconomic totem pole. It is also true, though, that the black middle class continues to suffer from a variety of impediments, rooted in racism, that put members of the black middle class in a position subordinate to their white counterparts. Middle-class black people bear injuries, often hidden, that stem in large part from racial mistreatment, injuries that are passed on from one generation to the next, injuries that warrant redress on a variety of grounds, including that of reparatory justice.[15]

The fact remains, however, that racial affirmative action plans typically offer more direct benefit to privileged, as opposed to disadvantaged, racial minorities. That differential does not stem solely from the actions of white authorities in higher education, business, and government. It also stems from the actions of racial-minority communities, more specifically the upper strata of those communities, which have greater access to resources—money, organization, connections, education, etc.—that enable them to advance their interests over those of their poorer racial counterparts. Every large affirmative action regime encounters the problem of relatively privileged sectors of beneficiary groups seizing an excessive portion of the affirmative action pie.[16]

The Left Critique of Affirmative Action

Detractors on the left have long attacked affirmative action for its class bias.* They charge that affirmative action benefits relatively privileged blacks while ignoring or benefiting only tenuously the black poor, that it is a glorified tokenism that buys off talented blacks who might otherwise provide leadership to a grassroots insurgency, and that it ruins the prospects for interracial populism.† Proponents of this critique prefer redistributive reforms framed by socioeconomic class boundaries. Their mantra is "class not race."

Key features of the Left Critique have long been voiced by figures on the right.[17] Sheer opportunism, however, frequently explains right-wing objections on these grounds. Figures who typically evince little or no constructive sympathy whatsoever for the black poor all of a sudden become their putative champions for the limited purpose of discrediting affirmative action. My suspicion is that when that mission is accomplished, they will renege on their promise to support nonracial, class-based

* See Richard Kahlenberg, *The Remedy: Class, Race, and Affirmative Action* (1996). See also William Julius Wilson, *The Bridge Over the Racial Divide: Rising Inequality and Coalition Politics* (2001); Michael Lind, *The Next American Nation: The New Nationalism & the Fourth American Revolution* (1995); Robert L. Allen, *Black Awakening in Capitalist America: An Analytic History* (1969).

† Since the early 1970s, some progressive critics of affirmative action have muted their complaints. Dismissive of affirmative action when more radical alternatives seemed possible, they have become more sympathetic toward affirmative action as it has come under increasingly hostile pressure from the Right. See Jennifer Hochschild, "Affirmative Action as Culture War," in Robert Post and Michael Rogin, eds., *Race and Representation: Affirmative Action* (1998), 348: "In the 1960s some on the left saw affirmative action as an individualistic sell-out, encouraging personal mobility . . . at the expense of structural transformation that would benefit the whole group. What happened to that view?"

reform and instead adopt their more usual posture: defending the current maldistribution of wealth, opportunity, and power in America. Even if that suspicion is correct, however, it does not address those who propound the Left Critique in good faith. It is to that task that I now turn.

I begin with a concession: the Left Critique contains strong points. Racial affirmative action is limited in that it often directly assists only those who are already positioned to take advantage of enlarged opportunities. To be sure, affirmative action is not solely a vehicle for elites. Tens of thousands of racial-minority firefighters, police officers, corrections personnel, craft workers, and lower-level office workers owe their positions to affirmative action.[18] But even these beneficiaries are situated in the higher ranks of the working class. Rarely does affirmative action directly embrace the lower ranks of the working class or those who have lost a grip on employment altogether.

Furthermore, there is considerable power to the claim that the campaign to promote and defend affirmative action has absorbed an inordinate amount of limited resources. Consider the remarkable amount of ink, attention, money, and energy that has been spent on racial affirmative action in higher education, even though the people who directly benefit reside in the most privileged strata of racial minorities. To be a candidate for admission to medical school or law school or merely college, one must first be a high school graduate. But large numbers of minority youth do not finish high school. And among those who do, large numbers fail to receive educations that enable them to be plausible candidates for selective colleges or universities. Racial affirmative action in higher education, in short, has little direct bearing on the fate of most minority youth, even though it has consumed much of the energy available for dealing with problems confronting racial-minority youth. The plight of minority youth, particularly those trapped in black ghettos, is pointed to for the purposes of initiating or defending affirmative action. Yet the truly disadvantaged are not the primary beneficiaries of positive racial selectivity in higher education.

Another argument of the left critique of affirmative action is that the struggle to protect it not only absorbs excessive resources but, perhaps even worse, facilitates acquiescence to an inadequate response to ongoing inequities. "So long as the Band-Aid of affirmative action dominates the debate," Anne Hudson-Price observes, "policy makers are excused from confronting the wound underneath."[19] Defenders of affirmative action, she charges, tend to exaggerate its benefits to justify its existence. Moreover, their fear of losing affirmative action dissuades them from being sufficiently open to the experimentation that will be required to uncover better alternatives. "[R]eliance on old solutions may be handicapping us from developing new methodologies." To critics on the left, die-hard defenders of affirmative action have become all too conservative.

The complaint about excessive caution should be taken to heart. Affirmative action does have important drawbacks that can only be minimized or avoided by a process of experimentation. Experiments entail risks. Not only is it possible that envisioned improvements will prove to be mistaken. It is also possible that in the process one will lose the existing benefit one was seeking to enhance. Many proponents of affirmative action are especially sensitive to such risks in an environment in which affirmative action is surrounded by powerful enemies.

Sensible experiments that address weaknesses of conventional racial affirmative action ought to be tried so long as they pose no undue threat to the underlying program. Hence, no alarm should be triggered by efforts to supplement conventional racial affirmative action with efforts to extend it to poorer sectors of minority communities and to the disadvantaged generally, regardless of race. Proponents of racial equity should enthusiastically support initiatives aimed at securing more equity along the class divide. "Race *and* class" is thus a suitable banner for affirmative action reform.

There are, however, several reasons to eschew the "class *not* race" position.* Any solely class-based affirmative action program *that is likely to be enacted* in the current political environment will likely fail to meet adequately the requirements of racial justice. One problem stems from the fact that, in many contexts, blacks of modest means are not only outnumbered by whites of modest means but also far surpassed by them in terms of education, skills, and overall preparedness to take advantage of widened opportunities for schooling and employment. This is so in part because of observable (though oft neglected) differences in the circumstances of whites and blacks of the same income level. Frequently there is a large difference in *wealth* that distinguishes blacks and whites whose incomes are similar. A white family earning $50,000 per year may seem at first blush to be the socioeconomic peers of a black family earning the same income. When other considerations—value of housing, equity in housing, character of neighborhood, familial experience with higher education, access to valuable social networks, etc.—are taken into account, however, it becomes clear that, typically, whites of a given income level are considerably wealthier than blacks of that same level.[20] Blacks, moreover, are also often afflicted by

* Among commentators discussing the relationship of class to race in affirmative action policy, the one from whom I have learned the most is Professor Deborah Malamud. See "Class Privilege in Legal Education: A Response to Sender," *Denver University Law Review* 88 (2011): 729; "Affirmative Action, Diversity, and the Black Middle Class," *University of Colorado Law Review* 68 (1997): 939; "Class Based Affirmative Action: Lesson and Caveats," *Texas Law Review* 74 (1996): 1847.

a variety of hidden injuries that lead to circumstances in which, contrary to the usual socioeconomic pattern, whites who are poor outperform middle-class or even affluent blacks.[21]

One response is to create interventions sensitive to the racial dimensions of class stratification. At the UCLA School of Law, for example, in the aftermath of Proposition 209, officials instituted a program that one of its designers describes as "a system of race-neutral class-based preferences."[22] Aware of the special vulnerabilities of blacks and Latinos because of the intersecting influence of class and race, organizers of the UCLA program commendably devised indicia of socioeconomic status that measured more than mere income. Additional indicia included parents' educational attainments, parents' assets, and the zip code in which a youngster lived during high school. In other words, law school officials sought to identify blacks and Latinos, but without saying that expressly.

I applaud the effort to mitigate the racial damage caused by Proposition 209. I applaud, too, the aim to channel affirmative action more directly to poorer racial minorities. Racial affirmative action needs to be better targeted. But we also need to be clear that the program under discussion is a version of *racial* affirmative action regardless of efforts to hide that fact. That program, viewed realistically, is not an example of "class not race" but is instead an example of race-conscious, class-focused redistribution with racial indicia erased from its exterior.

Some proponents of "class not race" apparently believe that an absence of explicit racial selectivity will save their proposals from white backlash. They err. Eligibility rules that say nothing explicitly about race but are wealth sensitive will still draw fire from detractors who will claim that the rules camouflage a racial Trojan horse—a policy primarily aimed at helping racial minorities while helping needy whites as a cover. In some instances, such claims will be accurate. After all, some proponents of "class not race" have admitted that their main concern is to help the black needy. Convinced that racial affirmative action as conventionally designed is inadequate "to address the problem of [the] disadvantaged" in racial-minority communities, Professor William Julius Wilson once proposed—he has subsequently changed his mind[23]—a "comprehensive program that . . . features universal as opposed to race-or-group-specific strategies."[24] He called his alternative "the hidden agenda." That agenda, he noted, was "to enhance the chances in life for the ghetto [i.e., black] underclass by emphasizing programs to which the more advantaged groups of all class and racial backgrounds can positively relate."[25] In other words, some proponents of class-not-race admit that the absence of overt racial selectivity in programs they propose is merely strategic: the price to be paid for white support and the avoidance of white opposition.*

But even when concern with race is not the primary driving force behind a program, if it turns out to assist racial minorities disproportionately, one can expect it to be attacked as racial affirmative action in disguise. This is the fate that has befallen social assistance programs that were truly nonracial in origin and application—think of the racial stigmatization of "welfare" in the 1960s, '70s, and '80s.[26] It will surely be the fate of social assistance programs that are aimed at helping the racial-minority needy, albeit through so-called race-neutral means. Up to now, race-silent programs animated largely by a desire to assist racial minorities have fared well in the court of public opinion. I am thinking here of programs such as the one in Texas, which offers

* Shouldn't one wonder about the efficacy of publicly announcing "a hidden agenda"?

automatic admission to the state university system to anyone in the top 10 percent of his or her high school graduating class. I anticipate more controversy, however, as opponents publicize and attack the racial aims that lie just beneath these programs' ostensibly nonracial exteriors.

Let me summarize my main point: the single most powerful argument in favor of racial affirmative action is that it seeks to rectify, at least partially, injuries that continue to put certain racial minorities at a competitive disadvantage with white peers. It is a policy to which objections can sensibly be raised. On balance, though, the arguments in its favor should be deemed to outweigh those against. Making amends for past wrongs is not, however, the only basis for affirmative action. It is to other justifications and criticisms of them that I now turn.

Affirmative Action for "Diversity"

A second major rationale for affirmative action is "diversity." Devotees of diversity argue that teaching, learning, and decision making will typically be richer, more informed, and better received if a wide array of people affiliated with salient social groupings participate together in carrying out the missions of the nation's schools, workplaces, and governments. The catalytic event in the history of "diversity" is the Supreme Court's ruling in 1978 in *Regents of the University of California v. Bakke.* In *Bakke,* the pivotal opinion by Justice Lewis F. Powell declared that the goal of creating diversity, including racial diversity, on a university campus is a compelling justification for properly designed racial selectivity in admissions.* After *Bakke,* "diver-

* For a fuller discussion of *Bakke,* see pages 182–205.

sity" became deeply influential throughout American society, including academia, philanthropy, the military, and business. Indicative of this influence is the presence of leading figures in these sectors as amici curiae in affirmative action disputes before the Supreme Court.

In 2003, in the University of Michigan affirmative action litigation, sixty-five leading American businesses (including American Express, Coca-Cola, and Microsoft) submitted an amicus curiae brief to the Supreme Court in support of the university's affirmative action programs. They declared:

> In the experience of *amici,* individuals who have been educated in a diverse setting are more likely to succeed, because they can make valuable contributions to the workforce in several important and concrete ways. First, a diverse group of individuals educated in a cross-cultural environment has the ability to facilitate unique and creative approaches to problem-solving, arising from the integration of different perspectives. Second, such individuals are better able to develop products and services that appeal to a variety of consumers and to market offerings in ways that appeal to those consumers. Third, a racially diverse group of managers with cross-cultural experience is better able to work with business partners, employees, and clientele in the United States and around the world. Fourth, individuals who have been educated in a diverse setting are likely to contribute to a positive work environment, by decreasing incidents of discrimination and stereotyping. Overall, an educational environment that ensures participation by diverse people, viewpoints, and ideas will help produce the most talented workforce.[27]

In the same cases, a group of civilians and retired military officers deeply involved in national defense (including several former chairmen of the Joint Chiefs of Staff and two former secretaries of Defense) also submitted a brief in support of the University of Michigan affirmative action program, maintaining that:

> Based on decades of experience, *amici* have concluded that a highly qualified, racially diverse officer corps educated and trained to command our nation's racially diverse enlisted ranks is essential to the military's ability to fulfill its principal mission to provide national security. . . . The military must be permitted to train and educate a diverse officer corps to further our compelling government interest in an effective military.[28]

In 2012, in litigation involving affirmative action at the University of Texas, the deans of the Harvard and Yale schools of law submitted a brief to the Supreme Court urging it to reaffirm the legitimacy of tailored affirmative action in the service of diversity. They declared:

> In our educational judgment, law students who pursue careers both within and outside the legal profession will inevitably interact with increasingly diverse clients, managers, and colleagues. Our commitment as educators is to create the educational environment best suited to prepare our students to succeed in this new world. In our view, diversity is associated with better educational outcomes.
>
> Diverse teams are better at solving a variety of problems when compared with homogeneous groups, even when rated higher on standard ability measures.[29]

While these distinguished figures may be sincere in their attestations, other considerations also play a role in their statements. Most important is the tremendous sway over thought and speech exerted by a Supreme Court that has been willing to accept affirmative action for purposes of diversity but not for other purposes, such as the rectification of societal discrimination. The Court's rulings have given authorities a strong incentive to engage in diversity talk.[30] The consequence of this incentive is especially evident in academia. Inasmuch as the Supreme Court upheld affirmative action plans based on diversity grounds, academic officials have become practiced in explaining such plans in terms of diversity, regardless of their actual aims.

There are other reasons that account for the popularity of the diversity rationale. It is widely seen as answering the felt need to ensure the presence of appreciable numbers of racial minorities in strategic positions of influence while apparently damping down toxic side effects of racial selectivity. One unadvertised attraction is that the diversity rationale is nonaccusatory. Affirmative action based on grounds of compensatory justice always entails an assumption or a finding of culpability for some past or present wrong. The diversity rationale, by contrast, depends on no predicate of misconduct or unfairness and thus minimizes the anger ignited when whites are accused of complicity in wrongdoing as the heirs of oppressors, the beneficiaries of racial privilege, or the perpetrators of their own misdeeds.[31]

Another attraction is that the diversity rationale explains affirmative action not as a special aid to racial minorities or a requirement of distributive fairness but rather as a requirement for better goods, products, and services that will presumably benefit the organizations that see diversity as a boon to their self-interest as well as to the society as a whole. Businesspeople love to say that "diversity is good for the bottom line." Many of them would be ideologically allergic to a business practice based solely on notions of justice or altruism. They are much more comfortable supporting a program they can promote as reinforcing the principal mission of their enterprise. For them, diversity is no do-gooder effort to right wrongs but rather a pragmatic initiative to do what it takes to make organizations better able to carry out core functions.*

The diversity rationale is also alluring because it facilitates the evasion of prickly subjects. It allows whites to avoid grappling with their status as beneficiaries of past wrongs (although some observers are suspicious of the diversity rationale precisely because they see it as letting white society off the moral hook of a racist history). But the diversity rationale also facilitates the evasion of a subject that makes many blacks uncomfortable: the *fact*—not the biased perception, but the sometimes discouraging *fact*—that pursuant to affirmative action, blacks selected for valued positions often have records that are inferior to those of white competitors. This does not mean that black beneficiaries of affirmative action are "unqualified"—a flash word in the affirmative action wars. It simply means that, at least under conventional measures of assessment, affirmative action plans select qualified blacks who are less qualified than at least some of their white competitors.

Many proponents of affirmative action detest discussing this aspect of the controversy; when it arises in college or law school classes, a silent, bitter, embarrassed pall often envelops the room, with black students feeling and exuding a special sense of shame and anger. Few things grate more on the sensibilities of blacks, especially those in the upper echelons, than hearing whites in authority talk about how far down they must reach to obtain minority individuals who are merely satisfactory. Even if the white

---

* The management of Coca-Cola has said that it regards "diversity in the background of talent of [its] associates as a competitive advantage." Similarly, the management of the Chrysler Corporation remarked that "workforce diversity" was its "competitive advantage," cautioning that its "success as a global community [was] as dependent on utilizing the wealth of backgrounds, skills and opinions that a diverse workforce offers as it [was dependent] on raw materials, technology, and processes." Quoted in Sanford Levinson, *Wrestling with Diversity* (2003), 22.

person in question is a vocal supporter of affirmative action, the black auditor will often bridle upon hearing that standards had to be lowered to assure the selection of black candidates.

The diversity rationale moves the spotlight from the perceived deficiencies of blacks to their perceived strengths. Other rationales accentuate blacks' comparative weakness by defending the selection of racial-minority candidates even if they were, in conventional terms, inferior to competitors and even if choosing them required sacrificing some degree of efficiency in the carrying out of the institution's mission. The diversity rationale, by contrast, posits that racial-minority candidates chosen over *apparently* superior white candidates are actually better qualified than their white competitors when the special qualities of minority perspective, experience, and voice are properly taken into account.

Unlike other justifications for affirmative action that seek to justify *exceptions* to meritocracy, the diversity rationale is consistent with meritocratic premises.* It does not concede that for reasons extrinsic to the mission of an institution minority candidates should be chosen who are less capable or accomplished than white competitors. Rather, the diversity rationale contends that conventional indicia of talent, achievement, and potential must be supplemented by other indicators that have heretofore been overlooked. Under the diversity rationale, affirmative action is tied to meritocracy because, to paraphrase Harvard College, such racial selectivity brings to an enterprise (student body, faculty, board of directors, slate of honorary degree recipients, edi-

---

* "The diversity model offers a non-stigmatizing account of why members of targeted racial groups are preferred: they bring valuable features to the institution—epistemic diversity—that advance the institution's mission. This is a meritocratic rationale, which represents the targets of affirmative action as contributing, deserving agents rather than pitiful subjects of an institution's beneficence. It gives other participants positive reasons to value the presence of affirmative action's beneficiaries." Terry H. Anderson, *The Pursuit of Fairness: A History of Affirmative Action* (2004), 142.

torial board, etc.) something that white candidates cannot offer. Diversity is thus predicated on the idea that racial-minority status carries with it useful sources of information. Indeed, the most striking and historically significant aspect of the diversity rationale is that it enables coloredness for the first time in American history to be seen as a valuable credential. Instead of the presence of blacks or other racial minorities constituting a necessary punishment in expiation of past sins, the diversity rationale makes their presence a positive good.*

THE REACTION AGAINST "DIVERSITY"

In the marketplace of political culture, few terms have amassed more influence as quickly as "diversity." Were it tradable as stock, its price would have soared over the past three decades. Perhaps the most striking indication of its prestige is the way it is handled by influential *opponents* of affirmative action. Theodore Olson, the solicitor general of the United States during the George W. Bush administration, was a fervent foe who argued on behalf of the federal government that the programs at issue in the University of Michigan litigation violated the federal Constitution. Olson, however, took pains to defer to "diversity's" iconic status. "Ensuring that public institutions . . . are open and accessible to a broad and diverse array of individuals, including individuals of all races and ethnicities, is an important and entirely legitimate government objective," Olson averred. "Measures that ensure diversity . . . are important components of govern-

---

* Under the diversity rationale, the preferred applicant "does the *institution* a favor, enriches the institution, brings to it the positive asset of new perspectives. The diversity rationale thus frees affirmative action from its 'necessary evil' label. . . . When diversity is the rationale, the institution needs the applicant more than the applicant needs the institution." Rodney A. Smolla, "Affirmative Action in the Marketplace of Ideas," *Arkansas Law Review* 44 (1991): 935–36.

ment's responsibility to its citizens."[32] Like his solicitor general, President George W. Bush also opposed the affirmative action plans at the University of Michigan. Yet he, too, took care to genuflect to "diversity," declaring, "I strongly support diversity of all kinds, including racial diversity in higher education."[33]

There are those, however, who repudiate "diversity." They dispute claims that it demonstrably enhances learning, facilitates creativity, and inculcates a sense of cross-racial empathy. They note what they see as weaknesses in the empirical basis of these claims and point to studies that reach different conclusions.*

According to Justice Clarence Thomas, " 'diversity' . . . is more a fashionable catchphrase than it is a useful term."[34] Shelby Steele of the Hoover Institution scathingly remarks that "diversity" stands for a "spurious" notion that has given rise to a "parasitic" industry. Elaborating upon this critique, he says that "diversity" is "an administrative banality . . . an unexamined kitsch that whites (especially administrators and executives) use to dignify their use of racial preferences as they . . . engineer . . . a *look* of racial parity." Diversity, he concludes, "is a great American cynicism."[35] In *Diversity: The Invention of a Concept,* Professor Peter W. Wood argues that "it is time to retire diversity from the small company of concepts that guide our thinking about who we are as a people and how we might best reconcile our differences."[36] And that is the mild expression of his distaste. Elsewhere in his book, he mentions that he would like to be present at diversity's funeral. The critiques of "diversity" just noted arise from the right. An acerbic attack from the left is voiced by Walter Benn Michaels. In *The Trouble With Diversity:*

---

* See, e.g., Brief of Abigail Thernstrom, Stephen Thernstrom, Althea K. Nagai, and Russell Nieli as Amici Curiae in Support of Petitioners, *Fisher et al v. University of Texas at Austin,* Supreme Court of the United States (2012); Brian N. Lizotte, "The Diversity Rationale: Unprovable, Uncompelling," *Michigan Journal of Race and Law* 11 (2005): 625.

How We Learned to Love Identity and Ignore Inequality, Michaels argues that "the commitment to diversity is at best a distraction and at worst an essentially reactionary position."[37] Asserting disapprovingly that "diversity has become virtually a sacred concept," Michaels complains that all too many Americans "would much rather get rid of racism than get rid of poverty . . . would much rather celebrate cultural diversity than seek to establish economic equality."[38]

The diversity camp has long been dogged by allegations of insincerity or outright duplicity.[39] When Justice Powell announced his diversity rationale, detractors complained that he penalized the honesty of the University of California set-aside while valorizing the Harvard policy that reached essentially the same result under cover of an intentionally obfuscatory rhetoric. Furthermore, according to Professor Lino Graglia, Powell's opinion "was taken as little more than an invitation to fraud by nearly all colleges and universities."[40] Complainants have alleged that agents and facilitators of the diversity regime, including administrators, scholars, and judges, have knowingly misrepresented their handiwork. Critics charge that the extent of preference for racial minorities is greater than acknowledged, that the desired outcomes are more predetermined than admitted, and that the real animating force behind affirmative action has much more to do with other considerations—rectification, simply advancing the interests of beneficiary groups, or keeping social peace—than a true interest in "diversity." In a brief to the Supreme Court in the Michigan cases, a group of conservative, anti–affirmative action law professors complained that diversity talk "is generally used as a cover for direct racial decision-making."[41] Their charge was echoed by several of the justices, with Scalia and Rehnquist repeatedly referring to the affirmative action programs and their rationales as "sham[s]."[42] In the most recent affirmative action case to reach the Court, *Fisher v. University of Texas,* a loud refrain of those attacking the diversity rationale is that it is pretextual.[43]

Some proponents of affirmative action have reached the same conclusion. "I am increasingly dismayed," Professor Sanford Levinson reports, by "the costs to intellectual honesty of the felt need to shoehorn one's arguments into the language of 'diversity.'"[44] Professor Samuel Issacharoff remarks facetiously that "in the endless discussions of diversity, I have never heard the term seriously engaged on behalf of a Republican, a fundamentalist Christian, or a Muslim."[45] In an article entitled "Why No Preferences for Fundamentalist Christians or for Neo-Nazis?" Professor Jed Rubenfeld argues that the diversity rationale is mainly a ruse used to justify decisions that are actually made—and better made—on alternative grounds. "Everyone knows," Rubenfeld writes, "that in most cases a true diversity of perspectives and backgrounds is not really being pursued."[46]

I conclude this section with three observations about the debate over racial affirmative action for purposes of diversity. First, while there are some who invoke this rationale insincerely—I will turn to them in a moment—others genuinely believe what they say about diversity's virtues. Among these are people who initially embraced diversity only strategically but then, eventually, with the benefit of observation, came to realize that, in at least certain settings, diversity does indeed enhance teaching, learning, and decision making. I include myself in this group. I remain doubtful about social scientific "proof" of diversity's value; much of that seems exaggerated and pre-determined with litigation in mind. I am convinced, however, based on my own experience and the testimony of observers in whom I have confidence, that in at least certain settings learning is enriched by racial diversity. I have seen firsthand the intellectual deprivation suffered by white law students consigned to racially homogeneous classes. In the absence of black and Latino students, discussions regarding large swaths of law were obviously and painfully impoverished. Diversity, then, is a suitable justification for affirmative action so long as the demands and expectations imposed upon it are not too onerous. The diversity rationale is not as strong a justification as others that are propounded. But it is a valid justification nonetheless.

Second, with respect to insincerity, a candid word needs to be said about the limits of candor. "We would be dishonest," Guido Calabresi sagely declares, "if we failed to recognize that at times total candor is not desired or desired by society."[47] No decision rendered by the United States Supreme Court is more honored than *Brown v. Board of Education*. The *Brown* decision, however, is far from candid. Its author, Chief Justice Earl Warren, carefully avoided identifying forthrightly the evil that de jure segregation represented.* Moreover, the decision was positively misleading to the extent that it suggested that the historical record is unclear regarding whether the overwhelming majority of those who designed and ratified the Fourteenth Amendment intended to prohibit de jure racial segregation.[48] The Court found the historical record "inconclusive" not as a matter of scholarly accuracy but rather as a strategy aimed at easing the way to a ruling that would go far toward undermining a monstrous injustice.† A decade later, proponents of what

---

* Chief Justice Warren informed his colleagues that he planned to write an opinion that was "short, readable, unemotional and, above all, non-accusatory." Quoted in Dennis J. Hutchinson, "Unanimity and Desegregation: Decision-making in the Supreme Court, 1948–1958," *Georgetown Law Journal* 68 (1979): 1, 42.
† The Court's misleading handling of history is even more pronounced in its famous ruling in *Loving v. Commonwealth of Virginia,* 388 U.S. 1 (1967) invalidating state laws

became the Civil Rights Act of 1964 had to make a choice. On one hand they could state that the legislation they supported was primarily based on the Fourteenth Amendment's grant of Congressional authority to enforce the Equal Protection Clause. On the other hand, they could assert that the legislation they supported was primarily based on the Interstate Commerce Clause. The former explanation was truer but riskier. The latter was evasive but safe. The principal backers of the legislation chose the latter route, which won acceptance when tested by litigation.*[49]

All of those episodes should be saddening to some extent in that they show well-intentioned people engaging in subterfuge out of a felt need to skirt volatile issues that are the legacy of racist misconduct. But one ought not denounce them. One ought, instead, denounce the circumstances that made candor unduly costly in terms of jeopardizing reforms that advance social justice.† The most regrettable feature of the diversity controversy is not the dissimulation of certain proponents but the profoundly mistaken Supreme Court jurisprudence that pushed outside the pale of legitimacy rationales for affirmative action that are at least as sound as the diversity rationale.

Third, one ought be careful about charges of insincerity given the ambiguous and changing character of the diversity rationale itself. Although Justice Powell posited a definition of "diversity" that appeared to distinguish it from other, more familiar ratio-

---

that prohibited interracial marriage. See Randall Kennedy, *Interracial Intimacies: Sex, Marriage, Identity and Adoption* (2003), 249–54.

* Objecting to the Kennedy administration's decision to base constitutional authority for the Civil Rights Act on the Commerce Clause rather than the Fourteenth Amendment, Professor Gerald Gunther complained that the "proposed end-run . . . suggests an inclination toward disingenuousness, cynicism, and trickery as to constitutional principles [by the] Law Department of the United States." Quoted in Christopher W. Schmidt, "The Sit-Ins and the State Action Doctrine," *William & Mary Bill of Rights Journal* 18 (2010): 767, 811.

† See the excellent exploration of this subject by David L. Shapiro, "In Defense of Judicial Candor," *Harvard Law Review* 100 (1987): 731.

nales, perhaps that distinction was more apparent than real. Perhaps Powellian "diversity" in some of its facets always implicitly included ideas that it otherwise seemed to abjure. If that is so, then some who have been tagged as dishonest were not really being duplicitous but simply seizing upon a new rhetoric that continued to allow them to pursue aims consonant with those validated by Justice Powell in *Bakke* and then the Supreme Court as a whole in *Grutter*. If Justice Powell truly "invited" disingenuousness as some detractors of his diversity rationale charge, then perhaps the response received should be seen not as fraud but complicity in a subtle diplomatic choreography in which the Court itself is playing a leading part. A notable feature of Powell's *Bakke* opinion was its unspoken message. What it seemed to be saying to universities, Calabresi observed, was that "if you are not blatant, if you cause no scandal, if you let us reconcile what you are doing with grounds that can be acceptable to most, we will let you work out your own quiet compromise between our deeply held but irreconcilable ideals."[50] All that is lost by such an approach, Calabresi ventured, is candor.

Furthermore, it bears noting that Justice Powell's diversity rationale has been considerably broadened by the interpretation put upon it by Justice O'Connor in *Grutter*. To the extent that there was a difference between Powellian diversity and the actual (but muted) aims of administrators in the field, that difference has been substantially lessened by O'Connor's capacious reformulation of diversity's aims and justifications.

Affirmative Action for Integration

Some proponents of affirmative action justify it primarily as a means of facilitating the racial integration of American society.[51] They posit integration as a condition in which people of various races participate together equitably and harmoniously in all of the society's major activities. They are willing to use race-conscious measures to effectuate that condition. They aim to ensure that the multiracial character of the population is reflected in all key institutions. They approve of using race-conscious measures to bring into play people affiliated with groups that have long been excluded. But they also approve of using race-conscious measures to bring into play people affiliated with groups that have not faced historical exclusion but find themselves marginalized nonetheless—e.g., recent immigrants.

The sentiments animating champions of integrative affirmative action vary. Some are moved by a belief that fairness in a multiracial democracy requires the representative presence of all or at least many of the groups that make up society. This appears to be what President Clinton had in mind when he insisted that he wanted to appoint a cabinet that "looked like America." The goal was not to mirror the demographics of the country according to some precise formula of proportionality; that would be impossible, given the number of available cabinet positions (twelve) and the number of racial and ethnic groupings in America (hundreds). Rather, the goal was largely symbolic: to make the cabinet sufficiently multiracial to signal to the public that the president was concerned about and open to the counsel of *all* Americans, including those affiliated with minority groups that have for various reasons found themselves isolated or marginalized. Attentiveness to this expressive function of integration and its hoped-for dividend—enhanced legitimation in the eyes of potentially disaffected onlookers—also showed up in the Supreme Court's *Grutter* decision. While Justice O'Connor's opinion for the Court is primarily a paean to diversity, it is secondarily an ode to integration, though she never uses the term. Elaborating on why racial affirmative action at the University of

Michigan Law School is constitutionally permissible, notwith-standing the Court's heavy presumption against racial selectivity, O'Connor insisted that "effective participation by members of all racial and ethnic groups in the civic life of our Nation is essential if the dream of one Nation, indivisible, is to be realized."[52]

AFFIRMATIVE ACTION AS A SUPPLEMENT TO ANTIDISCRIMINATION EFFORTS

Affirmative action has been justified in some quarters as a supplement to antidiscrimination efforts. Local, state, and federal laws prohibit invidious racial discrimination in contracting, the workplace, housing, public accommodations, education, and other contexts. All such laws, however, suffer from under-enforcement. To invoke an antidiscrimination law, one must first sense mistreatment—a perception that many victims do not have in light of their inability to compare their treatment with that of others. Seeking to protect one's rights through litigation, moreover, is expensive emotionally, financially, and in terms of time and effort. The ordeal of litigation is enough to dissuade even hardy individuals.

An argument for affirmative action is that it can usefully serve as a prophylactic device in service against illicit discrimination, preemptively addressing blockages that antidiscrimination law alone is unable to dislodge. The argument recognizes "the difficulty of avoiding discrimination in contexts organized around discriminatory habits and pervaded by group stigmatization." It supposes that "to do the right thing in the face of a contrary inclination, we must drag ourselves in the opposite direction, as an archer must aim against the wind to hit the bull's-eye."[53]

The antidiscrimination model of affirmative action has received some scholarly backing and a dollop of presidential and judicial encouragement.[54] "If there is evidence that discrimination still exists on a wide scale in ways that are conscious and unconscious," President Clinton asked rhetorically in 1995, "then why should we get rid of [affirmative action]?"[55] Later in that same speech (his famous "Mend it, don't end it" address), Clinton remarked: "Affirmative action should not go on forever. . . . But the evidence [of continuing] discrimination suggests, indeed screams" that the moment for cessation has not come. "The job of ending discrimination in this country is not over." Justice Ginsburg has also stressed the importance of affirmative action in the campaign against invidious discrimination. Concurring in the Supreme Court's decision to uphold the affirmative action plan at issue in *Grutter,* Justice Ginsburg observed that "[i]t is well documented that conscious and unconscious race bias, even rank discrimination based on race, remain alive in our land . . ."[56] To a large extent, however, the idea of affirmative action as prophylactic has played only a marginal role in the debate.

The Problem of the Disappointed White Candidate Who Feels Mistreated by Racial Affirmative Action

Whites who are disappointed by their failure to win coveted positions that they see Latinos and blacks attain often complain that they are victims of "reverse discrimination." They are, they say, innocent of complicity in racial wrongdoings that have harmed people of color. They also say that they are entitled to competitions in which people are judged on the basis of individual merit, by which they mean skills and accomplishments attributable to themselves and independent of race. In their view, considerations of race should have no place in the assessment of merit. They assert that it is profoundly wrong for them to be disadvantaged by arrangements in which racial minority status is counted as a "plus" while whiteness receives no such preference.

This perception of mistreatment and the anger and bitterness that flows from it are significant social costs that should be taken into account in calibrating the social utility of affirmative action. The precise extent of those costs are difficult to gauge. But that they are substantial is clear, given the force of the backlash against racial affirmative action.[57]

Though deep feelings of aggrievement may be beyond the reach of argument for some, it is possible that for others negative sentiments may be amenable to change, especially if the arguments made to them are based on appeals to norms of justice. For what stokes the outrage of some opponents of affirmative action is not only their sense of personal loss, but also their sense that they have been victimized. They often see themselves as innocent victims who have been robbed to benefit undeserving competitors who are false victims of long extinguished wrongs in which contemporary whites had no role.[58]

The first and most important thing to be said to them is that, as characteristically practiced, racial affirmative action is not unjust or violative of political morality because the "discrimination" that differentiates between whites and other races in this context is not *invidious*. Though affirmative action entails a modest narrowing of opportunities for whites in competitions for scarce, highly valued positions, this is in no way the result of an effort to humiliate, ostracize, or stigmatize whites. No one can plausibly believe that an affirmative action program signals that whites are thought to belong to an inferior race and must be kept "in their place." The disappointed white candidate should be told that racial affirmative action—unlike segregation—is not a policy aimed at expressing racial contempt, fear, or any other negative prejudice toward her race. Rather, it is a collective effort to address a major social problem: the continuing trauma of racial division in America. It is not unfair to enlist, to some extent, all Americans in that large, complex, and costly effort, including those who have had no hand in perpetrating racial wrongs. Membership in a polity entails contributing to the alleviation of its woes, just as it means sharing in the riches of its benefits. Americans who had nothing to do with the terrible injustice the United States government imposed on people of Japanese ancestry during World War II were required nonetheless, and rightly so, to contribute toward paying reparations to rectify the wrong done by the society in which they enjoy membership.[59]

All persons, including whites, have a right to freedom from racial subordination. But it strains credulity to contend that affirmative action (as characteristically practiced) is a form of racial subordination. As a practical matter, affirmative action could not have been instituted and cannot survive without at least the passive permission of a large sector of politically engaged whites. The story of affirmative action is largely the story of whites choosing to enlarge the number of Latinos and blacks in key institutions, with the consequence of decreasing the number of whites.[60] This has been done for a wide variety of purposes—diversity, integration, rectification, the purchase of social peace, legitimation—none of which involve putting whites down because of their race.

In terms of political morality, affirmative action for the purpose of assisting racial minorities disadvantages whites in a fashion similar to the way in which preferences for veterans disadvantage non-veterans, the way in which preferences for alumni disadvantage candidates whose parents are not alumni, the way in which preferences for athletes disadvantage non-athletes, the way in which preferences for in-state students disadvantage out-of-staters, the way in which preferences for those who are scientifically inclined disadvantages those who dislike science but love literature. Those who are disadvantaged in each of these cases and countless kindred examples can dispute the wisdom of the institutional preference that favors competitors. But they cannot, as the late professor Ronald Dworkin memorably and persuasively argued, claim a *right* to be judged absent consideration of the traits or circumstances that the preferences noted take into account.[61] They have a right to be judged according to the publicized criteria that advance the permissible goals determined by a given institution. But they do not have a right to set those goals unilaterally and thus determine for themselves what should count as "merit" for purposes of selecting the persons deemed to be most apt to further institutional goals.[62]

Disappointed opponents of affirmative action often tout their test scores and grade point averages as if those indicia of merit exhaust the spectrum of considerations that a school might properly take into account. If a college or university determines, however, that its institutional mission includes contributing to the task of racial rectification, inculcating within students a sense of multiracial solidarity, or facilitating transracial learning, then the race of a candidate would correctly be deemed to count as a feature relevant to assessing the comparative value of his or her likely contribution to a given student body.

Disappointed candidates sometimes evince an especially venomous antipathy for affirmative action because they see it as depriving them not only of valuable opportunities but also cheating them of their just deserts on behalf of those less deserving. They believe that if they have done better than a competitor in terms of conventional meritocratic criteria, fairness mandates that they prevail in the allocation of valued positions. They voice what the distinguished philosopher Michael Sandel describes as "the smug assumption . . . that success is the crown of virtue," that those on top are on top because they are more deserving than those below.[63] As another leading philosopher, John Rawls, observed, "no one deserves his greater natural capacity nor merits a more favorable starting place in society."[64] Many of the traits we most admire—intelligence, knowledge, creativity, insight—are not solely, often not even mainly, the fruit of our own effort but are instead offshoots of circumstances beyond one's control: inborn genius, health, caring parents, attentive teachers, a decent neighborhood. That is why discussions of university admissions and similar mechanisms of allocation need to be scrubbed clean of the excessively self-congratulatory individualism in which they tend to be steeped.* Affirmative action can assist with that task by making clear that "admission is not about an honor bestowed to reward superior merit or virtue. Neither the student with high test scores nor the student who comes from a disadvantaged minority group morally deserves to be admitted. Her admission is justified insofar as it contributes to the social purpose the university serves, not because it rewards the student for her merit or virtue, independently defined."[65]

Two additional points should be noted. One is that whites innocent of racial wrongdoing remain beneficiaries of it to the extent that they profit, albeit involuntarily, from historically embedded racial inheritances and the many privileges that accrue with the mere status of being white in a society that remains to a large extent a white-oriented pigmentocracy. Vocal

---

* I have contributed to the "excessively self-congratulatory individualism" to which I refer. See Randall Kennedy, "My Race Problem—and Ours," *The Atlantic Monthly*, May 1977, and "Racial Critiques of Legal Academia," *Harvard Law Review* 102 (1989): 1745.

about the ways in which they perceive themselves to be victims of reverse discrimination, whites angered by affirmative action rarely concede the advantages they enjoy by dint of their white-skin privilege.

The second point is that disappointed whites often overestimate the extent to which affirmative action decreases their chances of success and exaggerate the degree to which affirmative action played a role in a particular failure that they suffered. In university admissions, many white rejected applicants believe that they would have been admitted (1) if there had been no pro-minority affirmative action program and/or (2) if they had been non-white. Goodwin Liu demonstrated years ago, however, that that belief is frequently mistaken.[66] He calculated that with respect to certain selective schools, half of all rejected white applicants would have been turned down in the absence of affirmative action and would also have been turned down had they been non-white. Another large contingent of rejected whites would have been rejected in the absence of affirmative action but would have gained admission if they were racial-minority candidates.

Liu confirmed that affirmative action does substantially enhance the chances of racial minorities gaining admission to selective schools. What he also convincingly showed, however, is that often affirmative action does not substantially decrease the chances of any given white applicant, for the simple reason that there are many such applicants for each particular seat in a class that goes to someone helped by affirmative action. He found that "the admission of minority applicants and the rejection of white applicants are largely independent events."[67]

Though it may be comforting to proclaim that one would surely have been admitted had it not been for the minority candidate (or the legacy candidate or the athlete), the odds disagree.

Such proclamations, however, will continue to be voiced. While it is fallacious to assert that racial affirmative action causes the displacement of large numbers of rejected white applicants, the claim is nonetheless potent. It focuses resentment against an important vehicle of redistributivist reform and provides as well an all-purpose salve for the hurt feelings of disappointed whites.

DOES AFFIRMATIVE ACTION HELP OR HURT ITS BENEFICIARIES?

A damning argument, potentially, against affirmative action is that it hurts its putative beneficiaries more than it helps them. The argument features several claims. One is that affirmative action cripplingly stigmatizes its beneficiaries and, indeed, anyone affiliated with groups that are perceived as eligible for affirmative action assistance. A second is that affirmative action systematically overpromotes beneficiaries, putting them in positions for which they are ill-prepared, setting them up for destructive defeat in competition against better-prepared peers.

These objections are weighty. Some defenders of affirmative action, fearful of making any concessions, argue as if affirmative action poses no costs, entails no risks, involves no dangers. The reality is far different. Barbara Bergman rightly observes that "just as all potent medications have side effects, affirmative action may [also] have some results that are bad." The issue "is the balance of good and bad: are the bad effects . . . so pervasive and harmful that they outweigh whatever good might be accomplished?"[68]

THE STIGMA OBJECTION

The most well-known basis for claiming that affirmative action is more hurtful than helpful to its supposed beneficiaries is that it stigmatizes them.[69] Several Supreme Court justices have made allusion to this asserted cost. In his *Bakke* opinion, Justice Powell declared, "Preferential programs may only reinforce common stereotypes holding that certain groups are unable to achieve success without special protection based on a factor having no relationship to individual worth."[70] Echoing Powell, Justice O'Connor averred, in *City of Richmond v. J. A. Croson Co.*, "Classifications based on race carry a danger of stigmatic harm . . . they may in fact promote notions of racial inferiority."[71] Dissenting in *Metro Broadcasting v. FCC,* Justice Kennedy maintained that "special preferences can . . . foster the view that members of the favored group are inherently less able to compete on their own."[72]

It is Justice Clarence Thomas, however, who has voiced this theme most persistently, aggressively, and personally, stating that affirmative action "programs stamp minorities with a badge of inferiority" and complaining that "so-called 'benign' discrimination teaches many that . . . minorities cannot compete with them without their patronizing indulgence."*[73] His animosity toward affirmative action is wildly ironic in that it is hard to imagine anyone who has benefited more than he has from affirmative action. President George H. W. Bush intimated that race had nothing to do with the decision to select Thomas to fill the

---

* Inveighing against an affirmative action plan at the University of Michigan Law School, Justice Thomas wrote: "It is uncontested that each year, the Law School admits a handful of blacks who would be admitted in the absence of racial discrimination [by which Thomas means affirmative action]. Who can differentiate between those who belong and those who do not? The majority of blacks are admitted to the Law School because of discrimination, and because of this policy all are tarred as undeserving." Generalizing his point, Thomas asserted that when blacks take positions in the highest places of government, industry, or academia, it is an open question today whether their skin color played a part in their advancement. The question itself is the stigma. *Grutter v. Bollinger,* 539 U.S. 306, 373 (2003) (Thomas, J., dissenting).

seat vacated by the retirement of Justice Thurgood Marshall. But that can be believed only by dint of the most willful and stupid naïveté. *Of course* Thomas's race played a role, a major role, in his selection. It is not accidental that he was selected to fill the seat vacated by the first black member of the Court, the great Thurgood Marshall.*[74]

Social scientists have performed experiments that have produced results that are consistent with the stigma hypothesis. In one array of studies, experimenters asked volunteers to evaluate the qualifications of individuals selected for employment or for admission to higher education. Researchers informed one set of evaluators that the selecting institution had an affirmative action program but made no mention of affirmative action to a second set of evaluators. When affirmative action was mentioned, evaluators consistently gave lower grades to minorities and women than when no mention was made of affirmative action—even though the files for all of the purported candidates were identical.[75] In another investigation, volunteers paired five résumés with five newly "hired" employees. When told that affirmative action had affected the selection, the volunteers paired the one African American among the candidates with the weakest résumé at a rate that was significantly higher than when no mention was made about affirmative action.[76] These and similar research findings suggest, according to Professor Linda Hamilton Krieger,

---

* Race also played a part in President Lyndon B. Johnson's decision to nominate Marshall. Publicly, Johnson refrained from saying expressly that race mattered in the selection, maintaining simply that Marshall was "the right man at the right time." In private, Johnson was more candid. Responding to an aide's suggestion that he consider another black jurist, Judge A. Leon Higginbotham, Johnson reportedly declared: "The only two people who have ever heard of Judge Higginbotham are you and his momma. When I appoint a nigger to the [Supreme Court] I want everyone to know he's a nigger." Quoted in Robert Dallek, *Flawed Giant: Lyndon Johnson and His Times, 1961–1973* (1998), 44.

"that in many contexts, members of majority groups will assume that individual women and minorities selected in connection with preferential forms of affirmative action are less qualified and less capable than others."[77]

Commentators, too, have referred to stigma as a cost of affirmative action—in the eyes of some, a *prohibitively* expensive cost. The conservative polemicist Midge Decter asserted this proposition decades ago, charging that "affirmative action itself is creating a new wave of racism and sexism that is no longer based on fear, or hatred, or on guilt, but rather on contempt." According to Decter, "whatever people think about the justice or injustice of making special allowances for blacks and women, what they feel is that the objects of these allowances are somehow inferior. . . . By means of a policy intended to shortcut past discriminatory practice, the American populace will have been encouraged to a kind of prejudice that, if more subtle, will also for that reason be infinitely more difficult to overcome."[78]

I have seen affirmative action leave a stigma on its beneficiaries and anyone in the class of potential beneficiaries (whether or not they were actually assisted) by prompting a depreciation of their credentials. The concern, of course, is that credentials gained with an affirmative action boost are somewhat unreliable as signals of expertise. This leads to a certain dimming of the halo created by a prestigious appointment, promotion, or award. I offer two autobiographical examples. When I won a Rhodes Scholarship in 1977, a cousin asked whether I had won a "real" or merely "an affirmative action scholarship." He was joking. But, as with many jokes, this one delivered a sting. My other example is drawn from my experience as a professor at Harvard Law School. I have often received calls from partners in law firms inquiring about certain student candidates. They have been duly impressed by the students' credentials but have wanted to know whether the students were "really" good. The students for whom I have received such calls have invariably been black students. The partners calling (who have also been black) have said nothing about affirmative action expressly. But my strong impression is that apprehension over affirmative action inflation is what prompted their calls. They seemed to have wanted to peek beneath what to them were depreciated paper credentials in order to get a closer, more assuring, more "real" assessment of the candidates' abilities.*

A number of beneficiaries or potential beneficiaries have noted their sense of being diminished, underestimated, devalued, or condescended to at least in part because of the shadow cast by affirmative action. Consider the case of Stephen L. Carter, the distinguished professor-novelist-pundit at Yale Law School. A central feature of his *Reflections of an Affirmative Action Baby* (1991) is his agonized grappling with the collateral damage inflicted by efforts to promote high-achieving African Americans, like himself, who are locked in competition with high-achieving peers of all backgrounds. "Affirmative action has been with me always," he observed. "No matter what my accomplishments, I have had trouble escaping an assumption that often seems to underlie the worst forms of affirmative action: that black people cannot com-

---

* One might retort that the exploratory phone call, though reflective of skepticism exacerbated by affirmative action, still constitutes real progress. The candidates I recommended did get the jobs. But for the halos put over their heads with the help of affirmative action, they might not have received any serious consideration. After William T. Coleman, Jr., graduated from Harvard Law School at the top of his class and worked as a clerk to Supreme Court Justice Felix Frankfurter, he still found it difficult to secure employment, notwithstanding his outstanding record, because of the stigma attached to his status as a Negro. The stigmatization of blacks competing for highly valued positions far predates the modern affirmative action controversy. See William T. Coleman, Jr., *Counsel for the Situation: Shaping the Law to Realize America's Promise* (2012): 73–74.

pete intellectually with white people."[79] What Carter decried as particularly debilitating is "the 'best black' syndrome." He complained that high-achieving blacks who are assumed to be beneficiaries of affirmative action

> are measured by a different yardstick: *first black, only black, best black*. The best black syndrome is cut from the same cloth as the implicit and demeaning tokenism that often accompanies racial preferences: "Oh, we'll tolerate so-and-so at our hospital or in our firm or on our faculty, because she's the best black." Not because she's the best-qualified candidate, but because she's the best-qualified *black* candidate.[80]

According to Carter, the best black syndrome generates within affirmative action beneficiaries "a peculiar contradiction." They are flattered in that those who praise them mean to bestow a compliment. At the same time, "flattery of this kind carries an unsubtle insult, for we yearn to be called what our achievements often deserve: simply the best—no qualifiers needed!"[81]

Perhaps the most poignant reflection of the affirmative action stigma is the indignation with which some beneficiaries (or merely perceived beneficiaries) respond when identified as recipients, or even potential recipients, of affirmative action assistance.[82] A black student at the University of California in the early 1990s complained: "I feel like I have AFFIRMATIVE ACTION stamped on my forehead."[83] Richard Robinson was a black musician hired by the Detroit Symphony Orchestra pursuant to a highly public episode of racial selectivity in auditions. His response afterwards was hardly joyful: "I would have rather auditioned like everybody else. Somehow this devalues the audition and worth of every other player." A bit later, when another black musician was offered the job of conducting the Detroit Symphony, he rejected the offer, citing the controversy over affirmative action. "You fight for years to make race irrelevant, and now they are making race an issue."*[84]

Negative reaction upon being identified as a beneficiary stems largely from the derogatory meaning placed upon affirmative action by its enemies. But it is due as well to the inescapable inference that those needing the boost of affirmative action are inferior, at least temporarily, in some relevant way to those without need of the boost.

One response is to repudiate "established" criteria of performance, deny that test scores, grade point averages, or kindred traditional means of sorting are indicative of merit, and resist the claim that those with better test scores and grade point averages are superior in any way that ought to bear significantly on who should be selected for scarce openings or positions. Those embracing this position see established criteria as illegitimate means of sorting that do not so much identify "merit" as reinforce illicit hierarchies designed by elites to perpetuate the ascendancy of people like them.[85] Hence, Professors Lani Guinier and Susan Sturm maintain that

> affirmative action, as it is currently practiced, supports an underlying framework of selection that is implicitly arbitrary and exclusionary. It does not challenge the overall operation of a conventional and static selection process; instead, it creates exceptions to that process. Those exceptions play into existing racial stereotypes, predictably generating backlash. By implicitly legitimizing a selection process that operates in the name of merit, affirmative action programs reinforce that backlash.[86]

---

* Perhaps there should be an opt-out mechanism available for those who would prefer to forgo the benefits and burdens of being an affirmative action beneficiary. The extent to which such an opt-out is invoked would provide useful information about calculations of potential beneficiaries.

Guinier and Sturm see affirmative action, as conventionally understood and practiced, as a validation of deeply misleading established criteria.

This response, to a large extent, is tantamount to shooting the messenger of bad news. The bad news is that racial minorities typically eligible for affirmative action—i.e., Latinos and blacks—consistently perform less ably than others across a wide range of standardized tests and other widely accepted markers of knowledge and skill. This is true at elementary, intermediate, and higher levels of schooling. It is also true in a wide range of occupational settings.

Guinier, Sturm, and like-minded observers—I call them testing deniers—assert that these gaps reveal only an apparent or artificial difference in performance—not a real difference. Sometimes they are correct. The disparate-impact prong of antidiscrimination law has revealed scores of tests and other sorting devices that are only tenuously related to the knowledge or skills needed for a particular job. Often, though, testing and other mechanisms of sorting do reveal something real, pertinent, and significant. They reveal that those who have inherited less in the way of human capital—education, skills, valuable social networks—often perform less ably in relevant respects than their advantaged peers. This ought not be surprising. Oppression hurts. Injuries have consequences. The glaring and persistent gap between whites and racial minorities eligible for affirmative action is a manifestation of the manifold injuries inflicted by racial mistreatment.

Deniers acknowledge that racial minorities have been victimized by racial injustice. They refuse to concede, however, that that victimization has actually diminished the performance levels of those who have been directly or indirectly victimized. They refuse that concession because they insist that the testing gap is a reflection of the arbitrariness or unfairness of the tests and other sorting devices—*not* a reflection of the lesser achievement, skill, or knowledge of minority candidates. My sense is that they are afraid that any acknowledgment of a real gap in performance levels will be seized upon by partisans of the status quo to justify the existing order. The deniers want to challenge what they see as the "myth of meritocracy" and seem to believe that essential to their case is a denial of the utility of virtually any traditional sorting mechanism.

I support investigating sorting mechanisms to make sure that they are testing for pertinent attributes. When examinations impose a disparate impact and fail to identify sufficiently the qualities supposedly being sought, they ought to be scrapped, as is required under the disparate-impact prong of federal antidiscrimination law. But some criteria are useful indicators of skill or achievement even when they do have the effect of excluding disproportionately larger numbers of racial-minority candidates. When that is so, reformers should aim not to abolish the test but to abolish the conditions that create the stark, predictable racial gaps that have become all too familiar. Proponents of affirmative action should avoid denying the obvious—that many racial-minority beneficiaries of affirmative action are behind their white peers in terms of the knowledge and skills rightly expected by schools, firms, or other institutions. Rather, proponents of affirmative action should see racialized gaps in performance as signs of a difficulty to be overcome—the ongoing effect of insufficiently remedied racial injustice. *That* is the problem—not the criteria that expose that problem.

Some proponents of affirmative action fear that onlookers will repudiate my definition of the problem and will instead see racialized gaps as manifestations of innate racial inferiority or virtually irremediable cultural deficiencies. That is the fear that, in part, prompts them to deny that, in certain settings, whites do in fact outperform racial minorities. They want by all means to avoid conceding that, at least at the moment of testing, white competitors for valued positions do tend to outdo their racial-minority peers, and often by wide margins.

Their fear is understandable. Rumors, insinuations, assertions, and purported demonstrations of colored people's alleged cognitive inferiority have a long lineage in American culture. In 1994, a modern version of the myth of blacks' intellectual inferiority was published to considerable acclaim. *The Bell Curve*, by Richard J. Herrnstein and Charles Murray, was not only a best seller; it received a respectful hearing among leading arbiters of elite opinion.[87] Entrenched as well is the notion that racial gaps stem not so much from past or present racial mistreatment as the collective character defects of colored people, especially blacks—improvidence, impulsiveness, laziness, concupiscence—abetted by government largesse, lowered expectations, and coddling.[88] In this view, the proper reaction to racial gaps in performance is patient resignation or exhortations that racial minorities exercise more personal responsibility—*not* the initiation or continuation of programs like affirmative action.

The proper response to the stigma objection is to (1) acknowledge its strength, (2) diminish avoidable harms through careful design of affirmative action programs, (3) argue against exaggerations of stigmatic harms, and (4) insist that, ultimately, in reaching a conclusion about the wisdom of affirmative action, its benefits must be weighed against its drawbacks. I have already recognized that affirmative action imposes a stigmatic cost on anyone perceived to be a beneficiary. Even the staunchly pro–affirmative action researchers Derek Bok and William G. Bowen recognize that "the very existence of a process that gives explicit consideration to race can raise questions about the true abilities of even the most talented minority students."[89]

It is difficult to quantify, however, with even a modicum of precision how much of a stigmatic cost stems from affirmative action. For one thing, the cost probably varies with the design of the affirmative action policy in question and according to the nature of the position in dispute. The more skilled, subject to objective testing, and historically meritocratic the position is, the more a preference regime and its beneficiaries are likely to be stigmatized. More stigma (and alarm) is likely to attend racial preference extended to, say, airline pilots than to trash collectors.[90]

There are reasons to believe that affirmative action is not as stigmatically burdensome as certain anti–affirmative action detractors suggest. Especially among racial minorities, relatively few complain about this cost, against the concomitant benefit. Some do, as we have seen. But most blacks and Latinos embrace affirmative action notwithstanding this drawback.

One thing they recognize is the notable unevenness of attitudes toward different sorts of preferences. *Racial* affirmative action is said to be highly stigmatizing. But the stigma objection is advanced much less strongly when the preference in question has to do with geography (collegiate in-state preferences) or alumni status (collegiate legacy preferences) or preferences for the wealthy or for those with connections.* A columnist sarcastically made note of this phenomenon in a piece about the

---

* "It is somewhat ironic to have us so deeply disturbed over a program where race is an element of consciousness, and yet to be aware of the fact, as we are, that institutions of higher learning . . . have given conceded preferences . . . to those possessed of athletic skills, to the children of alumni, to the affluent who may bestow their largesse on the institutions, and to those having connections with celebrities, the famous, and the powerful." Justice Harry Blackmun, concurring and dissenting in *Bakke,* 438 U.S. 265, 404 (1978).

emergence of Chelsea Clinton, Jenna Bush Hager, and Meghan McCain as television journalists under circumstances that suggest that their familial prominence played an outsize role in their hiring.

> That's the way it is in America. So let's just call it what it is: affirmative action. I know that term has been corrupted in the public realm as shorthand for being on the receiving end of unearned privilege. Someone beats you out for a job, a spot in Yale's freshman class? Blame affirmative action. The ones doing the blaming usually aren't referring to women or veterans or people with disabilities or students with a building on campus named for dad, mom, or other generations that made their mark. It's those minorities—you know, because minorities have always had it so great in America.[91]

A recurring complaint against the claim that, on balance, affirmative action more harms than helps its putative beneficiaries is that that argument flies in the face of the preferences expressed by racial minorities themselves—people who concur with the black student who said, "I'd rather be at [my elite law school] and feel stigmatized . . . than not be here at all."[92] Responding to one stigma critique, Sandra J. Mullings indignantly challenged what she saw as an assumption that "we [minorities] are too ignorant . . . to know what is good for us."[93] Bok and Bowen, in their important study *The Shape of the River,* also allude to the calculation that appears to have been made by most blacks in a position to accept affirmative action benefits. "The black matriculants themselves—who are, after all, the ones most affected by any stigmatizing effects—are presumably in the best position to weigh the pros and cons. The . . . data are universal. Black students do not seem to *think* they have been harmed as a result of attending selective colleges with race-sensitive policies."[94]

That adults know what is best for themselves is surely a widespread and often warranted presumption. It is important, moreover, to be on guard against the insidious and deeply rooted habit of thinking that colored people simply do not know what is good for them—a habit that manifested itself previously in the fight over slavery (with some claiming that blacks flourished in bondage) and the fight over segregation (with some claiming that blacks preferred their subordinate "places").[95] Still, individuals and groups can act in ways that run counter to their own professed goals. All too frequently, people are misdirected by ignorance, habit, prejudice, and the many routine misperceptions that subvert optimal decision making. It is not enough, then, simply to scoff at those who assert that, notwithstanding popular support among minorities, affirmative action is bad for them. Sometimes people do not know their best interest or how best to attain their goals. In this instance, however, backers of racial affirmative action, including beneficiaries, are not misled by a mistaken impression of where their best interests lie. They see the benefits that accrue from access to opportunities that have long been out of reach for people like them. They see whites deploying any edge available—familial contacts, legacy preferences, celebrity, or wealth—to attain the very opportunities that have made affirmative action a battleground: the selective college or the career-making job. They wonder why, all of a sudden, people who previously expressed little concern over their fate are now working so hard to save them from affirmative action's supposed perils.

The Mismatch Objection

A complaint of long standing against affirmative action is that it creates debilitating mismatches by overpromoting beneficiaries, putting them in positions in which they are doomed to suffer dramatic negative comparisons with better-prepared white peers.[96]

A recent, much-publicized presentation of the mismatch objection is posited by law professor Richard H. Sander, who maintains that "blacks are the victims of law school programs of affirmative action, not the beneficiaries."[97] He shows that the boost given by affirmative action to racial-minority applicants is large, and that many of these applicants end up at schools where they struggle academically, receive mediocre or poor grades, and fail the bar exam at much higher rates than their white classmates. He claims that many black students, misled by the academic establishment, have calculated wrongly the trade-off between attending a higher-prestige school and being saddled with a weaker academic record. He denounces the strategy of pushing minority students upward into higher-prestige schools than they would attend absent strong affirmative action because, he argues, a consequence of doing so is condemning those students to law school environments in which they learn less than they would at less prestigious institutions. According to Sander, the affirmative action trade-off between school prestige and weaker grades substantially harms black students. Thrown in above their heads, they fare poorly not only as students but as fledgling attorneys. Indeed, Sander goes so far as to maintain that "in the legal education system as a whole, racial preferences end up producing fewer black lawyers each year than would be produced by a race-blind system."[98] That is because, as he portrays it, the affirmative action mismatch prompts a substantial number of black students to attend schools that are simply too difficult for them—schools at which, mired at the bottom of the class, they develop all manner of self-defeating outlooks and habits that subvert efforts to capitalize on talents that might have been better nurtured at lesser schools.

Sander's intervention has received a large amount of polarized attention.[99] Some opponents of affirmative action cite him as if his hypotheses were incontrovertible. Much of the scholarly response, however, has been decidedly negative.[100] Three of the key criticisms are that Sander underestimates the benefits of affirmative action, that he exaggerates its role in the subpar performance of black law students, and that he unreliably forecasts what would happen if affirmative action were ended.

Let's begin with the complaint that Sander is insufficiently attentive to the bonus obtained by attending higher-prestige institutions. He portrays as unequivocally negative the situation of a student who is significantly outpaced by classmates. But Professors Ian Ayres and Richard Brooks note an aspect of the situation that Sander largely ignores—that, at least sometimes, "when students are overmatched by their classmates, they appear to be carried along to more success."[101] Ayres and Brooks observe:

> Overmatched students in more selective academic settings may be mentored and inspired by their better-credentialed peers or teachers, or obtain the advantage of greater institutional commitment of resources. . . . [I]t is not irrational for parents to want to get their kids into the best possible school (even if they are overmatched).[102]

Professor David Wilkins complains that Sander underestimates the full panoply of benefits that come with attending a higher-tier school even at the cost of lower grades.[103] Sander recognizes that attending a higher-tier school gains one a placement and wage premium—for instance, entry into fancier firms that pay higher salaries. In Wilkins's view, however, Sander grossly minimizes other benefits that come from attending higher-tier schools. Students attending elite schools, Wilkins observes, are *socialized* into the habits and possibilities of eliteness and granted a lifetime membership in the elite *networks* to which the graduates of such institutions automatically belong. . . . [E]lite school graduates also obtain a visible and durable *credential* that they can use to signal to employers that they have received *all* of the valuable goods that elite schools provide.[104]

Over time, and especially with respect to black lawyers, Wilkins concludes, "the socialization, networking, and credentializing benefits of a degree from an elite law school dominate the educational and placement advantages discussed by Sander."[105] According to Wilkins,

the network effects of elite schools are so obvious that one would think that they would have to be a large part of any examination of the benefits of attending such institutions. Yet Sander ignores them entirely. . . . Being a Harvard, Yale, or Stanford graduate means being inserted into an exclusive club. . . . [It] opens up opportunities for relationship building across generations and domains of expertise and interest.[106]

Detractors also charge that Sander underestimates what would happen in the absence of affirmative action. He concedes that without it, the most elite law schools would have very few black students—probably in the range of 1 to 2 percent, as opposed to 8 or 9 percent. He estimates, however, that at the lower tiers the racial demographics wouldn't much change: blacks boosted upwards by affirmative action would now return to "where they belonged" in terms of race-blind assessment of GPAs and test scores. Yes, there would be some blacks pushed out of law school education altogether by a race-blind regime, but many of them would have dropped out or failed the bar anyway. According to Sander, the improved performance of black students enjoying more compatible schools would actually lead to a net gain in the overall production of black lawyers.

There is reason, however, to doubt Sander's forecast. Some analysts maintain that without affirmative action, black enrollment at the first-tier schools would decline by more than four-fifths, and at each of the next two tiers by about two-thirds.[107] A consequence is that law would be a far less appealing career option. A dramatic shrinking of the number of black students in law schools might well dissuade other blacks from applying.

Several lessons can be drawn from the controversy surrounding Sander's mismatch hypothesis.

First, the character of the discussion exemplifies the crisis of trust that continues to beset American race relations, including the study of race relations.[108] Behind the scholarly jousting is a high level of suspiciousness and anger. Sander himself is well aware of this reality. That is why he began his initial scholarly pronouncement on mismatch with a remarkable autobiographical aside in which he informed readers that he is white, worked as a community organizer on Chicago's South Side, participated in struggles for fair housing, and has a biracial son.[109] This represented, at least in part, a preemptive effort to stave off charges of racism or insensitivity. It largely failed. Among many pro–affirmative action scholars and activists, Sander is seen as a wily, disingenuous enemy of affirmative action and treated accordingly.

Here, however, as elsewhere, feelings of besiegement on the part of affirmative action defenders has provoked conduct that undercuts their own self-professed goals. Some have tried to suppress Sander's intervention. They have ostracized him and pressured individuals and organizations to cease cooperating with his efforts to obtain pertinent information on the academic and occupational records of law students. The attempted suppression, however, has actually been a boon to Professor Sander, since he gets to enjoy enhanced publicity and the considerable benefits of being seen as "brave" as well as "politically incorrect." Furthermore, the attempts to stifle Sander suggest that he is onto something that his scholarly adversaries want to hide. The adoption of an excessively pugnacious attitude by affirmative action defenders is a big mistake. It facilitates the denial of important facts that warrant attention and discourages the valuable habit of reconsidering established practices that need reform.*

Sander has revealed and publicized sobering facts that display striking disparities in the grades, attrition rates, and bar-passage results of whites versus racial-minority law students. According to his calculations, in 2003, of black students starting law school, only about 47 percent were becoming lawyers, with one-third of those having to take the bar examination two or more times before passing. By contrast, 83 percent of entering white students were becoming lawyers, and only one in twenty of these required more than one attempt to pass the bar.[110] That glaring disparity calls out for explanation. Perhaps the reason resides more in factors that Sander downplays, such as racially poisonous environments, than in the mismatch hypothesis that he propounds. That question never gets answered, however, without unflinching investigation that takes seriously the explanation that Sander posits. Just suppose, moreover, that mismatch is shown to be a major contributor to attrition, poor grades, and bar failures. A defender of affirmative action should be willing to accept that possibility. Existing arrangements are surely far from

* Things could be worse. In Malaysia, criticizing that country's analogue of affirmative action is a criminal offense punishable by up to three years in prison. See Daniel Sabbagh, "Affirmative Action," in Michel Rosenfeld and Andra Saja, eds., *The Oxford Handbook of Comparative Constitutional Law* (2012), 1130.

optimal. Perhaps there does need to be a recalibration of affirmative action programs to minimize avoidable costs.

A second lesson from the controversy is that a large part of the dispute between Sander and his adversaries has to do with an unacknowledged conflict over goals. Sander's goal—the baseline against which he measures the current system of admissions in legal academia—is to create, each year, as many black attorneys as possible. An implication of that goal is that black attorneys are fungible—the person from a tier-five school who struggles as a modest lone practitioner and the major-firm litigation partner from a top-tier school who influences the hiring and promotion of scores of attorneys and episodically serves in the upper echelons of government. An alternative goal is to advance the black community *as a whole,* a goal that might be seen as better served by whichever admissions regime will assure the largest number of blacks at the most elite schools. Those who prefer the current regime to the one that Sander envisions might well continue to do so even if they believed he was correct in concluding that his regime would, on balance, generate more black attorneys. They might prefer the current regime on the grounds that attorneys are not fungible, that the cadre of black attorneys trained at the top-tier schools are more valuable to the black community than those trained at the lower-tier schools, and hence that, if necessary, maintaining the numbers at the higher-tier schools would be worth sacrificing marginal members or potential members of the black bar. To some, this train of thought will be distressingly elitist. It is in keeping, however, with the perspective of an important and commendable activist tradition dedicated to African American uplift. One contributor to this tradition is W. E. B. DuBois, who championed the idea of a talented tenth that would serve as a vanguard for African American advance-

ment.[111] Another contributor was the formidable foe of segregation, the mentor of Thurgood Marshall, and director of litigation
for the NAACP, Charles Hamilton Houston. In his pioneering
reorganization of the Howard University Law School, Houston
took several steps that lessened the numbers of blacks able to
gain access to a legal education (for example, he closed Howard's
night school and drastically toughened the grading) in order to
create a more selective, prestigious, and influential school that
would train social engineers capable of reforming the American
racial order.[112] Sander seems to believe that he is helping blacks
by pushing changes that would, he thinks, advance the fortunes
of average African American law students. Some of his adversaries contend, however, that the realization of his policy preferences would diminish Black America by lowering the number
of black students who now obtain the premium bestowed upon
those attending America's most elite law schools.*

AFFIRMATIVE ACTION FOR WHOM: THE PROBLEM OF INDIVIDUAL ELIGIBILITY

Affirmative action programs bestow valued benefits. But who
is eligible to be a beneficiary? What are the indicia of eligibility? And who, or what, decides contested cases? One might
have thought that the determination of individual eligibility
would emerge as a large and vexing problem for the administration of racial affirmative action. After all, when something
of value is being dispensed, fraud or the threat of fraud usually lurks nearby. A striking feature of the American affirmative action regime, however, is the relative paucity of disputation

---

* This position is suggested by, and consistent with, the riposte to Sander written
by Professor David B. Wilkins, "A Systematic Response to Systemic Disadvantage: A
Response to Sander," *Stanford Law Review* 57 (2005), 1915.

over the matter of individual eligibility. There have been scores of criminal cases involving the eligibility of firms for affirmative action assistance.* What I am concerned with here, however, are controversies involving natural persons. There exist notably few cases in which some authority has rejected an individual seeking racial affirmative action assistance on grounds of racial eligibility. Nor, thus far, has this subject been central to ongoing battles over American affirmative action (though it has generated a substantial corpus of scholarly examination).[113]

It is possible that controversy over racial identification and ascription will emerge as an important subject in the American affirmative action debate. Opponents of affirmative action tried hard to conjure up a scandal involving Harvard Law School professor Elizabeth Warren during her historic, successful bid in 2012 to become the first female United States senator from Massachusetts. During that campaign, it was revealed that Harvard listed Warren as a Native American in its reports to the federal government regarding the racial demographics of its workforce. Rumor portrayed Warren as having gotten ahead illicitly in her professional career by posing as a Native American. Although the rumor was false, it did provide a predicate for sneering gibes against affirmative action (and an upsurge in grossly racist mockery of Indians).†

Another recent outcropping of interest in the matter of indi-

---

* The federal government, states, and municipalities have established programs designed to boost the fortunes of firms owned by racial minorities and women. Some of these programs have been beset by fraud. Instead of claiming falsely that they are minorities or women, malefactors in this area fabricate minority or women fronts. See James Traub, *Too Good to Be True: The Outlandish Story of Wedtech* (1990).
† See, e.g., Sean Sullivan, "The Fight over Elizabeth Warren's Heritage Explained," *Washington Post*, September 27, 2012; Noah Bierman, "Scott Brown Launches Ad About Elizabeth Warren's Native American Controversy," *Boston Globe*, September 24, 2012; Gerance Franke-Ruta, "Is Elizabeth Warren Native American or What?" *The Atlantic*, May 20, 2012.

vidual racial identification was displayed at the oral argument of *Fisher v. University of Texas.* Several of the justices asked questions indicative of impatience with a social policy that authorities are reluctant, if not altogether unwilling, to police. Hence, Chief Justice John Roberts asked the lawyer representing UT, "Would it violate the [university's] honor code for someone who is one-eighth Hispanic . . . to check the Hispanic box?" Upon being told that that would not constitute a violation, the chief justice wanted to know whether the university checked the racial bona fides of affirmative action beneficiaries, how that was done, and, if it was not done, how the university could confidently posit the racial demographics of its student body.[114]

Despite these episodes, however, controversy over racial identification remains marginal in the American debate over affirmative action. By contrast, in the Brazilian debate, disputation over individual eligibility is front and center. In his excellent book *Race in Another America,* Professor Edward E. Telles maintains that, among other things, the multiracial lineage and complex physiognomic cues of Brazilians makes racial boundaries there much more complicated than in the United States. Racial ambiguity in Brazil, he writes, "could present a major challenge to the implementation of racial quotas."[115] Brazilian universities have established committees that screen applicants seeking affirmative action assistance. These committees have denied eligibility to an appreciable number of applicants. Courts have reviewed these assessments, disagreeing with some of them in highly publicized instances. In one infamous instance, fraternal twins sought affirmative action assistance in attaining admission to the University of Brasília. Separate committees ruled that one of the siblings was eligible but that the other was not—a peculiar judgment that prompted a court to invalidate the program and moved detractors to point to this episode as a vivid illustration of what they perceive as the fatuity of affirmative action.[116]

In the United States, public and private authorities have decided with striking uniformity to forgo intrusive policing of racial eligibility. Like the administrators of the federal census, they have depended upon an honor system of self-reporting pursuant to which individuals identify themselves racially. Nor do they typically question, refute, or otherwise look beneath individuals' responses. Usually a person is taken at his or her word: if you say you are black, that is generally determinative—you are deemed to be black (or Native American, Latino, etc.). Some observers criticize the laissez-faire, non-investigatory posture that most organizations have taken in this regard. They see the failure to check the authenticity of claimed identity as negligence that permits the misallocation of valuable resources: opportunities that go to faux blacks, Latinos, or Native Americans leave fewer opportunities for *real* blacks, Latinos, or Native Americans. Notwithstanding that criticism, however, most institutions have continued to maintain a simple honor system of self-designation.

There are, though, exceptional cases. The one that has received the most attention stemmed from the hiring in 1977 of two firefighters in Boston, twin brothers Paul and Philip Malone.[117] They initially applied in 1975, noting on their applications that they were "white." They were unsuccessful. Two years later, they reapplied. By then the Boston Fire Department was under a racial affirmative action plan to rectify anti-black racial discrimination. The second time around, they stated in their application that they were "black." Because of affirmative action bumps given to their scores on the civil service examination, they received the jobs they sought. A decade later, after receiving information that led them to believe that the Malones had falsely claimed minority status, officials moved to end the brothers' employment.

Justice Herbert P. Wilkins of the Supreme Judicial Court of Massachusetts upheld the termination, finding that there was substantial evidence to support the conclusion that the Malones, in indicating that they were black, had knowingly made a material false statement when they applied for their jobs. According to Justice Wilkins, the Malones could have prevailed by supporting their claim of being black in any of three ways: by (1) visual observation of their features; (2) documentary evidence establishing black ancestry; or (3) evidence that they or their families held themselves to be black and were considered to be black in the community. According to Justice Wilkins, substantial evidence supported a hearing officer's conclusion that the Malones had failed to meet any of these criteria. To the hearing officer, the Malones did not look black, meaning that to him, in terms of physiognomy, they did not have characteristics (complexion, hair, facial features) commonly associated with blacks. The Malones' birth certificates reported them to be white. The birth certificates of their parents and grandparents reported them to be white as well. The only indication of black ancestry offered by the Malones was a photograph that, they claimed, showed that one of their maternal great-grandmothers was black. According to the Malones, they discovered that they were black when they learned belatedly of the existence of this African-American ancestor. The hearing officer believed, however, that there was no reliable means of verifying the identity of the woman in the photograph.

Finally, the Malones' record was bereft of any indication that, outside of trying to attain affirmative action benefits, they ever identified themselves as black. They never, for example, sought to join the Vulcan Society, an organization composed mainly of minority firefighters.

Apart from the points mentioned above was a fourth that was related but independent. The personnel administrator who discharged the Malones stated that even in the absence of meeting other criteria, they would have prevailed if they could have shown that they had acted in good faith. Justice Wilkins ruled that here, too, there was a firm basis for the administrator's determination (though the justice's explanation on this point is rather conclusory).

Malone is a rarity; it is, thus far, the only adjudicated racial identification case that involves an individual in an affirmative action context. That other applicants have engaged in racial fraud to exploit affirmative action programs is beyond doubt. But the dearth of challenges reflects a deep hesitancy to police individuals' racial self-identification. That hesitation stems from a fear of investigation into such a deeply personal area. It stems from respect for individual autonomy, a sense that, at least vis-à-vis the government, people should be able to freely express themselves in terms of racial affiliation, just as they are able to freely express themselves in terms of religious affiliation. It also stems from revulsion against racial policing in the past, when a ruling that a person was colored invariably meant dire consequences: enslavement, prison, the annulment of a marriage.[118]

The doctrinal tools with which *Malone* was resolved similarly display an aversion to the policing of racial self-identification. Those tools gave the Malones an array of ways to justify their racial self-identification. The administrator stated that, notwithstanding the objective evidence that cut against the Malones, he would still rule in their favor if he could be convinced that they believed themselves to be black (even if observers rejected their self-identification). In other words, all the Malones needed to show in order to prevail was good faith in their racial self-description, an appropriately loose and low standard that gives generous leeway to personal autonomy.

Another reason for the relative paucity of affirmative action racial-identification disputes is the perpetuation of a distinctively American contribution to racial politics—a powerful tendency toward racial simplification that maintains a racial duality that sharply distinguishes white from black. Many multiracial societies have formally privileged fractional whiteness even while subordinating the intermixed to those "purely" white. In the United States, on the other hand, officials have been loath to reward formally the progeny of amalgamation. Rather, they have tended to promote and enforce a one-drop rule pursuant to which any discernible Negro "blood" makes one black. Under the one-drop rule, a person is either colored or white, a Manichean imposition that has made racial identification in America less complicated and contested than in other societies.[119]

Yet another reason for the marginality of racial self-identification disputes is that racial fraud, though undoubtedly present, has remained at a sufficiently low level that officials have felt comfortable disregarding it, chalking it up to a necessary business expense. But why is the level of fraud low? Perhaps because the perceived benefits of affirmative action are less impressive than the perceived detriment of being seen as a racial minority. I suspect that the prospect of being outed has dissuaded some people from "going black," even if doing so would open access to valuable preferences.

What groups should be eligible for affirmative action assistance? Opponents of affirmative action stress the difficulty of making persuasive judgments and the certainty that any judgments made will be controversial and embittering. They cite the prospect of divisiveness as a strong reason to avoid affirmative action altogether. They portray it as a Pandora's box of group conflict.[120]

As with other objections, this one contains substantial points that should be attended to carefully. Affirmative action has exacerbated racial tensions in many contexts. The United States has been spared the violence that has flared in other countries.* But a seemingly unavoidable side effect of affirmative action's presence everywhere is a certain quantum of resentment.

Much of the resentment in America is directed at blacks by whites. Many of the latter see themselves as innocent of any racial wrongdoing and see the former as undeserving opportunists bent on reaping a racial windfall. The anger escalates as affirmative action embraces additional groups, some of which have little or no connection with the history of American racial oppression. Some of the most derisive critiques of affirmative action mounted by Supreme Court justices are aimed at programs deemed to be overly broad. In the opinion for the Court striking down a minority set-aside program in Richmond, Virginia, Justice O'Connor noted that, in addition to blacks, the program preferred Eskimos and Aleuts, even though "it may well be that Richmond has never had an Aleut or Eskimo citizen."[121]

Conflict is not limited to disputes between whites and blacks; conflicts between different groups of colored people also sim-

---

* In 1990 opponents and proponents of a contested program of "compensatory discrimination" in India immolated themselves, massacred adversaries, rioted, boycotted classes, blocked traffic, and engaged in many other sorts of disruptive behavior. The protests and counter-protests played a large role in bringing down the government of Prime Minister V. P. Singh. See E. J. Prior, "Constitutional Fairness or Fraud on the Constitution? Compensatory Discrimination in India," *Case Western Reserve Journal of International Law* 64 (1996): 63–69.

Violence has bedeviled programs of positive discrimination in other countries as well including Malaysia, Sri Lanka, and Nigeria. See Thomas Sowell, *Affirmative Action Around the World: An Empirical Study* (2004). That is not to say that positive discrimination *caused* the violence. A response to racial and ethnic division, affirmative action in some places likely lessened violence that would have been worse in its absence.

mer and erupt. The prevailing plaintiff who triggered one of the
most anti–affirmative action judgments in American case law
was a Hispanic student who challenged the constitutionality of
a state-sponsored scholarship program that limited eligibility to
African Americans.*[122] This case is by no means idiosyncratic. In
affirmative action and elsewhere, blacks and Latinos are bump-
ing into one another jousting for power as blacks' status as the
largest ethno-racial–minority group is superseded by Latinos.

Some champions of Asian American uplift and protection
have complained that racial affirmative action, conventionally
designed, has slighted or even hurt their communities. The
slight is attributed to a tendency toward disregarding the breadth
and variability of the Asian American community in ways that
shortchange newer and poorer subgroups (e.g., persons of Lao-
tian, Cambodian, and Hmong ancestry) in contrast to the older,
more affluent subgroups (e.g., persons of Chinese, Japanese, and
Korean ancestry). Some institutions, for example, forgo making
affirmative action efforts on behalf of "Asian Americans," perceiving them as sufficiently represented by dint of regular procedures. This conclusion is predicated, however, on a conception
of Asian Americans that renders invisible discrete and vulnerable
subgroups in that community.

Other opponents of affirmative action maintain that representational baselines penalize "model minorities" like Jews and
established Asian Americans who often do disproportionately
well in open competitions for seats in the most selective spheres
of higher education. For such groups, affirmative action regimes
can be seen as threatening, in that they raise the prospect of
group-based ceilings pursuant to notions of "overrepresentation"

---

* It bears noting that in this case, *Podberesky v. Kirwan,* 38 F.3d 147 (4th Cir. 1994),
the Mexican American Legal Defense and Educational Fund (MALDEF) submitted
an amicus curiae brief supporting the defendant scholarship program.

and "underrepresentation."* Some Asian Americans have lodged formal complaints alleging that their numbers of admittances to highly selective institutions have been wrongfully depressed to make room for less qualified whites and blacks. The story of Asian Americans in this context is decidedly mixed.[123] Some Asian American intellectuals and activists strongly support affirmative action. Others see it as an impediment to their group's full flourishing and prefer the consequences of an individualistic, laissez-faire model of race relations in which indifference is the attitude adopted by government toward the racial demographics of competition.

Yet another locus of conflict involves the allocation of benefit between, on the one hand, the offspring of American-born black parents and, on the other, the offspring of interracial couples and foreign-born blacks. Apprehensive about this development, Professors Kevin Brown and Jeannine Bell observe that

> right now we are witnessing a historic change in the racial and ethnic ancestry of blacks who are the beneficiaries of affirmative action. Selective colleges, universities, and graduate programs are admitting increasing percentages of blacks with a white parent and foreign-born black immigrants and their sons and daughters. . . . As a result, blacks whose predominate ancestry is traceable to the historical oppression of blacks in the United States are likely more underrepresented in affirmative action than most administrators, admissions committees, or faculties realize.[124]

Professors Brown and Bell note, for example, that, at least according to one report, in 2003, two-thirds of Harvard's black under-

---

* See Deborah C. Malamud, "The Jew Taboo: Jewish Difference and the Affirmative Action Debate," *Ohio State Law Journal* 59 (1998): 915; Daniel A. Farber and Suzanna Sherry, "Is the Radical Critique of Merit Anti-Semitic?" *California Law Review* 83 (1995): 853.

graduate population, a substantial percentage of whom benefited from affirmative action, were children of mixed-race couples or of African or Caribbean immigrants.[125] To Professors Brown and Bell, these figures suggest a misallocation of assistance detrimental to the "descendants of blacks originally brought to the United States as chattel slaves."[126] They argue in favor of institutions eliciting more information about familial background and using that information to redirect resources to the sorts of blacks for whom affirmative action was initially envisioned and who are also, in the critics' view, best positioned to provide leadership in the continuing struggle against African American subordination. Professors Brown and Bell state that they are "mindful of the long and odious history . . . of classifications based on ancestry" and that they realize that distinguishing between blacks in the manner they suggest "calls into question black unity." Still, they proceed, asserting that to avoid this matter would itself be a choice with consequences they would prefer to avoid.

Determining which individuals should be eligible for affirmative action and which groups should receive special assistance poses difficult theoretical and practical problems. The absence of a fully worked-out blueprint for dealing with these problems, however, need not be viewed as an insuperable impediment to the continuation of racial affirmative action. Some of these problems are best dealt with by local authorities who, one hopes, will be attentive to the peculiarities of the given controversy. But some of these problems might prove to be irresolvable. If that is so, authorities should acknowledge the virtue, on occasion, of merely "muddling through" without theoretical clarity. That is essentially what has been done with respect to ascribing racial identity to individuals. There is no wholly satisfactory answer to the question of who is white or black or Latino for purposes of affirmative action. In the face of that deficiency, however, thousands of affirmative action programs nonetheless proceed, muddling through well enough.*

CONCLUDING THOUGHTS

I am in favor of sensibly designed affirmative action for reasons elaborated upon above. I recognize, though, that there are weighty counterarguments and that reasonable people might find them, on balance, more persuasive than the arguments supporting the position I advance. I say that I support *sensibly designed* affirmative action, which means that I eschew affirmative action programs that are prejudiced or stupid. I refuse to support any program that is appreciably tainted by animus against any nonpreferred groups. Similarly, I refuse to support any program that needlessly accentuates the costs of affirmative action. Hence, I disavow any initiative that knowingly or negligently over-promotes beneficiaries, placing them in settings in which they are conspicuously less prepared than nonpreferred peers, a situation rife with risks of demoralization and the creation or reinforcement of racist stereotypes. I have taught in classrooms in which there existed a clearly discernible difference between "regular" students and beneficiaries of excessively strong racial affirmative action. The consequence is ugly.

Not only is my support for racial affirmative action conditioned upon the suitability of particular program designs; it is

---

* "It is easy to get sidetracked by the problem of identity posed by the rich contemporary theoretical literature on the construction of identity and the amazing proliferation of mixed-race and mixed-identity families. However, one should not lose sight of the fact that there are many minority candidates—especially African Americans— whose cultural identity is not a matter of real dispute." Paul Brest and Miranda Oshige, "Affirmative Action for Whom?" *Stanford Law Review* 47 (1995): 855, 876–77.

also conditioned on the availability of alternatives.* I am in favor of sensibly designed racial affirmative action in the absence of a superior replacement. I champion it if it provides a more likely vehicle than other possibilities for the realization of worthy ends. Many observers have asserted over the years that it would be better to offer to all children excellent schooling, from pre-kindergarten through high school, than to offer preferences to graduating racial minorities who often have been shortchanged throughout their primary and secondary schooling. I concur. I would be willing immediately to trade university-level affirmative action for an ironclad guarantee, no matter what the expense, of excellent primary and secondary schooling through-out the country. That deal, however, is unavailable. By contrast, racial affirmative action, with all of its deficiencies, is available. I will take what I can get for the purposes of making amends for past injustice, tapping into "diversity," countering ongoing prejudice, and accessing the benefits of integration. It is pos-sible that settling for what seems possible in the near term will assist in sabotaging the possibility of attaining what is optimal in the long term. Sometimes it is wise to forgo compromise in favor of unbending support for one's preferred policy. These judgments are always difficult. My sense is that, under present circumstances, maintaining affirmative action is the best of the plausible options.

* "Supporters of affirmative action . . . would surely favor more extensive programs if they were politically feasible. The problem is that they are not politically feasible. At the moment affirmative action happens to be the best we can get." James P. Sterba, "Completing Thomas Sowell's Study of Affirmative Action and Then Drawing Dif-ferent Conclusions," *Stanford Law Review* 547 (2004): 657. Throughout this book I have leaned on the work of Professor Sterba, particularly his contribution (alongside Carl Cohen) to the outstanding volume *Affirmative Action and Racial Preference: A Debate.*

3

The Color-Blind Challenge to Affirmative Action

"Color blindness" is a key idea in American life. It is probably the most popular conception of what is thought to be commendable racial thought and conduct. It stands for the proposition that race ought to play no role in assessing individuals—that race ought to be absent from any calculation determining whether a person is detained by police or sent to prison, tapped for a promotion or picked for an orchestra, chosen for jury service or selected by a university. Some see color blindness as a long-range aspiration that should not be demanded immediately. They say that they yearn for the day when race has sunk into utter irrelevancy but contend that comprehensive color blindness immediately is premature. They associate themselves with Justice Harry Blackmun's statement that "in order to get beyond racism, we must first take account of race."[1] This is the camp of the color-blind gradualists. Other proponents of color blindness are immediatists. They insist that in order to make race irrelevant, one must make it irrelevant *now*. Chief Justice John Roberts reflected the sentiments of that camp when he and a majority of the justices voted to strike down a racially selective student assignment plan instituted to retain racial balance. "The way to stop discrimination on the basis of race," Roberts insisted, "is to stop discriminating on the basis of race."[2] Another color-blind immediatist, Professor William Van Alstyne, put it this way: "one gets beyond racism by getting beyond it now: by a complete, resolute, and credible commitment *never* to tolerate in one's own life—or in the life or practices of one's government—the differential treatment of other human beings by race." That, according to Van Alstyne, "is the great lesson for government itself to teach: in all we do in life, whatever we do in life, to treat any person less well than another or to favor any more than another for being black or white or brown or red, is wrong."*[3]

Immediatists come in at least two varieties. One views all forms of racial discrimination, including affirmative action, as having always been illicit. A second views affirmative action as having been useful as a needed expedient in the late 1960s and early 1970s, but also as an intervention that became disastrously entrenched, requiring uprooting.† There is a consensus among immediatists, however, that whatever the proper status of affirmative action in the past, it should have no place in American life today.

To take the measure of color blindness, especially as it relates to affirmative action, I chart its history, note its attractions, and posit its weaknesses. I conclude that, as an aspiration and strategy, color blindness is misconceived.‡

---

* Van Alstyne does not explicitly say that he would favor prohibiting private affirmative action. I am making the inference that he would, given the militancy with which he denounces *all* racial discrimination, positive as well as negative.

† "As we pull the plug on preferential policies, we should remind ourselves that such policies have done more to change the culture of employee recruitment practices and to change the composition of the workforce in a relatively short period than any other approach imaginable." Ward Connerly, "Affirmative Action Programs, Race Relations, and the CCRI," *Nexus* 1 (1996): 10.

‡ Writings on this subject I found to be especially instructive include Ian Haney-Lopez, " 'A Nation of Minorities': Race, Ethnicity, and Reactionary Colorblindness," *Stanford Law Review* 59 (2007): 985; Barbara J. Flagg, " 'Was Blind, But Now I See': White Race Consciousness and the Requirement of Discriminatory Intent," *Michigan Law Review* 91 (1993): 953; Neil Gotanda, "A Critique of 'Our Constitution is Color-Blind,' " *Stanford Law Review* 44 (1991): 1; David A. Strauss, "The Myth of Colorblindness," *Supreme Court Review* 1986 (1986): 99; Laurence H. Tribe, "In What Vision of the Constitution Must the Law Be Color-Blind?" *John Marshall Law Review* 20 (1986): 201.

History

The single most widely cited statement associated with the idea of color blindness is a declaration by Justice John Marshall Harlan:

> In respect of civil rights, common to all citizens, the Constitution of the United States does not . . . permit any public authority to know the race of those entitled to be protected in the enjoyment of such rights. . . . There is no caste here. Our Constitution is color-blind, and neither knows nor tolerates classes among citizens.[4]

Harlan made this statement in 1896 in dissenting from the Supreme Court's ruling in *Plessy v. Ferguson,* which upheld the constitutionality of a Louisiana law that required passengers of different races to occupy "equal but separate" cars on intrastate trains. The Court concluded that the compulsory racial separation was reasonable in light of custom and public opinion. Harlan, by contrast, saw the law as a stigmatizing brand inflicted on Negroes.

> Everyone knows that the statute in question had its origin in the purpose, not so much to exclude white persons from railroad cars occupied by blacks as to exclude colored people from coaches occupied by . . . white persons. . . . What can more certainly arouse race hate, what can more certainly create and perpetuate a feeling of distrust between these races than state enactments which, in fact, proceed on the ground that colored citizens are so inferior and degraded that they cannot be allowed to sit in the public coaches occupied by white citizens?[5]

Harlan's assertion that government ought not be allowed to make racial distinctions in the enjoyment of civil rights stemmed in part from a resilient but marginalized strand of thought and feeling in nineteenth-century America. Contributors to this tradition included the women dissidents who petitioned the Massachusetts legislature in 1839 "to repeal all laws . . . which make any distinction . . . on account of color."[6] Another contributor was Charles Sumner, who, in attacking racial segregation in the Boston public schools, maintained that any and all racial discriminations amounted to unacceptable manifestations of caste. More immediately, Justice Harlan's evocation of the color-blind Constitution echoed the brief of the losing lawyer in *Plessy*. Albion Tourgée remarked that "Justice is pictured blind and her daughter, the Law, ought at least to be color blind."*[7] Condensing that language, Harlan made it more memorable.†

Justice Harlan offered no historical or textual support for his claim that "our Constitution is color blind." There is little support to offer. Congressional framers of the Fourteenth Amendment declined to accept language that would have expressly

---

* Albion Winegar Tourgée was a remarkable figure who helped establish Bennett College, an historically black women's institution, wrote novels dramatizing the tribulations of Reconstruction, and initiated the National Citizen's Rights Association, which supported the challenge to segregation in *Plessy v. Ferguson*. See Mark Elliott, *Color-Blind Justice: Albion Tourgée and the Quest for Racial Equality from the Civil War to* Plessy v. Ferguson (2006); Otto Olsen, *Carpetbagger's Crusade: The Life of Albion Winegar Tourgée* (1965).

† Although Tourgée's color blindness trope is the most influential aspect of his brief, the most cogent (and, unfortunately, overlooked) is the part in which he urges the justices to trade places with blacks for purposes of assessing the real meaning of the "equal but separate" requirement for railway accommodations: "Suppose a member of this court, nay, suppose every member of it, by some mysterious dispensation of providence should wake up tomorrow with a black skin and curly hair . . . and in traveling through the part of the country where the 'Jim Crow Car' abounds should be ordered into it by the conductor. It is easy to imagine what would be the result, the indignation, the protests, the assertion of pure Caucasian ancestry. But the conductor, the autocrat of Caste, armed with the power of the State conferred by this statute, will listen neither to denial or protest. . . . What humiliation, what rage would then fill the judicial mind!" Brief for Plaintiff in Error, *Plessy v. Ferguson* (1896), Supreme Court of the United States, Philip B. Kurland, Gerhard Coasper, eds., *Landmark Briefs and Arguments of the Supreme Court of the United States: Constitutional Law,* volume 13 (1975), 62–63.

prohibited government from drawing racial lines. Wendell Phillips proposed a Fourteenth Amendment that would have proclaimed that "no state shall make any distinction in civil rights and privileges . . . on account of race, color, or descent."[8] If adopted, that proposal would have required, as a constitutional rule, color-blind immediatism. That proposal, however, was not adopted; what was adopted was a purposefully open-ended standard that says nothing about racial distinctions. Moreover, many of the framers and ratifiers of the Fourteenth Amendment countenanced laws that explicitly differentiated people on a racial basis. In a few instances, Congress enacted laws that benefited only "colored" persons. More widespread were state laws that separated people along racial lines. Most discussed at the time were laws that prohibited people of different races from marrying one another. When asked whether such statutes were inconsistent with the demand that states afford all persons "the equal protection of the laws," the principal framers of the Fourteenth Amendment replied that there was no such inconsistency: whites could not marry blacks, just as blacks could not marry whites—*all* were subject to the *same* law and thus treated *equally*. The Supreme Court ratified that understanding of the Equal Protection Clause in 1883 (thirteen years before *Plessy*), in a unanimous ruling that included Justice Harlan. In *Pace v. Alabama,* the Court upheld an Alabama law that punished interracial fornication more harshly than intraracial fornication.[9] Since the law applied the same set of punishments to whites as to blacks, the Court saw no constitutional infirmity in the statute. It was, in the Court's view, race-neutral. True, even at the dawn of the Equal Protection Clause, there were some who repudiated oppressive racial laws that were camouflaged by race-neutral formalism.[10] But that perspective was an outlier among those with political influence.[11]

In addition to the absence of any reference by Harlan to a textual or originalist constitutional basis for his famous declaration is another noteworthy feature—one often obscured by casebook editors and others who decline to quote what the justice stated immediately before his allusion to color blindness. He wrote,

> The white race deems itself to be the dominant race in this country. And so it is, in prestige, in achievements, in education, in wealth, and in power. So, I doubt not, it will continue to be for all time, if it remains true to its great heritage and holds fast to the principles of constitutional liberty.[12]

What Harlan seemed to be saying was that, to remain ascendant, "the dominant race" did not need to resort to ruses like "equal but separate," precisely because it was dominant and would "continue to be for all time" if it observed "the principles of constitutional liberty." These principles, he suggested, posed no real threat to white supremacy. Under the new regime of the Thirteenth, Fourteenth, and Fifteenth Amendments, white supremacy in American society could continue unabated, albeit in a new form. This reading of Harlan's color-blindness declaration comports realistically with the historical, as opposed to the romanticized, Justice Harlan—after all, he was a former slave owner, initially opposed the Thirteenth Amendment, and tolerated various forms of segregation, notwithstanding his *Plessy* dissent.*[13]

---

* According to Professor Neil Gotanda, Harlan "was arguing that the white race was clearly superior to the black race in civil society . . . and did not need the government support of Jim Crow segregation laws to maintain white racial hegemony. . . . He was content to allow racial privilege to continue, so long as basic civil rights were maintained on a nonracial basis." "Failure of the Color Blind Vision: Race, Ethnicity, and the California Civil Rights Initiative," *Hastings Constitutional Law Quarterly* 23 (1996): 1135, 1150. See also Gotanda, "A Critique of 'Our Constitution Is Color

Whatever its limitations, the Harlan dissent did challenge Jim Crow segregation. Perhaps unsurprisingly, therefore, it was absent from the pages of the *United States Reports* during the long period when segregation was seen as an innocuous racial distinction, as opposed to a dangerous form of racial discrimination. But the absence continued even after the Court began to view segregation critically. References to the Harlan dissent appear in neither *Brown v. Board of Education* nor any of the other Supreme Court decisions of the 1950s that invalidated state laws requiring racial segregation. The first time the Harlan declaration surfaces explicitly in a Supreme Court opinion subsequent to *Plessy v. Ferguson* is in a concurring opinion by Justice William O. Douglas in a 1961 case, *Garner v. Louisiana,* that invalidated the arrest of civil rights demonstrators.[14] That reference, however, is fleeting; for the remainder of the 1960s it does not reappear.

The Harlan declaration became an oft used rhetorical weapon only later, when it was deployed against affirmative action policies that would have been almost inconceivable when *Plessy* was decided.* Justice Potter Stewart (joined by William Rehnquist) inaugurated the practice in 1980, when he began a dissent to the Court's validation of a federal minority business set-aside pro-

---

Blind,'" *Stanford Law Review* 44 (1991): 1. Laurence H. Tribe, "In What Vision of the Constitution Must the Law Be Color-Blind?" *John Marshall Law Review* 20 (1986) ("Perhaps it is anachronistic and even unfair to stress too heavily the manifest racism in Justice Harlan's full statement").

* In 1868, when the Fourteenth Amendment was ratified, anti-black sentiment was rife, but leavened by egalitarian themes that seeded and reflected the reforms of Reconstruction. As noted previously, Congress enacted legislation during the era of Reconstruction expressly for the benefit of African Americans. By 1896, when *Plessy* was decided, new variants of Negrophobia had emerged. By then, special congressional solicitude for blacks had become passé. See Rayford Logan, *The Betrayal of the Negro: From Rutherford B. Hayes to Woodrow Wilson* (1965); Heather Cox Richardson, *The Death of Reconstruction: Race, Labor and Politics in the Post–Civil War North 1865–1901* (2001).

gram by quoting Harlan.[15] Elaborating, Stewart wrote that in *Plessy* the Court had upheld "a statute that required the separation of people on the basis of race . . . because it was a 'reasonable' exercise of legislative power and had been 'enacted in good faith for the promotion of the public good.'" Now, he complained, "the Court upholds a statute that accords a preference to citizens who are 'Negroes, Spanish speaking, Orientals, Indians, Eskimos, and Aleuts,' for much the same reasons. I think today's decision is wrong for the same reason that [*Plessy*] was wrong."*

In 1989, Justice Scalia invoked "our Constitution is colorblind" to explain his vote to invalidate a municipal business set-aside program analogous to the one to which Stewart had objected. According to Scalia:

> The difficulty of overcoming the effects of past discrimination is as nothing compared with the difficulty of eradicating from our society the source of those effects, which is the tendency—fatal to a Nation such as ours—to classify and judge men and women on the basis of their country of origin or the color of their skin.[16]

In 2007, Justice Clarence Thomas invoked the Harlan declaration in a case that was not precisely an affirmative action dispute but did involve the legality of state action challenged by whites who claimed that, on account of race, their children had been victimized by reverse discrimination. Supporting the plaintiffs, Thomas declared, "My view of the Constitution is Justice Harlan's view."[17]

* That some jurists before Justice Stewart were already using the Harlan declaration against affirmative action is suggested by Justice Brennan's preemptive refutation the previous year. According to Brennan, "the shorthand phrase 'our constitution is color blind' . . . has never been adopted by this Court as the proper meaning of the Equal Protection Clause." *Regents of the University of California v. Bakke,* 438 U.S. 265, 355 (1978) (Brennan, J., concurring and dissenting).

Apparent Attractions of Color Blindness

Constitutional color blindness has several apparent attractions. It offers a clear rule—disregard race altogether in assessing people—that is vivid, succinct, and simple: it enjoys the bumper sticker advantage.[18] It is understandable to all and amenable to accountability. It appears to promise a clean break with a long-standing and ugly practice.

Color blindness also offers the allure of heroic associations, at least until the 1970s. Above I quoted the color-blindness rhetoric of nineteenth-century radical racial egalitarian Wendell Phillips. His ideological heirs kept this rhetoric alive throughout the twentieth century. The first time racial "color blindness" surfaces in the pages of the *New York Times* is in a story on December 26, 1942, that begins

> Complete social, political and economic emancipation for the Negro in a world that is seeking true democracy was advocated here [in Black Mountain, North Carolina] by the Fellowship of Southern Churchmen in a statement which calls upon all followers of democracy and Christianity to become "color blind."[19]

In the next mention, a year later, the *Times* quotes scholar-diplomat Ralph Bunche, declaring that real democracy is "color blind."*[20]

Throughout the 1950s and '60s, in sermons, speeches, editorials, essays, letters, briefs, and conversations, opponents of

---

* Ralph Bunche (1903–1997) was an African American educator and diplomat who was awarded the Nobel Peace Prize in 1950. See Brian Urquhart, *Ralph Bunche: An American Life* (1998).

segregation raised high the banner of color blindness to shame, challenge, and overcome state-enforced racial separateness. Champions of conservative constitutional color blindness are not fabricating the quotations they cite in which the lawyers attacking segregation praised color blindness. The appellants in *Brown v. Board of Education* did declare in their brief: "that the Constitution is color blind is our dedicated belief."[21] During oral argument, the representatives of the appellants did assert, "we have one fundamental contention which we will seek to develop . . . and that contention is that no State has any authority under the equal protection clause of the Fourteenth Amendment to use race as a factor in affording educational opportunities among its citizens."[22] Judge Constance Baker Motley did state that the "Bible" to which the great Thurgood Marshall turned in his most depressed moments was the Harlan declaration.[23]

A major lesson articulated by leading figures in the Civil Rights Revolution was that assessing people without regard to race was the proper, enlightened, virtuous way to judge individuals. Of course, that view was always contested: the Civil Rights Revolution was a hydra-headed movement that contained large and influential strains of black nationalism.[24] But color blindness was one of its signature themes. That theme gained enormous prestige, and understandably so. It seemed to be the very antithesis of segregationist race consciousness. It voiced a healthy desire to break free from the suffocating anti-colored bigotry that had saturated every sphere of American life.* It expressed an urge

---

* Setting forth its racial policy in 1961, Hugh Hefner's Playboy Club declared:

> We believe in the acceptance of all persons in all aspects of life on the basis of individual merit and without regard to race, color, or religion. Do we mean that we are "tolerant" and that we believe in economic integration but not social integration? No, we mean we believe in being "colorblind"

to tear away the blinders that prevent people from appreciating fully the humanity of others.

Constitutional color blindness, at least certain versions of it, displays additional attractions. One is a healthy skepticism regarding the ability of individuals and institutions to distinguish between various sorts of racial distinctions—including the good, the bad, and the evil. After all, leading twentieth-century jurists—including Oliver Wendell Holmes, Jr., Louis Brandeis, Benjamin Cardozo—failed to recognize the reality of Jim Crow racial distinctions. And in *Korematsu v. United States,* a Supreme Court that decried invidious racial discrimination simultaneously affirmed it in an egregious ruling upholding the unwarranted internment of people of Japanese descent during World War II—a ruling supported by some of the leading civil libertarians and civil rights champions of the day.[25] A color-blind constitutionalist might well argue, with *Plessy* and *Korematsu* in mind, that in the presence of the entrancing race line, no one, including the judges, can safely be trusted. Where race is concerned, he might contend, we must lean over backwards to protect ourselves from ourselves.

Another case that lends support to skepticism regarding the capacity of courts to suitably distinguish between permissible and impermissible types of racial discrimination is *Swain v. Alabama* (1965).[26] In *Swain,* the Supreme Court upheld racially discriminatory peremptory challenges for purposes of trial tactics while banning racially discriminatory peremptory challenges for purposes of excluding a race wholesale from jury service. Over

---

straight down the line. We believe that any form of racial discrimination is illogical. . . .

Cited in Chris Jones, "The House of Hefner," *Esquire,* April 2013.

the next several decades, it became clear that courts were simply unable to police that differentiation; they routinely allowed both sorts of racially discriminatory peremptory challenges.[27] In *Batson v. Kentucky* (1986),[28] the Court finally conceded that failure and barred racially discriminatory peremptory challenges altogether.*

Another context that draws into question the capacity of courts to distinguish appropriately between permissible and impermissible racial distinctions is racial profiling—the use of race as a factor in police surveillance.[29] Defenders of racial profiling differentiate racial harassment, which they abjure, from the good-faith use of race for law enforcement, which they support. The latter, they argue, is defensible because it enables authorities to screen, at less expense, those sectors of the population that are more likely than others to contain the criminals for whom officials are searching. Proponents of this theory stress that resources are scarce, that dangers are grave, and that efficiently locating criminals helps everyone—including, sometimes *especially,* those in the groups subject to racially selective surveillance. They maintain that it makes good sense to consider whiteness if the search is for a Ku Klux Klan assassin, blackness if the search is for

---

* Actually, in *Batson* the Court only prohibited *prosecutors* from using race in peremptory challenges. In a later case, *Georgia v. McCollum,* 505 U.S. 42 (1992), the Court extended the *Batson* prohibition to defense attorneys. Interestingly, Justice Clarence Thomas dissented, maintaining that "black criminal defendants will rue the day that this Court ventured down this road that will inexorably lead to the elimination of peremptory strikes." Id. at 69. It seems odd that Mr. Color Blindness should care about the racial consequences of a legal rule so long as the rule was instituted and implemented with no intent to disadvantage or advantage any group because of race.

Some jurists believe that the *Batson* and *McCollum* responses are inadequate, because lawyers will continue to deploy racially discriminatory peremptory challenges, knowing that the ban against them will be underenforced, as virtually all antidiscrimination measures are underenforced. These critics argue that courts or legislatures should get rid of the peremptory challenge altogether, thus removing it as even a potential tool of racial discrimination. See *Batson v. Kentucky,* 476 U.S. 79, 107–8 (1986) (Marshall, J., concurring).

drug couriers in certain locales, and Arab ethnicity if the search is for agents of al Qaeda.[30]

Opponents, by contrast, resist the attempt to create a protected category of "good" racial discrimination for purposes of law enforcement. They see racial discrimination in surveillance as frightening and illegitimate across the board. Stressing the harm racial profiling generates (including the fear, resentment, and alienation felt by innocent people in the profiled group), opponents laud the virtues of a strict antidiscrimination rule.

A notable feature of this conflict is that many partisans of each of the racial-profiling positions embrace rhetoric, attitudes, and values that are completely at odds with those they adopt when confronting affirmative action. Supporters of racial profiling who trumpet the urgency of communal needs when discussing law enforcement suddenly become fanatical individualists when condemning affirmative action. Supporters of profiling who are willing to impose what amounts to a racial tax on profiled groups denounce affirmative action for betraying color blindness. A similar turnabout can be seen on the part of affirmative action supporters. Impatient with talk of communal needs when assessing racial profiling, they often have no difficulty with subordinating the interests of individual white candidates to communal missions such as overcoming past racial wrongs. Opposed to race consciousness in law enforcement, they demand race consciousness in deciding whom to admit to college or select for a job.[31]

There are still other controversies that highlight difficulty in determining the character of racial distinctions. One involves housing quotas.[32] Integrationists committed to preserving multiracial neighborhoods came up with the idea of controlling the racial demographics of residency to prevent the phenomenon of "tipping." Tipping occurs when a group (typically whites) flees an area en masse when they perceive that the number of newcomers from a different group (say, blacks) is sufficiently large to irrevocably change the racial character of the neighborhood. The number that provokes panic is known as the "tipping point." People flee fearing that the neighborhood will deteriorate rapidly, destroying their investment in their home. To stabilize integrated communities, reformers have recommended the imposition of racial quotas that prevent the influx of "too many" people of this or that group (though typically what that means in practice is preventing the influx of "too many" Negroes). Color-blind immediatists denounce such quotas. But so, too, do some proponents of affirmative action who see the quotas as demeaning impediments that prevent African Americans from obtaining the housing they need. At the same time, there are some proponents of affirmative action who defend housing quotas. They acknowledge that the quotas racially restrict housing resources but emphasize that the quotas preserve a delicate rarity in America: integrated residential arrangements.

Or consider race policy and adoption.[33] Until recently, many states practiced race matching. They encouraged prospective parents to adopt children of the same race as themselves, often discouraging or even barring interracial adoption. Officials and like-minded allies argued that same-race placements would put vulnerable children in settings in which their status as adoptees was less evident, in which they would avoid the prejudice that still targets multiracial families, and in which their own identities would perhaps be better supported by similarly situated parents. Was race matching good or bad? Opinions vary. Some who support affirmative action condemn race matching, while some who support affirmative action embrace race matching.

Such complexities challenge the notion that racial distinctions can confidently be sorted and policed. One solution is to ban all racial discriminations. That response stems from doubts about capacities to deal appropriately with the seductions of racial selectivity. The argument runs that "because neither legislators nor judges may be trusted to choose wisely in this vexed area, and because we know that racial classifications are often highly injurious, our only safety lies in foreclosing altogether a power of government we cannot trust ourselves to use for good."[34]

PROBLEMS WITH COLOR BLINDNESS

There are, however, problems with the proposition that "under our Constitution, the government may not make distinctions on the basis of race."[35] Few color-blind immediatists are actually committed to erasing *all* governmental racial distinctions. Most have a narrower commitment than that—color blindness in routine matters, but with a safety hatch that permits attentiveness to race when "necessary." In *Johnson v. California,* the Supreme Court adjudicated the constitutionality of a policy under which California prison officials racially segregated prisoners for their first several weeks of incarceration to prevent violence fomented by racial gangs.[36] The Court held that, despite the prison context, officials were still required to justify this racial discrimination to the same extent as any other governmental racial discrimination. Justices Thomas and Scalia dissented. The Court's leading color-blind immediatists argued that a due regard for the expertise of prison authorities and the reality of prison violence justified relaxing the normal rules regulating governmental racial distinctions. Their argument is reasonable, but at odds with the declaration that "our Constitution is color blind."

Thomas and Scalia say they believe that the Constitution should be color blind—except in an emergency. That raises the question of why the lingering destructive consequences of past racial wrongs do not count as "emergencies" that justify the use of racially selective measures. These circumstances could be deemed emergencies. What Professor Nathan Glazer observed decades ago continues to obtain today:

> General principles that mean justice are often suspended to correct special cases of injustice, as when the immigration laws are suspended to let in a body of political refugees, or moneys are made available to those suffering from floods or other disasters. Negroes are victims of a man-made disaster more serious than any flood.*[37]

Glazer is absolutely right: racial minorities, particularly blacks, have been hit by man-made disasters more serious than any flood. But Thomas, Scalia, and those of similar mind have decided to decline to designate those catastrophes as such.† By conceding, however, that in some circumstances the government may properly differentiate on a racial basis, color-blind constitutionalists confess that they do not believe literally that government must *never* make racial distinctions. Rather, they believe that only under exceptional circumstances may the government properly differentiate on a racial basis. The issue then becomes identifying those circumstances, a task that gives rise to the inescapable messiness of judicial line drawing. The vaunted simplicity and clarity of constitutional color blindness is not so

---

* For a revealing examination of differing governmental response to disaster see Michele Landis Dauber, *The Sympathetic State: Disaster Relief and the Origins of the American Welfare State* (2013).

† That judges, especially Supreme Court justices, make choices is important to recognize, because of widely believed myths regarding the supposed separateness of "law" and "politics." The justices maintain that, regardless of their personal views, they *must* reach a given result because a source above and outside of themselves—"the Constitution"—*compels* them. They claim, in so many words, that the Constitution makes them do what they do. That portrayal is erroneous, if not false. The justices are not without will. They make policy through disputable judgments that stem from a complex mixture of ingredients including ideology, inclination, and emotion. Norms of various sorts limit them in certain ways, to be sure. But judges and justices have considerably more freedom of action than they typically acknowledge.

simple and clear after all. There is no escape from the necessity and risk of judgment.

Previously, I noted that an allure of color blindness is its association with admirable figures who have used color-blindness rhetoric to oppose white supremacism. I think here of abolitionists, founders of the National Association for the Advancement of Colored People (NAACP), and the organizers of the Student Non-Violent Coordinating Committee (SNCC). One should recognize, however, another facet of the history of color blindness: false proponents who use its rhetoric only tactically. Enemies of *Brown v. Board of Education* long fought against it, only to embrace a narrow version of the landmark ruling to forestall the implementation of a broader conception of desegregation.[38] Similarly, white supremacists long fought against any and all versions of color blindness, only to embrace eventually a version serviceable for suppressing affirmative action.* This describes the trajectory of a number of influential figures, including Senators Sam Ervin and Jesse Helms.[39] It also describes the evolution of Supreme Court Justice (and later Chief Justice) William H. Rehnquist. A law clerk to Justice Robert H. Jackson when *Brown v. Board of Education* was before the Supreme Court, the young Rehnquist opposed invalidating segregation (though he later lied about this matter during confirmation hearings before the Senate).[40] Nothing that Rehnquist did prior to his elevation to the high court suggested that he had substantially changed

---

* This point, often ignored, is noted by Michael Kinsley: "Today's sanctimonious calls for color-blind equal opportunity for the benefit of whites come primarily from political elements that opposed the principle when it was enshrined, in the nineteen fifties and sixties, to help blacks. (Republicans as moderate as George Bush were against the 1964 Civil Rights Act.) And even today much of the political power of anti-affirmative-action rhetoric is based on its appeal to emotions that are anything but color-blind." "The Spoils of Victimhood, or the Case Against the Case Against Affirmative Action," *The New Yorker*, March 27, 1995. See also Nancy MacLean, *Freedom Is Not Enough: The Opening of the American Workplace* (2006), 225–64.

his mind as he matured. As a justice, he persistently sought to constrain *Brown*'s scope. He also resisted exporting to new areas antidiscrimination norms helpful to minorities. For example, when the issue arose whether racially discriminatory peremptory challenges should be prohibited as violative of the Equal Protection Clause, Rehnquist characteristically voted in the negative.[41] With remarkably few exceptions, he somehow managed to avoid detecting illicit discrimination against racial minorities in the many cases that came before him during his long tenure.[42] Just as consistently, he ruled in favor of whites claiming to be victims of reverse discrimination in affirmative action litigation. Rehnquist was a notably low-key justice. But in several affirmative action disputes, Rehnquist exhibited an indignation that seldom surfaced in other contexts. Indifferent to or tolerant of racial policies that wrongly disadvantage racial minorities, Rehnquist was keenly alert to racial policies he perceived as unfair to whites. Resistant to color-blind constitutionalism when open, invidious racial discrimination oppressed colored people, Rehnquist was all too willing to deploy color blindness against affirmative action that would benefit racial minorities.[43] I am *not* suggesting that racism infects all opposition to affirmative action. I am saying that racism does infect some—indeed, a substantial element—of the opposition. Indeed, antagonism toward affirmative action has been a signature symptom of "color blind" racism.*

---

* I define color-blind racism as a manifestation of racial prejudice against a given group notwithstanding denials of bias on the part of the actor in question. For other, typically broader, sometimes excessively expansive, formulations of color-blind racism, see Eduardo Bonilla-Silva, *Racism Without Racists: Color-Blind Racism and the Presence of Racial Inequality in the United States* (third edition 2010); Michael K. Brown, Martin Carnoy, Elliott Currier and Troy Duster, et. al, eds., *Whitewashing Race: The Myth of a Color-Blind Society* (2003).

Immediatist color blindness is also marred by an insistence, on the part of some of its proponents, that affirmative action is the moral and legal equivalent of Jim Crow segregation and kindred forms of racial oppression. A striking example is found in the jurisprudence of Justice Clarence Thomas, who declares:

> I believe that there is a moral [and] constitutional equivalence . . . between laws designed to subjugate a race and those that distribute benefits on the basis of race in order to foster some current notion of equality. . . .
>
> That these programs may have been motivated, in part, by good intentions cannot provide refuge from the principle that under our Constitution, the government may not make distinctions on the basis of race. . . .[44]

Thomas's equating of racial distinctions intended to impose white supremacy with racial distinctions intended to undo white supremacy is one of the silliest, albeit influential, formulations in all of American law. As Professor Stanley Fish trenchantly remarks:

> to argue that affirmative action, which gives preferential treatment to disadvantaged minorities as part of a plan to achieve social equality, is no different from the policies that created the disadvantages in the first place is travesty of reasoning. Reverse Racism is a cogent description of affirmative action only if one considers the career of racism to be morally and medically indistinguishable from the therapy we apply to it.[45]

On the role of racial prejudice or a desire for racial group dominance in the struggle over affirmative action, see Jim Sidanius, Pem Singh, John J. Hetts, "It's Not Affirmative Action, It's the Blacks: The Continuing Relevance of Race in American Politics," in David O. Sears, Jim Sidanius, and Lawrence Bobo, eds., *Racialized Politics: The Debate About Racism in America* (1999) ("the desire for group dominance is among the important motives underlying opposition to race-specific policies").

When the University of Texas practiced Jim Crow segregation, it excluded *all* blacks categorically because they were black, pursuant to a state policy that was based on a belief in the contaminating inferiority of African Americans and a desire to express and propound that belief. When the University of Texas practices affirmative action, the policy decreases by a relatively small amount whites' chances for admission. The large majority of seats continue to be occupied by whites. When affirmative action contributes to the rejection of a white candidate (who would have been accepted if he were black), the aim is not to express or propound disdain for him because of his race; the aim is to undo past racial wrongs or to foster integration or to facilitate diversity. Those who say that intent is immaterial are wrong. An accidental slap is altogether different from an intentional one. A sign declaring "Blacks Welcome!" means something altogether different from a sign declaring "Blacks Unwelcome!"—though both contain a racial distinction.

Color-blind constitutionalism does not *require* negating the obvious difference between segregation and affirmative action. One could concede, as one sensibly should, that invidious discrimination rests on a different moral and legal plane than positive discrimination (i.e., affirmative action) yet still conclude that the latter (like the former) is unwise and unlawful. Judge Thomas Gibbs Gee showed this to be so in an opinion voicing his disagreement with a Supreme Court decision upholding an affirmative action program. Gee said that, as a lower-court judge, he would follow what he perceived to be the Supreme Court's erroneous judgment because, to him, affirmative action was merely mistaken as opposed to evil. Judge Gee declared that if he thought affirmative action were evil—truly equivalent to slavery or segregation—he would have felt honor-bound to resign rather than enforce a malevolent social policy.[46] Justice Thomas and like-minded immediatists, however, refuse to make such distinctions and instead paint with excessively broad strokes, proclaiming all the while that their own personal policy preferences have nothing to do with their judicial rulings.

Fortunately, assertions of mistaken equivalence have provoked judicial critique, the most pointed and sustained of which is found in a dissent written by Justice John Paul Stevens (and joined by Justice Ruth Bader Ginsburg).[47] Contrary to what Thomas maintains, Stevens argues that there is a gaping difference "between a decision by the majority to impose a special burden on the members of a minority race and a decision by the majority to provide a benefit to certain members of that minority notwithstanding its incidental burden on some members of the majority." Striving to clarify a difference that he perceives to be virtually self-evident, Stevens first posits the difference abstractly and then offers examples that provide concrete particularity to his analysis. "There is no moral or constitutional equivalence," he writes, "between a policy that is designed to perpetuate a caste system and one that seeks to eradicate racial subordination." Whereas "invidious discrimination is an engine of oppression, subjugating a disfavored group to enhance or maintain the power of the majority, . . . remedial race-based preferences reflect the opposite impulse: a desire to foster equality in society." It does no good, Stevens remarks, to ignore the gulf that should be seen as separating positive from negative racial distinctions. To do so, he complains, is to

disregard the difference between a "No Trespassing" sign and a welcome mat. It would treat a Dixiecrat Senator's decision to vote against Thurgood Marshall's confirmation in order to keep African

Americans off the Supreme Court as on a par with President John-son's evaluation of his nominee's race as a positive factor. It would equate a law that made black citizens ineligible for military service with a program aimed at recruiting black soldiers.

Using the equivalence of negative and positive racial discrimi-nation as a predicate, purveyors of color-blind immediatism threaten to devour public policies much needed in the ongoing struggle against racial hierarchy that the color-blind slogan once aided. If race-conscious public policy is verboten (except in the event of the sort of emergencies that Justices Thomas and Scalia are willing to recognize), then the legitimacy of affirma-tive action is nonexistent. Color-blind immediatism, moreover, threatens not merely hard forms of affirmative action but soft forms, too, including disparate-impact antidiscrimination law.

The central case in disparate-impact law is *Griggs v. Duke Power Co.* (1971), the Supreme Court's first substantive adjudi-cation of a suit arising from Title VII of the Civil Rights Act of 1964.[48] The defendant in *Griggs* organized its workforce in a way that perfectly mirrored Jim Crow etiquette: the lowest-ranking "white" job was higher than the highest "Negro" job. When the Civil Rights Act took effect, the defendant ended its two-tier system but simultaneously imposed new requirements for hiring and promotion. These new requirements—a high school diploma and minimal scores on a standardized aptitude test—made no reference to race and were administered even-handedly to applicants of all races. Still, they had an adverse effect on a considerably larger percentage of black as opposed to white applicants. Black workers who were denied positions on account of the new requirements sued under Title VII. Lower courts ruled against them, finding that the defendant had not imposed the new requirements for the purpose of excluding a disproportionate number of blacks. The plaintiffs asserted, however, that even if the defendant had acted with no racial purpose, its conduct still amounted to illegal racial discrimination under Title VII, because (1) the employment requirements generated a "disparate impact" (i.e., excluded a considerably greater percentage of blacks than whites) and (2) the employer could not show that the requirements in question actually revealed the presence or absence of skills or knowledge that the business truly needed employees to have. Somewhat surprisingly, the Supreme Court embraced the plaintiffs' argument. Without dissent and with President Richard Nixon's appointee, Chief Justice Warren Burger, writing for the Court, the justices agreed that the new requirements created disparate impact. The justices also agreed that the defendant had failed to justify adequately its reliance on requirements that generated disparate impact. After all, in previous times, (white) employees seemed to have done just fine without obtaining a high school diploma. As for the standardized test, the defendant had failed to have it validated, meaning that Duke Power Co. had failed to have experts examine the test to make sure that it looked for the precise skills needed by the business, as opposed to mere general knowledge.

"What is required by Congress," Chief Justice Burger wrote, "is the removal of artificial, arbitrary, and unnecessary barriers to employment when the barriers operate invidiously to discriminate on the basis of racial or other permissible classification."[49] Burger's definition of barriers "operat[ing] invidiously to discriminate" included more, however, than purposefully treating certain people worse or better than others on account of race. It also included using, without adequate justification, nonracial indicia that have a disproportionate adverse effect on a plaintiff's racial group. In other words, the Court interpreted Title VII as prohibiting not only unjustified direct discrimination but also

unjustified *indirect* discrimination—exclusions stemming from
disabilities presumed to arise from past racial mistreatment, for
instance, as was the case in *Griggs,* inferior education caused by
segregated schooling. The prohibition on criteria causing disparate impact is not unequivocal. It does not necessarily bar criteria
that, because of past racial wrongs, disproportionately burden
vulnerable groups. If a business needs workers who know trigo-
nometry, it is not disabled by Title VII from testing for that
knowledge, even though the consequence of doing so disproportionately excludes blacks on account of historical racial inequities regarding education. *Griggs* simply demands that the need
cited by the business be real. "If an employment practice which
operates to exclude Negroes cannot be shown to be related to job
performance," Burger declared, "the practice is prohibited."[50]

Griggs was an interpretation of a statute—Title VII. But some
jurists thought that the methodology of *Griggs* should be con-
stitutionalized so that, even in the absence of a racial motivation, public practices or policies that impose a disparate impact
on racial minorities without adequate justification could still
be invalidated. In the early 1970s, several courts did constitu-
tionalize *Griggs.*[51] The lesson of these rulings was that satisfy-
ing the Equal Protection Clause required more than merely
the absence of an intention to disadvantage racial minorities as
such. These rulings maintained that officials must also take the
affirmative step of refraining from imposing avoidable harms
on racial minorities. Imagine a municipal employer seeking to
fill ten openings for positions on the police force. One thousand people apply for the job. Officials whimsically, but with
no consciousness of race, decide to make knowledge of poetry a
job requirement. That requirement knocks out a disproportionate number of racial-minority applicants. Under the disparate-

impact theory, that requirement is racially discriminatory unless it can be shown to be job-related, despite the fact that officials used it with no attentiveness to race whatsoever. Indeed, under the *Griggs* model, lack of attentiveness to race is part of the problem. The *Griggs* regime demands that decision makers be concerned with race insofar as they can refrain from imposing avoidable burdens upon racial minorities. Under *Griggs,* it is not enough to be innocent of intending to harm for racial reasons. Under *Griggs,* even if the decision maker is innocent in terms of intention, it must still minimize any harms imposed if those harms bear down disproportionately on racial minorities. *Griggs* insists that decision makers take that extra step.

By extending *Griggs* from its statutory origins to the broader field of federal constitutional law, some courts ruled that, for public authorities, a soft form of affirmative action was required— not merely allowed, but actually mandated. In 1976, however, the Supreme Court repudiated the constitutionalizing of *Griggs*. In *Washington v. Davis* and subsequent cases,[52] the Court held that in order to make out a racial discrimination claim under the Fourteenth Amendment, a plaintiff must prove discriminatory intent. The Court ruled that it is not enough to show that a challenged policy imposes disparate impact and that the defendant cannot set forth a good justification for the challenged decision or policy. The Court insisted upon proof that the defendant, for racial reasons, intended to bring about the adverse effect.[53]

Washington v. Davis and its progeny have been harshly criticized for inhibiting courts from acting on constitutional grounds against all but the most blatant types of racial mistreatment. The *Washington* court, however, clearly indicated that legislative bodies seeking to address more subtle or structural forms of racial subordination were free to enact statutes deploying the disparate-impact theory. Color-blind immediatists have opposed that grant of judicial permission.

During the Reagan years, Attorney General Edwin Meese orchestrated an attack on the disparate-impact theory of discrimination that emanated from the Department of Justice's Office of Legal Policy. Revealingly titled "Redefining Discrimination: 'Disparate Impact' and the Institutionalization of Affirmative Action," the department produced a Report to the Attorney General, which charged that "discrimination" as traditionally understood had been "redefined." As traditionally understood, "discrimination" entailed conduct motivated by illicit considerations (i.e., race, gender, religion, etc.). As redefined by disparate impact, "discrimination" now also forbade a much wider array of conduct: (1) decisions or policies in which character of the motive behind the conduct is not dispositive; (2) conduct generating statistically disproportionate adverse effects; and (3) conduct found to be wanting in justification in light of the disparate impact created. The Reagan-Meese Department of Justice objected to this expanded conception of "discrimination":

> As a result of this redefinition . . . many of the nation's laws incorporating the non-discrimination principle of equal treatment have, in Orwellian fashion, been turned on their heads to effectively *require* the very behavior that they proscribe—the color and gender-conscious treatment of individuals—so that statistically proportionate representation or results for groups might be achieved. In short, through this redefinition of discrimination, the rights of individuals to equal treatment have been subordinated to a new right of proportional representation for groups.*[54]

---

* The Report to the Attorney General is scathing in its assessment of *Griggs,* which it refers to as "an epochal case . . . by virtue of its contrivance of the disparate impact standard." The decision, the report declares, "represented a U-turn in civil rights

Despite its sharp criticism of disparate impact, the Report to the Attorney General posited no corrective action to be taken. The critique, however, proved to be an influential force in its own right. Several years later, the Supreme Court cut back on disparate impact, animated by anxieties of the sort expressed by the report. When Congress responded with legislation that essentially codified *Griggs,* President George H. W. Bush vetoed the legislation, calling it a "quota bill" on the very grounds articulated by the report to Attorney General Meese. President Bush subsequently signed a legislative compromise. But that, of course, did not still the color-blind immediatist attack on disparate impact.*

The Supreme Court has thus far avoided confronting the constitutionality of disparate impact. But, as Justice Scalia notes, it has "merely postpone[d] the evil day on which the Court will have to confront [that] question."[55] His position is no secret. "Title VII's disparate impact provisions place a racial thumb on the scales," he notes,

> often requiring employers to evaluate the racial outcomes of their policies, and to make decisions based on (because of) those racial outcomes. That type of racial decisionmaking is . . . discriminatory. . . . The government must treat citizens as individuals, not as simply components of a [racial] class. . . . And, of course, the purportedly benign motive for the disparate-impact provisions cannot save the statute.[56]

Color-blind immediatism could end up devouring more than explicitly racial affirmative action and disparate-impact

---

jurisprudence, back to race-conscious decision-making." Office of Legal Policy, U.S. Department of Justice, Report to the Attorney General, "Redefining Discrimination: 'Disparate Impact' and the Institutionalization of Affirmative Action" (November 4, 1987), 14.
* See pages 67–69.

antidiscrimination law. It theoretically threatens old-fashioned disparate-treatment antidiscrimination law as well as programs like Texas's Top Ten Percent Plan that say nothing about race on their face but were proposed for the purpose of assisting racial minorities. Many observers see traditional antidiscrimination laws as fundamentally different in kind from affirmative action and thus wholly insulated from the objections of immediatist color-blind constitutionalism. Like affirmative action, however, the ban on racial-disparate treatment—intentionally disfavoring a person because of his race—also requires race consciousness. A simple charge of racial-disparate treatment requires a court or other adjudicator to identify the race of the plaintiff, or at least the perceived race of the plaintiff. Furthermore, the aim to redistribute resources along racial lines was the primary legislative purpose behind Title VII and similar statutes. Prior to Title VII, racially unregulated employment markets severely disadvantaged black workers even when they possessed skills and education comparable to white competitors. To assist black workers, within the confines of equal opportunity competition, was the primary aim animating the coalition that ultimately succeeded in passing Title VII. Some in this coalition might have been more interested in other things—economic efficiency, social stability, the international image of the United States, appearing to be enlightened, electoral calculation, paying off a political debt, etc., etc., etc. But the main publicly expressed purpose of the law was specifically to assist black Americans. Yet that aim is illicit according to certain strains of color-blind immediatism. There is little chance that immediatists will challenge, much less dislodge, disparate-treatment antidiscrimination law. Regardless of the collective intent with which it was conceived, disparate-treatment law is widely viewed now as color blind, or at least race neutral, and uncontroversial. It is simply too deeply embedded for anyone to attack without incurring discredit.*[57]

More vulnerable are policies, like the Texas percentage plan, that are race-silent on their face but established primarily for reasons of racial redistribution. Following a court decision barring racial affirmative action at the University of Texas, the Texas legislature enacted a plan under which any student in the top 10 percent of his or her high school graduating class became automatically eligible for admission to any Texas public university. This legislation was proposed and passed for the publicly expressed purpose of recovering at least some of the racial diversity lost on account of the abolition of the more conventional affirmative action program under which race had been explicitly counted as a plus by admissions officials.†

The Top Ten Percent Plan is widely dubbed "race neutral," in that race is absent from criteria of eligibility. More whites than Latinos or blacks obtain entry to the university through this program. But is it "race blind"? It is difficult to see how that label can be applied to a program that was established for the purpose of doing in a roundabout way what the invalidated affirmative action plan had done more directly by explicitly counting minority status as a plus in the admissions competition. The Top Ten Percent Plan arose from a keen concern with

---

* The impulse to see antidiscrimination as affirmative action was put on striking display during oral argument on February 27, 2013, in *Shelby County v. Holder*, involving the constitutionality of a key provision of the Voting Rights Act. Justice Antonin Scalia referred to that provision derisively as a "racial entitlement" immune to normal political pressure and thus perhaps warranting judicial invalidation. See Adam Liptak, "Voting Rights Law Draws Skepticism from Justices," *New York Times*, February 27, 2013. Fortunately, Scalia's remark received apt and widespread criticism. See "Antonin Scalia's Uber-Activism," *Economist*, February 28, 2013; Linda Greenhouse, " 'A Big New Power,' " New York Times Online, March 6, 2013.

† See pages 221–239.

the racial demographics of admitted students at the University of Texas, not from a race-blind indifference to those demographics. Moreover, if under present conditions the racial shoe were on the other foot, if the Texas legislature passed a law for the purpose of increasing the number of white students admitted to the university system, opponents would rightly label the law an exercise in illicit racial discrimination. Race would be absent from the face of the policy but deeply present right beneath the surface, as intended by the law's authors. We have seen such laws before: they were a staple of the Jim Crow era. The "grandfather" clauses in disenfranchising voting laws, for example, said nothing expressly about race when they excused from new registration requirements people whose grandfathers had been eligible to vote before the Civil War. Everyone knew, however, the purpose of the grandfather clause: to excuse whites (whose grandfathers could vote prior to the Civil War) while subjecting to new burdens blacks (whose grandfathers were ineligible to vote prior to the Civil War).[58]

Policies that are silent as to race but initiated for the purpose of establishing or maintaining a racial advantage for whites are invalidated nowadays on the grounds that they violate the constitutional prohibition against government action motivated by race that cannot meet the standard of judicial strict scrutiny.[59] Why, then, are policies like the Texas Top Ten Percent Plan allowed to stand? The reason is that rigorous immediatist color-blind constitutionalism is not yet fully ascendant. Even some immediatists are willing to countenance racially motivated percentage plans so long as in form they are silent as to race. President George W. Bush's solicitor general objected to the affirmative action programs at the University of Michigan that explicitly used racial selectivity to achieve diversity but welcomed "race neutral" programs designed to accomplish the same goal.[60] Justice O'Connor condemned the racially explicit set-aside program that was invalidated in *City of Richmond v. Croson,* complaining of, among other things, the absence of "any consideration of the use of race-neutral means to increase minority business participation in city contracting."[61] Returning to this point in *Grutter,* O'Connor, on behalf of the Court, declared that narrow tailoring of affirmative action programs requires "serious, good faith consideration of race-neutral alternatives that will achieve [diversity]."*[62] The Court voiced the same belief in *Parents Involved v. Seattle School District No. 1.* Invalidating the racial classification in dispute, the Court noted disapprovingly that the defendants had "failed to show that they considered methods other than explicit racial classifications to achieve their stated goals."[63] Clearly, in other words, the Court, including even its most conservative members, has suggested that there are no equal protection problems raised by policies that aim to assist racial minorities but deploy no express racial classifications in doing so.

On the other hand, some color-blind immediatists are already laying siege to policies such as the Texas percentage plan— policies they see as racially motivated affirmative action that is merely disguised. Hence, Professor Brian T. Fitzpatrick contends that "when government actors attempt to gerrymander racial results by race-neutral means . . . these efforts are often no more legal than the explicit racial discrimination that they are trying to avoid."[64] Ward Connerly objects as well. "It is not the legitimate business of government in America," he writes, "to promote 'diversity.'"

---

* In *Grutter* the Court upheld the explicit racial selectivity of the affirmative action program in question, maintaining that its designers had sufficiently considered workable race-neutral alternatives. *Grutter v. Bollinger,* 539 U.S. 306, 339–340 (2003). ("Narrow tailoring [of racially selective affirmative action] does not require exhaustion of every conceivable race-neutral alternative.")

When the government uses "race-neutral" means to achieve a desired racial outcome instead of explicit race preferences, the two approaches become a distinction without a difference. The deliberate pursuit of racial diversity by either race-neutral means or "quotas'" is the antithesis of ensuring that individuals are guaranteed freedom from government discrimination and then letting the chips fall where they may.[65]

Similarly opposed is Roger Clegg, an immediatist activist who is general counsel of the Center for Equal Opportunity, a leading proponent of color-blind constitutionalism. Most percent plans, he complains, are discriminatorily motivated ruses featuring "jiggled admissions criteria with an eye on racial outcomes." That attentiveness to racial outcomes, he maintains, is their flaw, because "decisions should be made without regard to racial and ethnic winners and losers." In his view, "the benign neglect of race is long overdue."[66]

The espousal of racial laissez-faire expressed by Gregg and Connerly highlights the biggest drawback of immediatist color blindness: its equanimity in the face of a social structure still terribly disfigured by past and ongoing racial wrongs. In every aspect of American life, racial differentials in well-being don't just exist—they erupt, showering the social landscape with stark, familiar patterns: average white life spans that are four to six years longer than those of blacks, black infant mortality rates that are twice those of whites, black poverty rates that are double those of whites; a black-white ratio of incarceration that is eight-to-one; a situation in which, for every dollar of wealth held by a typical white family, the typical black family holds a dime.[67]

Ward Connerly says, "Let the chips fall where they may," as if where they will fall is a mystery unconnected to the past and dependent only upon individuals' pluck and luck. Clarence Thomas says much the same thing. At the beginning of his dissent in the University of Michigan Law School affirmative action case, Justice Thomas espouses a social Darwinist message that he fashions in words spoken in 1865 by Frederick Douglass:

> What I ask for the negro is not benevolence, not pity, not sympathy, but simply *justice*. The American people have always been anxious to know what they shall do with us. . . . I have had but one answer from the beginning. Do nothing with us! . . . If the apples will not remain on the tree of their own strength, if they are worm-eaten at the core, if they are early ripe and disposed to fall, let them fall! . . . And if the negro cannot stand on his own legs, let him fall also. All I ask is, give him a chance to stand on his own legs! Let him alone! [Y]our interference is doing him positive injury.*[68]

We know, however, where the chips will fall in a laissez-faire regime governed by benign neglect of racial inequity: they will fall in favor of whites who continue to benefit in innumerable

---

* Justice Thomas's reference to Douglass is misleading. He omits what Douglass said immediately after the language cited above, statements that make clear that Douglass was referring to discriminations *against* blacks not in favor of them.

> If you see [a black person] on his way to school, let him alone, don't disturb him! If you see him going to the dinner table at hotel, let him go! If you see him going to the ballot box, let him along, don't disturb him! If you see him going into a work-shop, just leave him alone—your interference is doing him positive injury.

At times, Douglass did make statements consistent with the approach Thomas favors. Douglass once declared, for example, "we utterly repudiate all invidious distinctions, whether in our favor or against us, and only ask for a fair field and no favor." Douglass also made statements, however, that cut in precisely the opposite direction. "Whenever the black man and the white man [are] equally eligible, equally available, equally qualified for an office," he declared in 1871, "the black man at this juncture of our affairs should be preferred." Or consider this remark from 1894: "It is not fair play to start the Negro out in life, from nothing and with nothing, while others start with the advantage of a thousand years behind them." Clearly Douglass's thinking on this matter was more complex than Justice Thomas's attribution suggests. See Waldo E. Martin, Jr., *The Mind of Frederick Douglass* (1984), 69–72; Eric J. Segall, "Justice Thomas and Affirmative Action: Bad Faith, Confusion, or Both," Wake Forest Review Online, February 15, 2013.

ways from a long train of beliefs, habits, practices, and institutions that systematically privilege Euro-Americans and that
systematically disfavor "others," especially blacks, Latinos, and
Native Americans. In the face of that daunting reality, more is
required than adherence to a merely procedural color blindness.
What is required is a commitment to racial justice that unavoidably entails the racial redistribution of scarce resources.

My remarks thus far have mainly addressed immediatist color
blindness, the version that would abolish affirmative action
now. What about the version that grudgingly tolerates affirmative action for now but views it distastefully as morally and
legally tainted? That is the version of color blindness that Justice O'Connor expressed in her *Grutter* opinion, asserting that
"race-conscious admissions policies must be limited in time"
because, after all, "a core purpose of the Fourteenth Amendment
was to do away with all governmentally imposed discrimination
based on race." That version of color blindness ought also to be
rejected. What should be recalled—though it is difficult to do so,
given the salience, popularity, and prestige of the color-blindness
mantra—is a point made by Professor Paul Freund years ago:
that the constitutional mission of the Fourteenth Amendment is
the establishment of equal protection, not of color blindness.[69]

The strategy of disregarding race—color blindness—is a
methodology that can, in appropriate circumstances, serve as a
tool helpful for attaining equal protection. It should not, however, be elevated to the rank of a purpose, a principle, a goal
in and of itself. The strategy of disregarding race can be used
for good. But it can also be used for bad, to cover up injustice. Recall that, textually, the United States Constitution of
1787–1864 said nothing expressly about race. It was thus, in an
important sense, race blind—even while it countenanced racial

slavery and all manner of other forms of racial mistreatment. Only when race was expressly mentioned in the revolutionary legislation and constitutional provisions of Reconstruction did the U.S. legal order challenge American pigmentocracy.

Finally, I note that it is odd that so many have staked so much on a figure of speech that celebrates a disability.* Some people are truly color blind: they cannot distinguish colors. But they ought not be happy about this; their incapacity is a bane. It is past time to come up with a new metaphor that will better serve our desire to create within our multiracial society a more perfect union—one decidedly more fair than what we have today.

---

* That Justice is a blind goddess
  Is a thing to which we blacks are wise.
  Her bondage hides two festering sores
  That once perhaps were eyes.

"Langston Hughes, Justice," in Arnold Rampersad and David Roessel, eds., *The Collected Poems of Langston Hughes* (1994): 31. See also Bennett Capers, "On Justitia, Race, Gender, and Blindness," *Michigan Journal of Race and Law* 12 (2006): 203.

4.

The Supreme Court and Affirmative Action
The Case of Higher Education

The Supreme Court's handling of the controversy over affirmative action in higher education mirrors the thinking and sentiments of the nation's governing elite. Hence, over the past thirty years the Court's jurisprudence has been marked by ambivalence and confusion, obfuscation and inconsistency. The Court has made a series of ambiguous, ad hoc rulings that reflect the country's racial anxieties. That this is so ought not generate disappointment, for this outcome was entirely predictable. Seldom does the Court depart far or long from "the mainstream" of elite public opinion. When the mainstream is divided, so, too, is the Court.

The Supreme Court's reckoning with racial affirmative action in higher education is a drama with three main acts thus far: (1) *Regents of the University of California v. Bakke* (1978); (2) *Grutter v. Bollinger* and *Gratz v. Bollinger* (2003); and (3) *Fisher v. Texas* (2012).

Bakke

In 1974, Allan Bakke sued the University of California–Davis School of Medicine. The locus of his complaint was a policy under which Davis had set aside sixteen out of one hundred seats for qualified "disadvantaged" "blacks," "Asians," "Indians," or "Chicanos." Applicants who were not deemed to be affiliated with those groups were ineligible for consideration for the seats set aside.* Bakke was a white man who applied for a place in the medical school. Twice rejected by the Davis "regular" admissions program, he was turned down by all twelve medical schools to which he applied. These rejections were probably due in part to his age: a Marine Corps veteran in his thirties, Bakke was older than most entering medical students.

Bakke suspected, and it was subsequently confirmed, that applicants with lesser records than his, in terms of standardized test scores and grades, had been accepted at Davis through its "special" admissions program. Bakke's science grade point average (GPA) was 3.44; the average GPA of special admittees was 2.62. His Medical College Admission Test (MCAT) score for science was 97; the average MCAT score for science among special admittees was 37. This program was overseen by a separate committee to which were sent the applications of those who wished to be considered "disadvantaged" members of a "minority group." The special committee relaxed Davis's typical standards. While regular candidates with grade point averages below

---

* The goals and criteria set forth initially by the Davis authorities are notably confusing. In 1973, applicants to Davis were told the following about the special program. "A special subcommittee of the Admissions Committee, made up of faculty and medical students from minority groups, evaluates applications from economically and/ or educationally disadvantaged backgrounds. The applicant may designate on the application form that he or she requests such an evaluation. Ethnic minorities are not categorically considered under the [special program] unless they are from disadvantaged backgrounds." *Regents of the University of California v. Bakke*, 438 U.S. 265, 272 (1978). One plausible interpretation was that the special program was open to all, regardless of race, but that racial minorities would be given a preference within it. Several whites did indeed apply via the special program. None obtained admission, and subsequently courts found that, in fact, the special program considered only racial-minority applicants. Ibid. at 276, 289. ("The special admissions program is undeniably a classification based on race and ethnic background. . . . [W]hite applicants could compete only for 84 seats . . . rather than the 100 open to minority applicants.")

2.5 were summarily rejected, there existed no grade point average cutoff for special applicants. Moreover, the difference in the grade point averages and standardized test scores distinguishing regular admits from special admits was conspicuous. In 1974, the science GPA of regular admits was 3.36; for special admits, 2.42. The average MCAT scores for regular admits were 69 (verbal), 67 (quantitative), and 82 (science); for special admits, 34 (verbal), 30 (quantitative), and 37 (science).

Prior to the institution of the special program, the number of racial minorities admitted to Davis had been negligible. When the school opened in 1968, with a class of fifty, it had admitted three people of Asian ancestry, but no blacks, Chicanos, or American Indians. The special program was inaugurated in 1970, and in 1971 the entering class was enlarged to one hundred. In 1971, four blacks, nine Chicanos, and two Asian Americans gained admission through the special program; at the same time, one black, no Chicanos, and eight Asian Americans gained admission through the regular program. In 1972, five blacks, six Chicanos, and five Asian Americans gained admission through the special program; no blacks, no Chicanos, and eleven Asian Americans gained admission through the regular program.

In 1974, the year of Bakke's second rejection, the sixteen seats in the special admissions program were allocated to six blacks, seven Chicanos, and three Asian Americans. In the regular admissions program, no blacks were accepted, four Chicanos were accepted, and five Asian Americans were accepted. The remaining seats in the entering class in 1974 were presumably occupied by whites.

Bakke claimed that by favoring minority candidates on a racial basis through its special admissions program, the university had violated, among other things, his right to the equal protection of the laws under the Fourteenth Amendment. A California trial court deemed the medical school's special program to be a racial quota that violated the Fourteenth Amendment (as well as the state constitution and the federal Civil Rights Act of 1964). The court refused, however, to order Bakke's admission, concluding that he had failed to show that he would have been admitted but for the existence of the special program. The California Supreme Court agreed with the trial court's constitutional ruling in an opinion written by Justice Stanley Mosk. He acknowledged the argument with which he would ultimately disagree:

> To achieve the American goal of true equality of opportunity among all races, more is required than merely removing the shackles of past formal restrictions; in the absence of special assistance, minorities will become a "self-perpetuating group at the bottom of our society who have lost the ability and the hope of moving up."[1]

Indeed, Mosk stated that the persuasiveness of that argument "cannot be denied." He quickly added, however, that there are even "more forceful policy reasons against preferential admissions based on race."

> The divisive effect of such preferences needs no explication and raises serious doubts whether the advantages obtained by the few preferred are worth the inevitable cost to racial harmony. The overemphasis upon race as a criterion will undoubtedly be counterproductive: rewards and penalties, achievements and failures, are likely to be considered in a racial context through the school years and beyond. Pragmatic problems are certain to arise in identifying groups which should be preferred or in specifying their numbers, and preferences once established will be difficult to alter or abolish; human nature suggests a preferred minority will be no more willing than others to relinquish an advantage once it is bestowed. Perhaps most important, the principle that the Constitution sanctions racial discrimination against a race—any race—is a dangerous con-

cept fraught with potential for misuse in situations which involve far less laudable objectives than are manifest in the present case.[2]

With respect to remedy, the California Supreme Court reversed the lower court, ordering that Bakke be admitted to Davis forthwith. It concluded that, insofar as the special admission program was invalid, the university bore the burden of proving that even in the absence of the program Bakke would not have been admitted. Since the university stipulated that it could not make that showing, the Court held that Bakke was entitled to admission.

The University of California then appealed to the federal Supreme Court, setting up one of the most eagerly anticipated, closely observed disputes in American constitutional history.*[3] The Court's resolution mirrored the fractured state of public opinion. Four justices—John Paul Stevens, Warren Burger, Potter Stewart, and William H. Rehnquist—agreed with the California Supreme Court's judgment in favor of Bakke but declined to reach the constitutional issue. That faction asserted that by favoring certain candidates on a racial basis, the special program violated the Civil Rights Act of 1964. Four justices— William J. Brennan, Byron White, Harry Blackmun, and Thurgood Marshall—maintained that the special program violated neither the Civil Rights Act nor the Fourteenth Amendment.

With the Court evenly split, four to four, Justice Lewis F. Powell cast the deciding vote, explaining it in an opinion that was joined by no other justice. He agreed with the California

---

* Four years before *Bakke,* the Supreme Court considered a reverse discrimination case arising from an affirmative action program at the University of Washington Law School. The Court avoided reaching a decision on the substantive merits of the case by holding that it was moot given that the law school had allowed the plaintiff to enroll and earn a diploma. Notwithstanding this procedural dodge, Justice William O. Douglas issued a dissent denouncing the defendant university's racially selective admissions program. See *DeFunis v. Odegaard,* 416 U.S. 312 (1974).

Supreme Court that the Davis medical school's special program violated the federal Constitution and that Bakke was entitled to admission. He disagreed with the California Supreme Court's belief that federal law forbade any consideration of race in selecting students. Powell concluded that the Civil Rights Act prohibited only what the Fourteenth Amendment proscribed. He then concluded that while the Fourteenth Amendment prohibited most racial selectivity—including the special program at issue—it did not prohibit *all* racially selective decision making. Powell maintained that a properly designed racial affirmative action program aimed at attaining "diversity" would be constitutional. He then sketched the acceptable sort of program that he had in mind.

Powell disappointed those who argued that "benign discrimination" favoring racial minorities should be given wide leeway and viewed as something wholly different from the "malign discrimination" that has long menaced racial minorities. At the same time, Powell expressly declared that race could be a factor in a properly designed affirmative action plan. He thus also disappointed those who sought the *total* exclusion of racial selectivity from college and university admissions as part of a broader effort to bring about immediately a color-blind legal regime.

Justice Powell's pivotal opinion has provoked a wide range of responses.

Scholars of varying ideological perspectives have found it wanting in terms of judicial craft. Professor (later Judge) Harry T. Edwards gave the opinion "poor marks."[4] Professor (later Judge) Guido Calabresi derided it as "misguided."[5] Professor Vincent Blasi said that it constituted "a disturbing failure . . . to give coherent, practical meaning to our most important constitutional ideals."[6] Professor Ronald Dworkin complained that Powell's opinion was "without sound intellectual foundation."[7]

Some proponents of affirmative action initially interpreted the Powell opinion as a major defeat. The Reverend Jesse Jackson called for demonstrations against it. Lerone Bennett, Jr., charged that it would send blacks "back to the end of the line."[8] The venerable chair of the NAACP Legal Defense and Educational Fund, William T. Coleman, Jr., complained that *Bakke* "turns the Fourteenth Amendment on its head. . . . It invokes an amendment which was adopted primarily and principally to benefit blacks to overturn state action which does just that."[9]

Other proponents of affirmative action accentuated what they perceived as the essential positive feature of the decision: its holding that, properly cabined, race could play a legitimate role in the admissions process for institutions of higher education. United States Attorney General Griffin Bell portrayed *Bakke* as "a great gain for affirmative action. It's the first time the Supreme Court ever upheld affirmative action and it did so in as strong a way as possible."[10] The attorney general's remarks put a good face on disappointment. After all, in its brief to the Supreme Court, the Department of Justice had supported the affirmative action program that Powell invalidated. But pragmatic proponents of affirmative action realized that it made little sense, given their aims, to emphasize what they disliked in the ruling. Instead they trumpeted what they saw as its upside. "The most important thing," Vernon Jordan, then the president of the National Urban League, declared, "is that a majority of the Supreme Court backed the use of race as a permissible factor."[11]

Stalwart opponents of racial affirmative action decried *Bakke* when it was announced, as they have done ever since. Professor (later Justice) Antonin Scalia mordantly remarked that while Powell's opinion reads like "an excellent compromise between two committees of the American Bar Association on some insignificant legislative proposal," it is "thoroughly unconvincing as an honest, hard-minded, reasoned analysis of an important provision of the Constitution."[12]

Others, however, have praised the opinion as a feat of judicial statesmanship that produced a "Solomonic" compromise that reconciled antagonistic and deeply felt yearnings.[13] Speculating that an outright victory for the university would have triggered an overwhelming legislative backlash, Professors Kenneth Karst and Harold W. Horowitz suggest that "Powell may have rescued affirmative action from death at the hands of the political process."[14] Another notable plaudit is offered by Professor Paul J. Mishkin, one of the authors of the *Bakke* brief for the University of California. Though Powell's decision dealt a defeat to his client, Mishkin nonetheless concluded that the Court had reached a good result.

> I consider the Court's stance in *Bakke*—the ambivalent posture made possible by Justice Powell's opinion . . . —to be a wise and politic resolution of an exceedingly difficult social problem. The Court took what was one of the most heated and polarized issues in the nation, and by its handling defused much of the heat. To lower the boil in the intense cauldron of race issues was . . . no mean nor easy achievement.[15]

Before I offer my take on Powell's opinion, I shall describe it in more detail, an investment warranted in light of its significance.

Powell maintained that "racial and ethnic distinctions of any sort [by public authorities] are inherently suspect and thus call for the most exacting judicial examination."[16] He insisted that *any* and *all* racial distinctions should trigger the *same* searching judicial inquiry—"strict scrutiny." Pursuant to strict scrutiny, judges jettison their usual deference to governmental conduct, their usual presumption that such conduct is legitimate. Applying strict scrutiny, judges are skeptical of the governmental conduct in question and indeed presume it to be illegitimate. Under strict scrutiny, a policy or decision is valid only if it is supported by a "compelling" justification and narrowly tailored to attain that goal.

Powell rejected the idea that racial distinctions benefiting racial minorities ("benign discrimination") should be appraised differently, more tolerantly, than racial distinctions burdening them ("malign discrimination"). One theory that justifies distinguishing benign from malign discrimination in constitutional law is that the Equal Protection Clause of the Fourteenth Amendment was established specifically to benefit blacks, most of whom in the 1860s were just emerging from enslavement. Powell acknowledged that "many of the Framers of the Fourteenth Amendment conceived of its primary function as bridging the vast distance between members of the Negro race and the white 'majority.' "[17] He countered, however, that "it is not unlikely that among the Framers were many who would have applauded a reading of the Equal Protection Clause that states a principle of universal application and is responsive to the racial, ethnic, and cultural diversity of the nation."[18] Moreover, the text of "the Amendment itself was framed in universal terms, without reference to color, ethnic origin, or condition of prior servitude."[19]

Furthermore, as far as Powell was concerned, whatever the situation was at the dawn of the Fourteenth Amendment, the country had moved on demographically, morally, politically, and legally. It was "no longer possible to peg the guarantees of the Fourteenth Amendment to the struggles for equality of one racial minority," he maintained, because "the United States had become a Nation of minorities."[20] Powell portrayed America as a congery of minorities in which "each had to struggle . . . to overcome the prejudices not of a monolithic majority, but of a 'majority' composed of various minority groups of whom it was said . . . that a shared characteristic was a willingness to disadvantage other groups."[21] As the country filled "with the stock of many lands," Powell contended, the reach of the Equal Protection Clause of the Fourteenth Amendment was gradually, and rightly, applied to all seeking protection from official racial discrimination. Dismissing originalist arguments in favor of an asymmetrical interpretation of the Fourteenth Amendment that would accord special solicitude to racial minorities, particularly blacks, Powell averred that "the clock of our liberties . . . cannot be turned back to 1868. . . . It is far too late to argue that the guarantee of equal protection to *all* persons permits the recognition of special wards entitled to a degree of protection greater than that accorded to others."[22]

Another justification for treating racial distinctions benefiting racial minorities more tolerantly than racial distinctions benefiting whites rests on the belief that whites as a group can fend adequately for themselves in the arena of regular politics, while blacks and other discrete, insular, and historically stigmatized groups need judicial protection against prejudiced majorities.[23] Powell rejected the sociology on which that theory rests. He saw no overweening white racial hegemony, instead perceiving that "the white 'majority' itself is composed of various minority groups, most of which can lay claim to a history of prior discrimination at the hands of the State and private individuals."[24] According to Powell, not only is it impossible to envision all of these groups receiving preferential treatment; more problematic for courts is the absence of any "principled basis for deciding which groups would merit 'heightened judicial solicitude' and which would not." Powell feared that "courts would be asked to evaluate the extent of the prejudice and consequent harm suffered by various minority groups." He anticipated that "as these preferences began to have their desired effect . . . new judicial rankings would be necessary." He believed that "the kind of variable sociological and political analysis necessary to produce such rankings simply does not lie within judicial competence." He thought that "by hitching the meaning of the [Fourteenth Amendment] to these transitory considerations, [the Court] would be holding, as a constitutional principle, that judicial scrutiny of classification touching on racial and ethnic background may vary with the ebb and flow of political forces."[25] That, Powell concluded, would be wrong.

Having determined that *all* official racial discriminations are suspect, meaning presumptively invalid, Powell proceeded to acknowledge, in accordance with previous case law, that, under certain circumstances, some kinds of racial discrimination are justifiable. But the circumstances in which such justifications apply are exceptional. The state must show that it has a "compelling" reason to use a racial classification and that the use of the racial classification is narrowly tailored to accomplish the end that is sought.

Canvassing the rationales proffered by Davis to justify its special admissions program, Justice Powell rebuffed all but one. Davis asserted that its special admissions program was justified as a strategy for remedying the effects of past societal discrimination. This rationale is entitled to concentrated attention, because it was the one that the University of California and most observers saw as the principal justification for racial affirmative action.

Its priority is clear in the brief for the Regents of the University of California:

> I. The Legacy of Pervasive Racial Discrimination in Education, Medicine and Beyond Burdens Discrete and Insular Minorities, as Well as the Larger Society. The Effects of Such Discrimination Can Not Be Undone by Mere Reliance on Formulas of Formal Equality. Having Witnessed the Failure of Such Formulas, Responsible Educational and Professional Authorities Have Recognized the Necessity of Employing Racially-Conscious Means to Achieve True Educational Opportunity and the Benefits of a Racially Diverse Student Body and Profession.[26]

Elaborating, the principal writers of the brief, Paul Mishkin and Archibald Cox, observed that "the dismantling of the formidable structures of pervasive discrimination requires great endurance and the courage to maintain the necessary great effort." They portrayed special assistance to racial minorities as an essential aspect of this dismantling of racial oppression. There is, they argued, "no substitute for the use of race as a factor in admissions if professional schools are to admit more than an isolated few applicants from minority groups long subjected to hostile and pervasive discrimination." They contended that the outcome of the case would determine whether racial minorities "are to have meaningful access to higher education and real opportunities to enter the learned professions, or are to be penalized indefinitely by the disadvantages flowing from previous pervasive discrimination." Repeatedly and insistently, the university's lawyers championed the policy of showing special solicitude to racial-minority applicants to enable them to escape limitations imposed by deprivations rooted in past historical wrongs.

The brief of the United States as amicus curiae also stressed remedying historical societal discrimination as the main justification for affirmative action, asserting in pertinent part:

> I. Race may be taken into account to counteract the effects of prior discrimination . . .

> II. The University could properly conclude that minority-sensitive action was necessary to remedy the lingering effects of past discrimination.[27]

The brief averred that "the effects of racial discrimination are not easily eliminated," that the Court had recognized "that simple elimination of future discrimination may well be insufficient to rectify what has gone before," and that "mere neutrality often is inadequate." In other words, like the university petitioner, the United States solicitor general gave priority to rectification as a justification for the special admissions program at Davis.

Powell rejected the rationale that justified affirmative action as a remedy for *societal* discrimination. The state, Powell maintained, certainly has a "substantial interest in ameliorating, or eliminating where feasible, the disabling effects of identified discrimination."[28] Here, however, the discrimination complained about had not been "identified" by legislative, judicial, or administrative findings of constitutional or statutory violations. Rather, on its own, Davis sought to assist in redressing what it perceived to be the general, systemic, ubiquitous discrimination that racial minorities have long confronted. To this Powell objected, writing that " 'societal discrimination' is an amorphous concept of injury that may be ageless in its reach into the past."[29] He asserted, moreover, that the Court had never before "approved a classification that aids persons perceived as members of relatively victimized groups at the expense of other innocent individuals in the absence of judicial, legislative, or administrative findings of constitutional or statutory violations."[30] Here there were no such findings. Davis did not purport to have made any, and, according to Powell, it lacked the institutional capacity or authority to do so. Courts and legislatures can make such determinations, Powell maintained, but not educational institutions acting on their own. As Powell saw it,

> the purpose of helping certain groups whom the faculty of the Davis Medical School perceived as victims of "societal discrimination" does not justify a classification that imposes disadvantages upon persons like [Bakke], who bear no responsibility for whatever harm the beneficiaries of the special admissions program are thought to have suffered. To hold otherwise would be to convert a remedy heretofore reserved for violations of legal rights into a privilege that all institutions throughout the Nation could grant at their pleasure to whatever groups are perceived as victims of societal discrimination.[31]

Another justification asserted by Davis but rejected by Powell was the aim of improving the delivery of health care to underserved black communities. The theory was that the training of more black physicians would enhance health care in the black communities in which these physicians were expected to practice. Powell found this rationale inadequate. Davis conceded that it could not assure that beneficiaries of the special admissions program would, in fact, "give back" by practicing in minority communities especially needful of their services. Furthermore, quoting Justice Mosk of the California Supreme Court, Justice Powell stated that

> there are more precise and reliable ways to identify applicants who are genuinely interested in the medical problems of minori-

ties. . . . An applicant of whatever race who has demonstrated his concern for disadvantaged minorities in the past and who declares that practice in such a community is his primary professional goal would be more likely to contribute to alleviation of the medical shortage than one who is chosen entirely on the basis of race and disadvantage.[32]

This brings us to the justification asserted by Davis that Powell accepted: the goal of attaining a diverse student body. Asserting that the authority of a university to select its own student body is an entailment of academic freedom that is protected by the First Amendment, Powell expressly championed granting deference on this score to the judgments of academic administrators. A university, he insisted, "must have wide discretion in making the sensitive judgments as to who should be admitted."[33] He recognized that that deference must be bounded, since "constitutional limitations protecting individual rights may not be disregarded."[34] But he believed that what he deemed to be a right to be assessed regardless of race could be subordinated somewhat by a university's aim to create what it viewed as an optimal academic environment. Several universities, most notably Harvard and Princeton, argued that an optimal academic environment required the presence of various sorts of diversity, including racial diversity. Powell accepted this argument, saying that, as against Fourteenth Amendment Equal Protection concerns, a university's desire for "diversity" "invokes a countervailing [First Amendment] constitutional interest."[35] Lauding "diversity," Powell averred that "the atmosphere of speculation, experiment and creation—so essential to the quality of higher education—is widely believed to be promoted by a diverse student body." Further, he maintained that, "in this light, [Davis] must be viewed as seeking to achieve a goal that is of paramount importance to the fulfillment of its mission."[36] Attempting to give specificity to this "diversity" value, Powell stated that

> an otherwise qualified medical student with a particular background—whether it be ethnic, geographic, culturally advantaged or disadvantaged—may bring to a professional school of medicine experiences, outlooks, and ideas that enrich the training of its student body and better equip its graduates to render with understanding their vital service to humanity.[37]

Having determined that "the interest of diversity is compelling in the context of a university's admissions program,"[38] Powell turned to whether Davis's program was acceptably structured. He concluded that on this front it had failed. Recall what the Davis special admissions program did: it set aside sixteen of one hundred seats for qualified disadvantaged racial-minority candidates who were evaluated separately from the candidates competing for places in the regular admissions program. Powell found this arrangement to be inconsistent with the goal of attaining what he termed "genuine" diversity. "Genuine" diversity—"the diversity that furthers a compelling state interest"—encompasses "a far broader array of qualifications and characteristics of which racial and ethnic origin is but a single though important element."[39] Powell complained that insofar as Davis's special program focused *solely* on racial and ethnic diversity, it hindered rather than furthered genuine diversity. Powell also objected to other features of the Davis program, such as the separate assessment of "special" as opposed to "regular" candidates and the fixed number of seats set aside for the affirmative action program.

Powell contrasted what he saw as Davis's flawed plan to attain diversity with an acceptable, indeed exemplary, plan—the Harvard College admissions program. Powell was so impressed with Harvard's description of its admissions philosophy that he appended it to his opinion. It read in pertinent part:

> In recent years Harvard College has expanded the concept of diversity to include students from disadvantaged economic, racial and ethnic groups. Harvard College now recruits not only Californians or Louisianans but also blacks and Chicanos and other minority students . . .
>
> In practice, this new definition of diversity has meant that race has been a factor in some admission decisions. When the Committee on Admissions reviews the large middle group of applicants who are "admissible" and deemed capable of doing good work in their courses, the race of an applicant may tip the balance in his favor just as geographic origin or a life spent on a farm may tip the balance in other candidates' cases. A farm boy from Idaho can bring something to Harvard College that a Bostonian cannot offer. Similarly, a black student can usually bring something that a white person cannot offer.[40]

Powell admiringly observed that in such a program,

> race or ethnic background may be deemed a "plus" in a particular applicant's file, yet it does not insulate the individual from comparison with all other candidates for the available seats. The file of a particular black applicant may be examined for his potential contribution to diversity without the factor of race being decisive when compared, for example, with that of an applicant identified as an Italian American if the latter is thought to exhibit qualities more likely to promote beneficial educational pluralism.[41]

This sort of program, Powell declared, "treats each applicant as an individual." Hence,

> the applicant who loses out on the last available seat to another candidate receiving a "plus" on the basis of ethnic background will

not have been foreclosed from all consideration for that seat simply because he was not the right color or had the wrong surname. It would mean only that his combined qualifications . . . did not outweigh those of the other applicant. His qualifications would have been weighed fairly and competitively, and he would have no basis to complain of unequal treatment under the Fourteenth Amendment.[42]

Powell cites his *Bakke* opinion as the most important he produced during his tenure as a justice. It has been highly influential. It has served as a key blueprint for racial affirmative action in higher education. It is, alas, deeply flawed.

Powell's most consequential and regrettable misjudgment was his determining that remedying societal discrimination is an inadequate justification for racial affirmative action.* He briefly mentioned that the United States is "a Nation confronting a legacy of slavery and racial discrimination."[43] But his statement is cursory and appears to carry little weight in his analysis. Powell's apparent lack of appreciation of the distinctive historical mistreatment of colored people, particularly blacks, is put into sharp relief by Justice Thurgood Marshall's opinion, which set forth in detail and with feeling the burden of America's racial past, starting with the Founding Fathers, who "made it plain that 'we the people' . . . did not include those whose skins were the wrong color."[44] Marshall recalled the status of Negroes in antebellum America as beings with "no rights which the white man was bound to respect," and recalled, too, the disenfranchisement and segregation of Negroes after Reconstruction. "The combined actions and inactions of the State and Federal Governments," he observed, "maintained Negroes in a position

---

* The point is driven home powerfully by an excellent article that has strongly shaped my thinking. See Colin S. Diver, "From Equality to Diversity: The Detour from Brown to Grutter," *University of Illinois Law Review* (2004): 691.

of legal inferiority for another century after the Civil War."[45] Marshall acknowledged the lineaments of racial hierarchy that continue to be reflected in every index of well-being from life expectancy to infant mortality to income to wealth to occupational attainment, noting that in the 1970s, while blacks accounted for around 11.5 percent of the population, they constituted only 1.2 percent of the lawyers and 2 percent of the physicians. "The relationship between those figures and the history of unequal treatment afforded to the Negro cannot be denied," Marshall declared. "At every point from birth to death the impact of the past is reflected in the still disfavored position of the Negro."[46]

Marshall delivered a sobering, realistic portrayal of an America long ruled illegitimately by an ideology and practice of white supremacy. Powell, by contrast, obscured the reality of white supremacy—the wholesale monopolization of power, wealth, prestige, and influence by Caucasians—with his invocation of "a Nation of minorities" in which various religious and ethnic groups (Jews, Catholics, the Irish, et al.) have all had to face base prejudices. True, social prejudices of all sorts have afflicted a wide variety of groups throughout American history. But it is misleading to suggest that social prejudices have been equally persistent, confining, or damaging. Although whites of various sorts have encountered bigotry in America, only with respect to people of color has bigotry enlisted the force of formal state power in effectuating exclusion and subordination. Private parties told the white Irish, Jews, and Catholics to "Stay out!" But, at least among residents, colored people are the only ones who have been told to "Stay out" by dint of law. White ethnics have been sadly mistreated. In contrast, however, to African Americans, Asian Americans, and Native Americans, white ethnics never had to contend with the peculiarly demeaning force of removal, enslavement, segregation, ineligibility for naturalization, prohibitions on land ownership, and antimiscegenation statutes.

Justice Powell contended that remedying societal discrimination did not warrant being deemed a "compelling justification." His position would be easier to swallow if he had, at any point, set forth the indicia that determine what is "compelling." He made no such offering. Justice Powell dismissed societal discrimination as "amorphous." Yet he embraced "diversity" as a compelling justification for racial selectivity. Why should anyone be persuaded that the latter is weightier and more urgent than the former? As Professor Vincent Blasi asks, with appropriate skepticism, "Can there be any validity to a conclusion . . . that a state may make race-conscious decisions regarding university admissions in order to enrich its academic dialogue, but not injustices of three centuries?"[47]

In the course of making the case for "diversity," Powell averred that "the atmosphere of 'speculation, experiment and creation' . . . is widely believed to be promoted by a diverse student body." Notice that he did not say that diversity actually enriches the collegiate atmosphere of speculation, experiment and creation. He only said that those benefits are "widely believed" to be promoted by diversity—hardly a foolproof recommendation, given the number of erroneous propositions that are "widely believed" to be true. To substantiate his assertion of a wide belief in the value of diversity, Powell cited one person—the formidable then-president of Princeton University, William G. Bowen. Powell quoted Bowen declaring that

> a good deal of learning occurs informally. It occurs through inter-
> actions among students of both sexes, of different races, religions,

and backgrounds; who come from cities and rural areas, from various states and countries; who have a wide variety of interests, talents, and perspectives; and who are able, directly or indirectly, to learn from their differences.[48]

This statement supports the assertion that educational benefit is derived from a diverse student body. But Bowen went on to remark, in a passage also quoted by Powell, that "in the nature of things, it is hard to know how, and when, and even if, this informal 'learning through diversity' actually occurs. It does not occur for everyone."[49] That attaining "diversity" could be deemed by Justice Powell to be a *compelling* justification on the basis of such a fragmentary, anecdotal, and tentative record should be disturbing.

It is not at all clear that Justice Powell's "diversity" is less amorphous and more compelling than the aim to remedy societal discrimination. After all, to repeat Bowen's concession: in the nature of things, it is hard to know how, and when, and even if "learning through diversity" actually occurs. The diversity rationale hardly seems more solid as a basis for racial affirmative action than seeking to rectify societal discrimination. It isn't. Powell simply treated it more deferentially. He applied a searching gaze to the societal-discrimination justification but a much less demanding eye to the diversity justification, even though he claimed to subject both to the same exacting standard of strict scrutiny.

Justice Powell, as we have seen, rejected societal discrimination as a suitable justification for racial selectivity in university admissions. However, as Professors Kenneth Karst and Harold Horowitz recognized decades ago, "underlying Justice Powell's approach is the unspoken assumption that the history of racial discrimination in this country inevitably makes race a valid consideration in the diversity formula."[50] Numerous observers have asked why—if "genuine diversity" encompasses all sorts of potentially instructive differences—racial difference, or, more specifically, racial difference in a colored skin, seems *always* to be an especially important factor in university admissions. The reason is that it is "the history of racial subordination, above all, that makes race socially significant."[51] When Harvard alludes to a black student bringing to the school something that a white person cannot offer, it is referring, primarily, to that student bringing "an inheritance from past societal discrimination."[52] Despite its formal packaging, Harvard's diversity rationale was thoroughly shaped by a remedial purpose. This is true to such an extent that some observers see the diversity justification as largely an elaborate pretext meant to cover the real aim of Harvard's program and the many others like it, an aim that Powell invalidated and thus drove underground—namely, the aim to remedy societal discrimination.

Powell's astute biographer, Professor John Jeffries, argues that one reason the justice eschewed the societal-discrimination rationale is that he saw "little prospect [that that] rationale would place any meaningful limit on the duration of such preferences."[53] According to Jeffries, "Powell thought of affirmative action as a transition, a short-term departure from the ideal of color-blindness justified only by pressing necessity. Allowing minority set-asides to continue until all effects of past societal discrimination had been eliminated might mean they would last forever." It is hard to see, however, how the diversity rationale addresses Powell's anxiety over duration. Presumably, universities will *always* want to obtain the "educational pluralism" said to stem from diverse student bodies. If that is so, the diversity rationale could be used as a predicate for affirmative action indefinitely. As George Will observes, "preferences as recompense for past discrimination must eventually become implausible, but the diversity rationale for preferences never expires."[54]

Although *Bakke* is formally one case, in actuality it is two: the appeal brought by the University of California–Davis and the shadow appeal that Justice Powell created, featuring the admissions program at Harvard College.[55] While Powell deemed the process at Davis to be objectionable, he deemed the process at Harvard to be palatable. The distinctions that Powell drew between them, however, were squishy and misleading. According to Powell, the Davis program displayed "a facial intent to discriminate," while "no such facial infirmity exists in an admissions program where race and ethnic background is simply one element—to be weighed fairly against other elements—in the selection process."[56] Powell insinuated that racial discrimination was absent from a Harvard-style admissions process because the race factor was "simply one element" in the program. But race was also only one element in the Davis special program. Both programs were racially discriminatory. If a racial factor is present at all, then racial discrimination is taking place. It may be "positive," "benign," or "affirmative" instead of "malign," "exclusionary," or "invidious," but it is a species of "discrimination" nonetheless.*

Powell railed against the Davis program's set-aside of a fixed number of seats (sixteen of a hundred), comparing it unfavorably with the seeming fluidity and open-endedness of the Har-

---

* In controversies involving racial profiling by police, "some courts argue that there is nothing to be concerned about if race is only one of several factors taken into account by police in determining suspiciousness. Indeed, some courts are suggesting that decisions which distinguish between persons on a racial basis do not even constitute racial discrimination when race is not the *sole* or dominant consideration prompting disparate treatment. This is a profoundly wrong view. Even if race is only one of several factors behind a decision, tolerating it at all means tolerating it as potentially the *decisive* factor." Randall Kennedy, *Race, Crime, and the Law* (1997), 148.

vard program. Justice Harry Blackmun correctly noted, however, that "the line between the two is a thin and indistinct one."[57] The self-description of the Harvard admissions policy is more opaque than the self-presentation of the Davis policy. It is thus more acceptable to some observers. But beneath the apparent differences, they overlapped on the essential point—they both used race to boost the fortunes of racial-minority applicants, with no intention of excluding whites out of any animus or indifference to them on racial grounds. Justice Powell maintained that the difference in form amounted to an important substantive divide: Harvard's program would be less objectionable to public opinion than Davis's program. This mattered, Powell insisted, because appearances matter: "Justice must satisfy the appearance of justice."[58] Critics rightly maintain, however, that Powell's concern with appearances devolved into mere public relations, facilitating the crafting of a "diversity" compromise that persists largely on the basis of winks and nods.

GRUTTER V. BOLLINGER AND GRATZ V. BOLLINGER

The second big act in the higher-education affirmative action drama involved Supreme Court rulings stemming from two challenges to admissions programs at the University of Michigan. A full appreciation of those rulings, however, requires a bit of backtracking. Toward the end of the post-*Bakke* quarter century, some judges disenthralled themselves from Powell's opinion. The most important example is *Hopwood v. Texas,*[59] a case in which rejected white applicants to the University of Texas Law School sued, claiming that they were victims of reverse discrimination. The plaintiffs argued that they had a constitutional right to be assessed by the University of Texas Law School in a process from which racial considerations were absent altogether. The United States Court of Appeals for the Fifth Circuit agreed.

When Justice Powell's *Bakke* opinion was advanced as a predicate for allowing the school to use race as one factor in selecting a "diverse" entering class, Judge Jerry E. Smith responded that, for him and his colleagues, diversity was *not* a compelling state interest. This conclusion, Smith maintained, rested on three arguments. First, Justice Powell's view in *Bakke* is not binding precedent on this issue, because no other justice joined it. Second, Supreme Court case law subsequent to *Bakke* cast doubt over the validity of Powell's diversity theory. In 1990, the Supreme Court had upheld congressional programs that, for the purpose of "diversity," gave an expressly racial boost to racial-minority entrepreneurs seeking to obtain licenses for radio and television broadcasting.[60] But in that ruling, the Supreme Court evaluated the racial distinction in question under only an "intermediate" level of judicial scrutiny. Later, the Court held that "intermediate" scrutiny was insufficient and that only "strict" scrutiny would suffice to validate racial classifications.[61] As Judge Smith saw it, no case subsequent to *Bakke* had accepted diversity as a compelling state interest under a strict scrutiny analysis.

The third prong of Judge Smith's repudiation of Powell's *Bakke* opinion was a full-bore attack on the idea that public institutions can validly count race as a credential symbolizing a quality valuable to an educational enterprise. "Justice Powell's conception of race as a 'plus' factor," Smith complained, "would allow race always to be a potential factor in admissions decisionmaking," indefinitely postponing "the ultimate goal of the Fourteenth Amendment: the end of racially motivated state action."[62] Smith also denounced the credentializing of race as just a new form of stereotyping, asserting that "the use of a racial characteristic to establish a presumption that the individual also possesses other, and socially relevant, characteristics, exemplifies, encourages, and legitimizes the mode of thought and behavior that underlies most prejudice and bigotry in modern America."[63]

Although *Hopwood* provoked howls of protest, the Supreme Court declined to review it. The Court waited seven more years before revisiting the matter of racial selectivity in university admissions. It finally did so in 2003, in the University of Michigan cases.

Jennifer Gratz and Patrick Hamacher had applied to the University of Michigan's College of Literature, Science, and the Arts (LSA), encountered rejection, and sued in 1997. Barbara Grutter had applied to the University of Michigan Law School, failed to get in, and also sued in 1997. Both sets of plaintiffs claimed that, as whites disadvantaged by the university's minority-friendly diversity program, they were victims of unconstitutional reverse discrimination. In *Gratz,* a United States district judge, heeding Justice Powell's *Bakke* opinion, ruled that "diversity" is a compelling justification for racial selectivity in university admissions. The district court also ruled that the then-existing admissions policy at LSA was suitably tailored to meet constitutional requirements, though the previous version, which the plaintiffs had faced, had not been suitably tailored. In short, the district court upheld the current LSA admissions process.

In *Grutter,* the United States district court sided with the plaintiffs but was reversed by the Sixth Circuit United States Court of Appeals. The opinion of that court, written by Chief Judge Boyce F. Martin, Jr., declared Justice Powell's *Bakke* opinion to be controlling and found the University of Michigan Law School admissions process to be consistent with it. The opinion was rather conventional and masked whatever emotions were felt by its author. The concurring and dissenting opinions were more revealing. Notable among them is a dissenting opinion by

Judge Danny Julian Boggs that rejected the idea that *Bakke* precluded consideration of the diversity issue, mocked the notion that diversity could possibly justify racial selectivity by a public university, and assailed what he saw as the egregiously loose design of the university's program. He also questioned the good faith of the law school's administration, academic experts cited by the defendants, and even his court's chief judge. Boggs alleged that the chief judge had manipulated procedures to increase the probability that pro–affirmative action judges would prevail. This charge of judicial malfeasance provoked a strong response. Judge Eric L. Clay described Boggs's allegation as "an embarrassing and incomprehensible attack on the integrity of the Chief Judge and this Court as a whole."[64] Similarly, Judge Karen Nelson Moore complained that Boggs and those joining his opinion had "done a grave harm not only to themselves, but to this Court and even to the Nation. . . . [T]heir conduct . . . is nothing short of shameful."[65]

Having savaged one another in *Grutter,* the judges of the Sixth Circuit were preparing to do battle over *Gratz* (remember that it had only received consideration by a trial judge) when the Supreme Court short-circuited the usual process by deciding to review both cases together without further intermediate appellate adjudication.*

With the precedential authority of *Bakke* in question, with judicial tempers flaring, and with all of higher education awaiting nervously, the Supreme Court heard arguments on April 1,

---

* An internal report by the Sixth Circuit Court of Appeals found that Chief Judge Martin had acted improperly in his handling of the case but recommended no disciplinary action. The Sixth Circuit's handling of the matter was subsequently criticized by a report of the Judicial Conduct and Disability Act Study Committee, chaired by Justice Stephen Breyer. See *Implementation of the Judicial Conduct and Disability Act of 1980: A Report to the Chief Justice* (September 2006), 76–78; Adam Liptak, "Court Report Faults Chief Judge in University Admissions Case," *New York Times,* June 7, 2003.

2003, and issued decisions on June 23, 2003. The result mimicked *Bakke*. A majority of the justices for the first time expressly embraced the proposition that "diversity" is a compelling justification for racial selectivity in admissions to higher education. The Court also affirmed Powell's strictures regarding narrow tailoring. That led to victory for the law school in the *Grutter* litigation, and to defeat for the LSA in the *Gratz* litigation.

Let's take a closer look at these cases.

Justice Sandra Day O'Connor wrote the Court's opinion in *Grutter*. One might well have expected her to condemn the law school's diversity program. She had denounced governmental racial selectivity in aid of racial minorities in previous cases.* In 1990, in *Metro Broadcasting v. FCC*, the United States had defended a racially selective program that aimed to assist racial-minority broadcasters (or prospective broadcasters) for the purpose of enhancing broadcast diversity. The Court upheld the program, relying substantially on Justice Powell's opinion in *Bakke*. Speaking for the Court, Justice William J. Brennan wrote that "just as a 'diverse student body' contributing to a 'robust exchange of ideas' is a 'constitutionally permissible goal' on which a race-conscious university admissions program may be predicated, so too is it constitutionally permissible to use tailored racial selectivity to facilitate diversity among broadcast licensees since doing so would enhance the diversity of views and information on the airwaves which also serve important First Amendment values."[66] Justice O'Connor disagreed. Explicitly addressing the diversity rationale, she wrote that "the interest in increasing the diversity of broadcast viewpoints is clearly not a

---

* For commentary on Justice O'Connor's affirmative action jurisprudence, see Earl M. Maltz, "Ignoring the Real World: Justice O'Connor and Affirmative Action in Education," *Catholic University Law Review* 57 (2008): 1045; Thomas R. Haggard, "Mugwump, Mediator, Machiavellian, or Majority? The Role of Justice O'Connor in the Affirmative Action Cases," *Akron Law Review* 24 (1990): 47.

compelling interest. It is simply too amorphous, too insubstantial, too unrelated to any legitimate basis for employing racial classifications."[67]

In *Grutter,* however, O'Connor flipped, replacing Powell as the indispensible conservative champion of "diversity." Writing on behalf of the slimmest of majorities, she articulated two main propositions. First, she quieted (at least temporarily) debate over the status of Powell's *Bakke* opinion, declaring, "We endorse Justice Powell's view that student body diversity is a compelling state interest that can justify the use of race in university admissions."[68] The educational benefits of diversity, O'Connor maintained, are "substantial" and "laudable." In her view, diversity promotes cross-racial understanding, helps break down racial stereotypes, and enables students to better understand persons of different races. She accepted the claim, posited by the university, that "classroom discussion is livelier, more spirited, and simply more enlightening and interesting when the students have the greatest possible variety of backgrounds."[69]

In deferring to the judgment of educators that "diversity" is essential to optimal learning on their campuses, O'Connor was staying within the parameters established by Powell. But O'Connor then innovated, stating that diversity was valuable not only to on-campus learning, and thus not only to schools but to post-university settings. Numerous studies show, she related, that student body diversity "better prepares students for an increasingly diverse workforce and society, and better prepares them as professionals."[70] These benefits, she insisted, "are not theoretical but real, as major businesses have made clear that the skills needed in today's increasingly global marketplace can only be developed through exposure to widely diverse people, cultures, ideas and viewpoints."[71] Furthermore, O'Connor averred, "high-ranking retired officers and civilian leaders of the United States military assert that, based on their decades of experience, a highly qualified racially diverse officer corps . . . is essential to the military's ability to fulfill its principal mission to provide national security." At present, though, "the military cannot achieve an officer corps that is *both* highly qualified and racially diverse unless the service academies and the ROTC use limited race-conscious recruiting and admissions policies."[72] To fulfill its mission, the military amici argued, "the military must be selective in admissions . . . *and* it must train and educate a highly qualified, racially diverse officer corps in a racially diverse educational setting."[73] "We agree," O'Connor declared on behalf of the Court, that "it requires only a small step from this analysis to conclude that our country's other most selective institutions must remain both diverse and selective."[74]

Having advanced the virtues of diversity in universities, in business enterprise, and in the military, O'Connor went further. She championed the value of diversity for a robust, unified, legitimate polity. According to the justice, "to cultivate a set of leaders with legitimacy in the eyes of the citizenry, it is necessary that the path to leadership be visibly open to talented and qualified individuals of every race and ethnicity."[75]

Second, O'Connor announced the Court's approval of the manner in which the law school had sought to attain diversity. She portrayed a process that was a rigorous sifter, receiving around 3,500 applicants for a class of around 350. Describing its aspirations, the law school said that it sought to admit candidates with "substantial promise for success in law school" and "a strong likelihood of succeeding in the practice of law and contributing in diverse ways to the well-being of others." The school also said that it sought "a mix of students with varying backgrounds and experiences who will respect and learn from each other."[76] In deciding whom to invite into its ranks, admissions officials at the law school considered applicants' undergraduate grade point averages, Law School Admission Test (LSAT) scores, and other indicia of accomplishment and promise, including recommendations and the applicants' personal admissions essays.

According to the law school, "diversity" was an important consideration in assessing each and all of the applicants. It aimed to "achieve that diversity which has the potential to enrich everyone's education and thus make [the] class stronger than the sum of its parts."[77] The school did not limit the types of diversity that might receive "substantial weight" in the process of evaluation. It expressly recognized "many possible bases for diversity admissions." The school did reaffirm, however, a commitment to "one particular type of diversity," namely "racial and ethnic diversity with special preference to the inclusion of students from groups which have been historically discriminated against, like African-Americans, Hispanics and Native Americans, who without this commitment might not be represented in our student body in meaningful numbers." To bring about the diversity envisioned, the school tried to enroll a "critical mass" of racial-minority students to "ensure their ability to make unique contributions to the character of the law school."[78]

The Court found, in Justice O'Connor's words, that the law school's admissions program bore "the hallmark of a narrowly tailored plan."[79] It provided "truly individualized consideration" in which race was used in a "flexible, non-mechanical way." All applicants, O'Connor noted, had "the opportunity to highlight their own potential diversity contributions," and the law school showed that it actually gave substantial weight to diversity factors besides race, accepting nonminority applicants with grades and test scores lower than those of some underrepresented minority applicants who were rejected. All candidates competed against one another for all of the available seats in the class, and no fixed number or proportion of places was reserved exclusively for any particular minority group. Responding to objections to the law school's aim of enrolling a "critical mass" of minority students, O'Connor assured her audience that the school's goal did not transform its program into a quota. A "quota," she wrote, "is a program in which a certain fixed number or proportion of opportunities are reserved exclusively for certain minority groups." By contrast, "a permissible goal . . . require[s] only a good-faith effort . . . to come within a range demarcated by the goal itself . . . and permits consideration of race as a 'plus' factor in any given case while ensuring that each candidate 'compete[s] with all other qualified applicants.'"[80] The law school's program sought a permissible goal, O'Connor concluded, noting that between 1993 and 1998, the number of racial minorities in each entering class varied from 13.5 to 20.1, a range she deemed "inconsistent with a quota."[81]

Chief Justice Rehnquist wrote for the Court in *Gratz*, which posed similar issues as *Grutter* but against the backdrop of a different selection scheme. As with the law school, the college declared that it sought "diversity" broadly conceived and in accordance with the guidelines set forth in Justice Powell's *Bakke* opinion. Unlike the law school, however, which purportedly subjected all students to the same holistic, individualized assessment, the college accorded underrepresented racial-minority applicants special treatment in a vivid way: it automatically bestowed upon any minority applicant twenty points in the selection competition, a number, Rehnquist noted, that amounted to one-fifth of the points needed to virtually guarantee admission. The effect, Rehnquist observed, was to make the factor of race decisive for almost every minimally qualified minority applicant.

The Court majority—which included Justices O'Connor and Breyer—gagged on the twenty points. Rehnquist complained that the automatic, class-wide benefit for all underrepresented racial-minority applicants was in conflict with Justice Powell's requirement of flexible, individualized assessment. He complained, too, of the uniform and, in his view, excessively large scope of the minority "plus." Under the college's admissions protocol, even a student with "extraordinary artistic talent" would receive, at most, five points as a bonus. Yet every underrepresented minority applicant received twenty bonus points simply on account of his or her racial status. The Court saw these features of the college's admissions process as flaws indicating the absence of the narrow tailoring needed to pass strict scrutiny. The Court therefore reversed the district court that had decided in favor of the college.

In sum, in *Gratz* and *Grutter,* the Court ratified Justice Powell's *Bakke* opinion. It held that race could serve as a "plus" for purposes of diversity but that any process using race would have to be narrowly tailored. The Court found that the University of Michigan Law School admissions program met its requirement but that the college program did not. The Court's disposition of *Gratz* and *Grutter* provoked internal criticism. In *Gratz,* Justices Souter and Ginsburg dissented from the Court's invalidation of the college admissions process. In *Grutter,* Justices Rehnquist, Scalia, Thomas, and Kennedy dissented from the Court's validation of the law school's admissions process.

Among this welter of critiques, three are particularly noteworthy. The first is that the Court has made a mess of "strict scrutiny." The purpose of strict scrutiny is to arm the judiciary with a mechanism with which to smoke out illicit purposes. It prompts judges to take special steps to make sure that the governmental action in question is actually being taken for the reasons officially expressed, to make sure that that reason is compelling, and to make sure that the action is no broader than necessary to accomplish its ends. The animating sentiment behind the strict-scrutiny doctrine is distrust. After all, strict scrutiny is invoked when the government does something—e.g., draws a race line—that prompts judicial anxiety, upending the presumption of legitimacy normally enjoyed by the government.

Both wings of the Court dissented, for different reasons, from the majority's handling of strict scrutiny as applied to affirmative action. Justice Ginsburg restated her opposition to applying "strict scrutiny" to *all* official race-dependent decision making— Jim Crow laws and affirmative action alike. "Once again," Ginsburg objected, the Court "maintains that the same standard of review controls judicial inspection of all official racial classifications."[82] In her view, "government decisionmakers may properly distinguish between policies of exclusion and inclusion."[83]

O'Connor responded by saying that, contrary to what was once thought, strict scrutiny does not represent a death sentence for governmental racial distinctions. It is not fatal, in fact, but only a signal that the Court wishes to investigate all racial distinctions seriously. If, upon investigation, the government can show the benignity and necessity of the challenged policy, then fine, it survives. If the government fails to make that showing, the policy is rightly invalidated. This does not mean that in the Court's view all racial distinctions are equivalently bad, only that all are toxic and should, at the outset, be examined searchingly.

A difficulty with the O'Connor brand of moderated strict scrutiny is that it flies in the face of a widespread inclination to associate strict scrutiny with governmental action that warrants not merely skepticism but hostility. Given what "strict scrutiny" connotes for many jurists, its invocation generates a heavy pull of presumptive illegitimacy that is exceedingly difficult to dissipate. True, O'Connor and the Court ostensibly subjected the Michigan Law School's affirmative action plan to the rigors of strict scrutiny and concluded that it passed this exacting test. But careful observers have expressed doubts about the Court's grading. They charge that in *Grutter,* O'Connor went easy on the law school's affirmative action plan and in so doing eroded the strict-scrutiny firewall.* If she and her colleagues, though purporting to apply strict scrutiny, were this willing to defer to educational authorities, one can only imagine with alarm the deference they would be willing to show to military or police officials desiring to investigate or detain individuals on a racial basis à la *Korematsu.*

There is considerable force, then, to the complaint that, in *Grutter,* O'Connor's strict scrutiny is a troublingly diluted strict scrutiny. Echoing Powell's *Bakke* opinion, she expressly accords deference to university officials based on their presumed expertise as educators. Instead of rigorously cross-examining the law school administration, O'Connor's Court accepted its claims at face value. But O'Connor's deference does not stop with the law school authorities; it extends as well to amici and scholarship supportive of those authorities.

> In addition to the expert studies and reports entered into evidence at trial, numerous studies show that student body diversity promotes learning outcomes, and better prepares students for an increasingly diverse workforce and society, and better prepares them as professionals. . . . These benefits are not theoretical but real.[84]

---

* "Although the Court recites the language of our strict scrutiny analysis, its application of that review is unprecedented in its deference." *Grutter v. Bollinger,* 539 U.S. 306, 380 (2003) (Rehnquist, C.J., dissenting). "The Court . . . does not apply strict scrutiny. By trying to say otherwise, it undermines both the test and its own controlling precedents." Ibid., 387 (Kennedy, J., dissenting).

Perhaps what the experts claim is accurate. O'Connor's opinion, however, displays virtually no engagement with the substance of that claim. The justice positively cites studies that purportedly "show that student body diversity promotes learning outcomes" without showing any awareness that at least some of these studies have been sharply challenged. She refers neither to critiques nor to studies that reach different conclusions. Ostensibly engaged in strict scrutiny, O'Connor validates a wide range of scholarship— some of it academic, some of it advocacy-inspired—with no hint of critical skepticism, no impulse to test propositions, no apparent realism about the politics of knowledge.[85]

A second critique of the Court's opinion in *Grutter* has to do with bad faith: detractors charge that proponents of affirmative action are so committed to it that they brook no impediments, not even the law, or commitments to roles as officials, scholars, or judges. They charge that the Court facilitates this heedlessness. This allegation is a central feature of Chief Justice Rehnquist's dissent in *Grutter*. Openly labeling the defendant as deceptive and the Court as gullible, Rehnquist complains that "the ostensibly flexible nature of the Law School's admissions program that the Court finds appealing, appears to be, in practice, a carefully managed program designed to ensure proportionate representation of applicants from selected minority groups."[86] Justice Kennedy is similarly damning, asserting that the law school's argument in favor of admitting a "critical mass" of minority students is nothing more than "a delusion used by the Law School to mask its attempt to . . . achieve numerical goals undistinguishable from quotas."[87]

Allegations of disingenuousness, or, indeed, outright deceptiveness, have long shadowed the affirmative action debate. A criticism of Powell's opinion in *Bakke* is that it rewarded obfuscation over forthrightness. A criticism of academic culture on many campuses is that it stifles robust debate regarding affirmative action, preferring instead rote acquiescence. A criticism of many defenders of affirmative action is that they dishonestly rally behind the banner of "diversity," though what truly animates them are other goals, such as reparations or integration.[88] Not only do opponents of affirmative action bemoan this evasiveness; some proponents do as well, even as they recognize that practicalities—e.g., receiving approval from courts—often prompt supporters to articulate justifications other than those they really most favor.* Hence, Justice Ginsburg voices a preference for "fully disclosed" affirmative action programs, as opposed to pretextual ones that proceed by dint of "winks, nods, and disguises."[89]

A third notable line of attack against the *Gratz/Grutter* validation of Powellian affirmative action issued from Justice Clarence Thomas. In addition to mounting his color-blindness critique, Thomas attacked the University of Michigan affirmative action programs for what he saw as their distracting and hollow elit-

---

* "Let's be honest: Many who defend affirmative action for the sake of 'diversity' are actually motivated by a concern that is considerably more compelling. They are not so much animated by a commitment to what is, after all, only a contingent, pedagogical hypothesis. Rather, they are animated by a commitment to social justice. They would rightly defend affirmative action even if social science demonstrated uncontrovertibly that diversity (or its absence) has no effect (or even a negative effect) on the learning environment." Randall Kennedy, "Affirmative Reaction," *The American Prospect,* March 1, 2003. See also Kent Greenawalt, "The Unresolved Problems of Reverse Discrimination," *California Law Review* 67 (1979): 87, 122 ("I have yet to find a professional academic who believes the primary motivation for preferential admission has been to promote diversity in the student body for the better education of all students"); Alan Dershowitz, "Affirmative Action and the Harvard College Diversity-Discretion Model: Paradigm or Pretext," *Cardozo Law Review* 1 (1979): 379, 407 ("The raison d'être for race-specific affirmative action programs has simply never been diversity for the sake of education. The checkered history of 'diversity' demonstrates that it was designed largely as a cover to achieve other legally, morally, and politically controversial goals").

ism.* His thinking on this subject reflects a long-standing divide within black America—a conflict whose most outstanding protagonists were Booker T. Washington and W. E. B. DuBois. Washington was rewarded handsomely by powerful white conservatives who appreciated his willingness to forswear demanding civil and political rights that whites were loath to recognize.† Likewise, Thomas was handsomely rewarded for repudiating affirmative action and other polices resisted by today's conservatives.

W. E. B. DuBois, America's first black Ph.D., was one of the founders of the NAACP and an indefatigable opponent of white supremacy.‡ A reformer, he was also an elitist, famous for his assertion that black America needed a "talented tenth" that would serve as the vanguard of the black masses. DuBois was the ideological ancestor of the racial activists whom Thomas openly detests. Just as Washington accused DuBois of being excessively invested in advancing the interests of black elites to the detriment of the black masses, so, too, does Thomas reprove defenders of affirmative action who, in his view, fail to focus sufficiently on racial minorities with "real" problems—problems more severe than potential rejection from a top twenty law school;

* The vociferousness with which Thomas excoriated the University of Michigan is noteworthy. "All the Law School cares about," he announced, "is its own image among know-it-all elites, not solving real problems like the crisis of black male underperformance." *Grutter v. Bollinger*, 539 U.S. 306, 373 (2003) (Thomas, J. dissenting). He makes this attribution of institutional selfishness without substantiating evidence and with no hint of having considered that the law school's conduct might have been actuated at least in part by generous intentions.

† Booker T. Washington, born a slave, was the founder of the Tuskegee Institute. An advisor to leading politicians and philanthropists, he was probably the most influential African American at the dawn of the twentieth century. Derided for his apparent acquiescence to white supremacy, Washington secretly assisted challenges to it. See Robert J. Norrell, *Up from History: The Life of Booker T. Washington* (2011).

‡ See David Levering Lewis, *W.E.B. DuBois, 1898–1919: Biography of a Race* (1994); *W.E.B. DuBois, 1919–1963: The Fight for Equality and the American Century* (2001).

problems that preclude one from being even a plausible candidate to any law school; problems such as dropping out of high school or becoming enmeshed in criminality. Affirmative action at the University of Michigan Law School, Thomas noted, did "nothing for those too poor or uneducated to participate in elite higher education and therefore presents only an illusory solution to the challenges facing our Nation."[90]

As I noted previously, there is merit in calling attention to the limits of racial affirmative action for purposes of expanding the scope of egalitarian reform. But that is not what Thomas was up to. He was using a classic tactic of reaction: deploying against modest reform inflated aims and the disappointment that accompanies them.[91] No one claims that affirmative action, much less affirmative action in higher education, is a panacea for all of "the challenges facing our Nation." Thomas was just creating a straw man to knock down. He asserted that affirmative action does "nothing" for those unable to take advantage of elite higher education. "Nothing" overstates the case (as Thomas is wont to do). Black youngsters in Detroit who somehow manage to graduate from high school with educational skills that give them a chance at completing college will likely find a number of institutions of higher learning that will give them special assistance—educationally, socially, financially—because of the affirmative action ethos that Thomas disparages.

Grutter was embraced with relief by many who feared that the Court was about to repudiate *Bakke*. The ruling has also been applauded by some who believe that O'Connor's elaboration of "diversity" put the concept on a far broader and stronger basis than that which Powell had set forth. Powell's diversity was a pedagogical hunch, the hypothesis of educational authorities that schooling would be improved by heterogeneity on campus. O'Connor's diversity, by contrast, contained not only the pedagogical hunch, but ideas that the Court had seemingly eschewed in previous affirmative action rulings—the need for racial-minority role models, the importance of factoring in how racial minorities assess the fairness of institutions, attentiveness not only to justice regarding individuals but justice regarding groups, the imperative to facilitate racial integration. O'Connor's opinion recalled, for some, memories of the best of the Warren Court era, as when she intoned that "effective participation by members of all racial and ethnic groups in the civic life of our Nation is essential if the dream of one Nation, indivisible, is to be realized."[92]

O'Connor's expansive rhetoric in *Grutter* does provide the *potential* for a judicial breakout from the narrow confines in which affirmative action has long been stuck. That potential has been enhanced by the strong, instructive, and hopeful readings given to *Grutter* by formidable interpreters such as Robert Post, Jack Balkin, and Cynthia Estlund.[93] Judicial language, however, is never self-enforcing; its fate is determined by what others do with that language. The reelection of Barack Obama on November 6, 2012, increased the likelihood that in the future, newly appointed judges and justices will be disposed toward nurturing and building upon O'Connor's expansive *Grutter* rhetoric. But that is only a distant possibility. For now, O'Connor's rhetoric and, indeed, the very holding that that rhetoric sought to justify, are in the hands of a Supreme Court majority that is more likely to constrict rather than expand the current contours of affirmative action jurisprudence.

FISHER V. UNIVERSITY OF TEXAS

On February 21, 2012, the Supreme Court announced that it would review *Fisher v. University of Texas at Austin*. This case

featured Abigail Fisher and Rachel Michalewicz, white applicants who failed to gain admission to the University of Texas
(UT) in 2008. They sued, claiming that they were victimized
by a process that illicitly discriminated against them on account
of their race. Recall that in 1996, in *Hopwood,* the Fifth Circuit
Court of Appeals had ruled that UT would no longer be permitted to count race as a plus for purposes of attaining diversity.
The numbers of blacks and Latinos enrolling at UT plummeted.
Subsequently, legislation was enacted for the purpose of, among
other things, using "race-neutral" means to enlarge the presence
of blacks and Latinos in the student body. This legislation provided that, with exceptions irrelevant here, Texas high school
seniors in the top 10 percent of their class would gain automatic
acceptance to any Texas state university. An openly expressed
aim of this legislation was to assist the best racial-minority students. It would enable them to gain automatic admittance to a
Texas university by being the top students where they attended
high school, even if the academic level of their school was lower
than that of peer institutions and even if their standardized test
scores were lower than those of competitors. Since schools, mirroring residential patterns, are often racially distinct enclaves,
the legislators thought that the Top Ten Percent Plan would
allow the best racial-minority students to come to the fore in the
competition for places in Texas universities, whereas previously
they would have been submerged in a sea of better-credentialed
white applicants.

The Top Ten Percent Plan succeeded only modestly in rais-
ing the number of racial minorities at UT. In the plan's first
year, African American enrollment at UT rose from 2.7 percent
to 3 percent, while Latino enrollment rose from 12.6 percent
to 13.2 percent. In 2004, African American enrollment rose to
4.5 percent, while Latino enrollment rose to 16.9 percent. Whites,

too, were eligible for the Top Ten Percent Plan and reaped benefits from it. But it assisted racial minorities disproportionately. In 2004, among freshmen who were Texas residents, 77 percent of the enrolled black students and 78 percent of the enrolled Latino students had been admitted under the Top Ten Percent Plan. By contrast, only 62 percent of the white students had been admitted under the aegis of that plan.

In 2003, the Supreme Court's *Grutter* ruling superseded *Hopwood,* opening the door in Texas once again to using race explicitly as a plus in university admissions. The UT administration walked through that door. First, it commissioned studies to assist in determining whether the university should supplement the Top Ten Percent Plan with a *Grutter*-like layer of race-sensitive affirmative action. One study examined smaller classes (five to twenty-four students) and found that in 2002, 90 percent of such classes had zero or one black student, 43 percent had zero or one Latino student, and 46 percent had zero or one Asian American student. A second study surveyed undergraduates regarding their impression of life on campus and in the classroom. Many minority students reported feeling isolated, and a majority of all students said that in their view there was "insufficient minority representation" in classrooms for "the full benefits of diversity to occur."[94]

University authorities concluded that "diversity" was essential to the optimal realization of its missions, because diverse student enrollment "break[s] down stereotypes," "promotes cross-racial understanding," and "prepares students of an increasingly diverse workplace and society." According to UT's *Proposal to Consider Race and Ethnicity in Admissions,* Texas was failing to assemble the "critical mass" of underrepresented students needed to attain the full educational benefits of diversity. To remedy this perceived failing, UT began to include race as a factor to be considered in making selections. It is the reintroduction of race as a positive feature in an applicant's profile that the plaintiffs challenge in *Fisher*.

A United States district court ruled in favor of UT. A panel of the United States Court of Appeals for the Fifth Circuit upheld the district court. Writing for a unanimous three-judge panel, Patrick E. Higginbotham ruled that UT's counting of race as a plus was constitutional, even though it was layered upon the Top Ten Percent Plan, which was itself largely animated by a desire to achieve more "diversity." He warned that the "ever increasing number of minorities gaining admission under [the Top Ten Percent law] casts a shadow on the horizon to the otherwise-plain legality of the *Grutter*-like [race as a plus] admissions program."[95] Still, for Judge Higginbotham and his colleagues, the UT admissions process as a whole was consistent with *Grutter*.

The Fifth Circuit's ruling, however, was attended by expressions of misgivings. First, as noted above, Judge Higginbotham evinced some anxiety over the legality of the race-as-a-plus diversity program, since it sat atop the Top Ten Percent Plan, which itself had been begun to address perceived deficiencies of diversity. "That the Top Ten Percent [Plan] . . . threatens to erode the foundations UT relies on to justify implementing *Grutter* policies," he observed, "is a contention not lacking in force."[96] Second, another judge on the panel, Emilio M. Garza, wrote a special concurrence that complained bitterly about what he viewed as the wrongheaded Supreme Court precedent to which he had to conform. "I concur," he wrote, "because despite my belief that *Grutter* represents a digression in the course of constitutional law, [the panel's] opinion is a faithful, if unfortunate, application of that misstep. The Supreme Court has chosen this erroneous path and only the Court can rectify the error."[97]

Third, several judges on the Fifth Circuit moved to have the entire court, en banc, review the judgment of the panel.*[98] This effort was rebuffed. But the chief judge of the Fifth Circuit, Edith H. Jones, and four colleagues nonetheless penned a scathing dissent in which she charged that the panel had "essentially abdicate[d] judicial review."[99] The dissenting judges seeking en banc review complained, among other things, that the panel had authorized "the University's race-conscious admissions program although a race-neutral state law (the Top Ten Percent Law) had already fostered increased campus racial diversity."[100] According to the dissenters, "more than 20 percent of the entering freshmen [at UT] are already African American and Hispanic, resulting in real diversity even absent a *Grutter* plan." The additional diversity contribution of the university's race-conscious admissions plan, they asserted, was "tiny," and thus far from indispensable to creating a "critical mass" of underrepresented racial minorities. Under these circumstances, they argued, the UT plan amounted to merely "gratuitous racial preferences" and should not be deemed a narrowly tailored affirmative action program that met the requirements of strict scrutiny.

Although the dissenters failed to convince a sufficient number of Fifth Circuit judges to force a rehearing of *Fisher,* they probably played a role in attracting the Supreme Court's interest in the case. The Supreme Court's announcement that it would review the Fifth Circuit's handiwork alarmed defenders of affirmative action and buoyed opponents.

Interested parties deluged the Court with briefs. The peti-

---

* Three judge panels chosen randomly typically decide cases for the twelve federal circuit courts of appeal. If a sufficient number of judges vote to reconsider a panel's decision, the case is heard en banc by all of the circuit's active judges. If a majority of judges disagree with the panel, their judgment becomes the holding of the circuit.

tioner argued that the Fifth Circuit misapplied the requirement that any use of race by public officials in making admissions decisions must be subjected to "strict scrutiny." The Fifth Circuit had erred, the petitioner maintained, by allowing UT to pursue a goal of mirroring the racial demographics of the state—a goal the petitioner condemned as "racial balancing" that was "patently unconstitutional." The actual purpose behind UT's "racial engineering," the petitioner charged, was not diversity for pedagogical purposes but rather the effectuation of a racial formula that was "purely representational."[101] Having impugned what she perceived to be the state's real, as opposed to its merely nominal, goal, the petitioner next challenged the necessity for racial selectivity at UT. The defendant, the petitioner averred, "should not be permitted to employ gratuitous preference when a race-neutral policy has resulted in over one-fifth of University entrants being African-American or Hispanic."[102]

After arguing that the Fifth Circuit had erred, the petitioner next asserted that if the Fifth Circuit had applied *Grutter* rightly, that precedent itself warranted reconsideration. "If the Fifth Circuit's reading of *Grutter* is permissible," the petitioner declared, "that decision should be clarified or reconsidered to restore the integrity of the Fourteenth Amendment's guarantee of equal protection."[103]

Various individuals and organizations supported the petitioner as amici curiae. Lawyers representing several organizations, including the California Association of Scholars, the Reason Foundation, the Individual Rights Foundation, and the American Civil Rights Foundation, launched a frontal assault on *Grutter,* calling for it to be overruled. "The diversity rationale," former attorney general Edwin Meese III wrote, "is a mere pretext masking invidious discrimination."[104] Lawyers filing a brief on behalf of anti–affirmative action public intellectuals, including Abigail and Stephan Thernstrom, similarly called for the overruling of *Grutter*. According to them, research "indicates that diversity as generated by race-based admissions simply does not lead to [. . .] purported benefits. Quite the contrary, the evidence suggests that use of race-based admissions actually undermines race relations on college and university campuses . . . [and] negatively impact[s] black and Latino students."*[105]

UT's lawyers stressed the significance of stare decisis, emphasizing that the university's "admissions plan was modeled on the type of plan upheld in *Grutter* and commended by Justice Powell in *Bakke*."[106] They acknowledged that its racially explicit affirmative action program differed in certain ways from the program challenged in *Grutter*. But they insisted that those differences should make UT's program more, rather than less, palatable to affirmative action skeptics, particularly Justice Anthony Kennedy, to whom the respondent's brief repeatedly addressed itself beseechingly. Noting, for instance, that Justice Kennedy had objected to the Michigan Law School's affirmative action plan because, in his view, it used race "to achieve numerical goals indistinguishable from quotas," the respondent's brief in *Fisher* maintained that UT "[had] not set any 'target' or 'goal' for minority admissions."[107]

The petitioner argued that UT was engaged in "racial balancing" insofar as the state's racial demographics constituted part of the predicate of the institution's overall admissions strategy. UT countered, however, that it was not involved in racial bal-

---

* Others called for the overruling of *Grutter* as well. See, e.g., Brief Amicus Curiae of Pacific Legal Foundation, Center for Equal Opportunity, American Civil Rights Institute, National Association of Scholars, and Project 21 in Support of Petitioner ("*Grutter* is irredeemably flawed and should be overruled").

ancing and that its admissions officers neither monitored the racial composition of classes nor worked backwards from any explicit or implicit racial goals to reach any defined racial target. Eschewing any political commitment to racial representation, UT's lawyers insisted that the university's "objective in considering race was to achieve the educational benefits of diversity."[108] UT's attorneys conceded that officials had paid some attention to comparisons between proportions of racial groups in the state's population and proportions of racial groups in the university's student population. But the attorneys maintained that those comparisons had been consulted merely for the purpose of identifying problems, not for the purpose of designating solutions. "The point of considering such data," they wrote, "was not to ensure that the university reaches some representational target; it was to assess whether minority groups are underrepresented at the university because, among other things, they are systematically faring poorly in the admissions process."[109]

Petitioners argued that the racial diversity generated by the Top Ten Percent Plan obviated the need for an explicitly race-based affirmative action program. UT countered with several responses. It declared that in *Grutter* the Court had "specifically rejected the argument that percentage plans are a complete, workable, and constitutionally required alternative to the individualized consideration of race in holistic review."[110] Rebutting the belief in some circles that percentage plans constitute a costless process, UT's attorneys explained that "percentage plans have serious educational tradeoffs." The university "seeks to assemble a class that is diverse in innumerable ways—including race—that advance its mission of educating students and preparing them to be the leaders of tomorrow."[111] The percentage plan, however, "with its single-minded focus on class rank—makes such nuanced judgments impossible." Furthermore, the percentage plan "forecloses the consideration of other academic criteria, including the quality of the applicant's high school, the nature of her course load, and her performance on standardized tests."[112]

UT's lawyers also noted that the Top Ten Percent Plan substantially advantaged minority students at underperforming, racially isolated schools over minority students at stronger, racially integrated schools. Even when the latter were better prepared than their counterparts at weaker schools, they often found themselves left out of the top 10 percent category because of the relative strength of the schools they attended. Officials at UT wanted desperately to admit and recruit these minority students, whom they saw as having "great potential for serving as a 'bridge' in promoting cross-racial understanding, as well as breaking down racial stereotypes."[113] Emphasizing how the absence of an explicitly racial affirmative action plan would significantly diminish diversity even with the continuation of the Top Ten Percent Plan, UT posited in its brief:

> The African-American or Hispanic child of successful professionals in Dallas who has strong SAT scores and has demonstrated leadership ability in extracurricular activities but falls in the second decile of his or her high school class (or attends an elite private school that does not rank) cannot be admitted under the top 10% law. Petitioner's position would forbid UT from considering such a student's race in holistic review as well, even though the admission of such a student could help dispel stereotypical assumptions (which may be *reinforced* by the top 10% plan) by increasing diversity within the diversity.

Supplementing the university's brief were submissions by allied defenders of racial affirmative action. In *Grutter,* amicus curiae briefs from leading figures in the military and business seem to have made an important impression on Justice O'Connor; she cited them conspicuously in her opinion. In *Fisher,* similar groups voiced the same messages. Former senior officers and civilian leaders of the armed forces (including General Colin L. Powell, General Wesley K. Clark, and Admiral Bobby R. Inman) maintained that "a highly qualified and racially diverse officer corps . . . is a mission-critical national security interest."[114] They asserted that "race-conscious policies are vital to increasing and maintaining the pool of highly qualified minority military officers."[115] They insisted that "fulfillment of the national security interest in officer corps diversity must not be imperiled by a sweeping ruling against race-conscious admissions."[116]

In an amicus curiae brief on behalf of leading businesses, including American Express, Halliburton, and Wal-Mart, lawyers argued that the Supreme Court "should reaffirm . . . that the conscious pursuit of diversity in the admissions decisions of institutions of higher education . . . is a compelling state interest."[117] This mattered to these businesses, they said, because "the only means of obtaining a properly qualified group of employees is through diversity in institutions of higher education, which are allowed to recruit and instruct the best qualified minority candidates and create an environment in which *all* students can meaningfully expand their horizons."[118]

The most moving of all the briefs submitted to the Court in *Fisher* was the "Brief of the Family of Heman Sweatt as Amicus Curiae in Support of Respondents." It revisited the experience of Heman Marion Sweatt, who had been denied admission to the University of Texas Law School in 1946. The president of the university, Theophilus S. Painter, acknowledged that, except for one consideration, Sweatt was "duly qualified for admission." Sweatt was qualified, Painter declared, "except for the fact that he is a negro." Unwilling to admit Sweatt to the state's premier law school, state officials instead admitted him to a law school for Negroes that the state legislature conjured up virtually overnight. No one registered for any of the three classes offered by the law school for Negroes, and it closed within a week of its opening. Sweatt maintained that the instant makeshift state-sponsored law school to which he had been admitted was inferior to the venerable, influential, state-sponsored law school that had excluded him solely because of animus against his race. This, he charged, violated the "separate but equal" standard of *Plessy v. Ferguson* and justified an order commanding that he be admitted forthwith to the "white" University of Texas School of Law. State courts ruled against Sweatt, holding (to their eternal shame) that the two law schools were "substantially equal." The Supreme Court, however, ruled in his favor, noting that the white school was superior in tangible assets—number of faculty, scope of library, size of student body—and, more important, intangible assets: reputation, contacts, experience—features the Court described as "those qualities which are incapable of objective measurement, but which make for greatness in a law school."[119]

Sixty-two years later, the daughter and nephews of Heman Sweatt urged the Court to uphold the affirmative action program under attack at UT. Acknowledging that their relative had been commemorated at UT in a variety of ways (a named professorship, symposia, the naming of a part of the campus), the Sweatt family asserted that "it is [the university's] commitment to creating a genuinely diverse student body—one based on a holistic review of applicants' unique history and persona, not just their race—that best honors Heman Marion Sweatt."

More than any other submission to the Court, the Sweatt family brief accentuates what should be a central concern: the unfinished business of rectification. This is a point I made at the outset of this book when I mentioned that my own parents were refugees from the Jim Crow South: segregation is not far away historically. It directly impinged upon the parents of millions of Americans alive today, often diminishing their opportunities. Some, like Heman Sweatt's daughter, were able to forge ahead and prosper despite racist impediments. But many others found themselves stymied by inherited confinements that are mirrored by the stark patterns of racial disparity that attend every index of well-being and development in American society, including educational attainment.

The Sweatt family brief reminds readers that, forty-five years after *Sweatt v. Painter*, segregation continued to infect Texas higher education. In 1994, when rejected white applicants challenged affirmative action programs at the University of Texas Law School, a federal trial judge examined in detail the pathology of uncured segregation at every level of public education in Texas, remarking that "the problem of segregated schools is not a relic of the past."[120] Judge Sam Sparks cataloged the long history of segregation in Texas schooling, including egregiously stubborn resistance to desegregation. Judge Sparks noted that, even as he wrestled with the pending challenge to affirmative action at the University of Texas School of Law, there remained a serious question whether, with respect to educational desegregation, Texas had fully and finally complied with federal statutory and constitutional requirements.

In deference to Justice Powell's opinion in *Bakke*, Judge Sparks also upheld racial affirmative action at UT for the purpose of attaining diversity. But the need for remediation was the main thrust of his opinion. Discussing the plaintiff's contention that any racial preferential treatment is unconstitutional, Judge Sparks declared that "such a simplistic application of the Fourteenth Amendment would ignore the long history of pervasive racial discrimination in our society that the Fourteenth Amendment was adopted to remedy and the complexities of achieving the societal goal of overcoming the past effects of that discrimination."[121] Later, Judge Sparks returned to this theme, maintaining that "the reasoning behind affirmative action is simple—because society has a long history of discriminating against minorities, it is not realistic to assume that the removal of barriers can suddenly make minority individuals equal and able to avail themselves of all opportunities."[122] According to Judge Sparks, "until society sufficiently overcomes the effects of its lengthy history of pervasive racism, affirmative action is a necessity."[123] Applying this general idea to the specifics of the University of Texas Law School, Judge Sparks ruled that racial affirmative action, properly designed, was permissible there because "the legacy of the past . . . has left residual effects that persist into the present." According to the judge, "those effects include the law school's lingering reputation in the minority community . . . as a 'white' school. . . . An affirmative action program is therefore necessary to recruit minority students because of past discrimination."[124]

Judge Sparks invalidated the particular affirmative action program that was in place when the *Hopwood* plaintiffs applied for admission, ruling that it did not suitably follow the directives posited by Justice Powell in *Bakke*. But he emphatically endorsed appropriately tailored racial affirmative action at the University of Texas Law School, because "overcoming the effects of past discrimination is an important goal for our society."[125]

In an opinion written by Judge Jerry E. Smith, the United States Court of Appeals reversed, holding that UT could not use race at all in selecting students. Better known for its repudiation of diversity, the Fifth Circuit in *Hopwood* also expressly rejected desegregation as a valid basis for the UT affirmative action pro-gram.[126] It maintained that Judge Sparks's conception of a reme-dial predicate for affirmative action was overly expansive. He had pointed to invidious discrimination by public primary and secondary schools and by the University of Texas as a whole. In doing so, the Court of Appeals declared, Judge Sparks had cast his net too widely, addressing historical misconduct that, albeit regrettable, was too far afield from the law school to be a proper basis there for racial affirmative action. The Court of Appeals insisted that the only racial misconduct pertinent to assessing affirmative action at the law school was misconduct by the law school itself. The Court of Appeals also rejected Judge Sparks's conclusion that the effects of the law school's own past racial discrimination were sufficiently evident to warrant a racially selective remedy. Denying that the law school's poor reputation among blacks was a vestige of past misconduct warranting affir-mative action, the Court of Appeals remarked that "knowledge of historical fact simply cannot justify current racial classifica-tions. . . . [T]he very enormity of that [historic] tragedy [. . .] lends resolve to the desire to never repeat it, and [to] find a legal order in which distinctions based on race shall have no place."[127]

Denying that blacks' perception of a hostile racial environ-ment was a vestige of segregation warranting a racially selective remedy, the Court of Appeals declared that there had been no showing of action by the university that contributed to any racial tension. Indeed, according to the Court of Appeals, "any racial tension at the law school is most certainly the result of present societal discrimination and, if anything, is contributed to, rather than alleviated by, the overt and prevalent consideration of race in admissions."[128] Finally, denying that the paucity of blacks at the law school was a vestige of past misconduct, the Court of Appeals ruled that, inasmuch as that underrepresentation was mainly attributable to acts or omissions other than those directly chargeable to the law school, there was no basis for a racially selective remedy at the law school. "Past discrimination in education, other than at the law school, cannot justify the present consideration of race in law school admissions."[129]

The ruling by the Court of Appeals on the ongoing implications of past racial misconduct by state authorities in Texas has never been reviewed by the Supreme Court. The Supreme Court declined to review *Hopwood*. Then, seven years later, in the University of Michigan cases, the Court indirectly reversed *Hopwood* by ruling, in direct contravention to the Fifth Circuit, that Powell's opinion in *Bakke* was binding and, therefore, that race could permissibly be taken into account by properly designed affirmative action programs. But the Court never did grapple with the Court of Appeals' handling of *Hopwood* as a desegregation case. *Fisher* offers the Court that possibility insofar as it, like *Hopwood,* involves the University of Texas Law School. That institution, unlike the previous ones that have helped to generate the Court's affirmative action jurisprudence, did categorically exclude or discriminate against blacks on a racial basis until the 1950s and beyond. But with the exception of the Sweatt family brief and a few others, advocates in *Fisher* have avoided the theme of remediation. At the oral argument of *Fisher,* there was no discussion at all of historical invidious racial discrimination by Texas educational institutions and no allusion whatsoever to *Sweatt v. Painter*.

The Sweatt family brief usefully demonstrates that for the purpose of adjudicating *Fisher* rightly, the ordeal of Heman Sweatt is neither ancient nor irrelevant. Yet, for all its virtues, the Sweatt family brief also manifests problems that are pervasive in our race relations law. Although it is, in part, a plea for candor, the brief ultimately joins a discursive mode that evades a full reckoning with our burdensome past. For one thing, there is no hint in the brief that the Supreme Court ruling in *Sweatt v. Painter* was itself complicit in the baleful racist fiction of segregation. After all, *Sweatt* did not invalidate racial segregation but merely held that Texas authorities had failed to meet the standard of "separate but equal" and that the Negro complainant was thus entitled to the extraordinary remedy of admission to a "white" institution. *Sweatt* was surely a step forward for racial justice. But it was a step forward within a legal environment in which the lie of segregation's innocence still held sway. Recall that when *Sweatt* was announced, *Brown v. Board of Education* remained four years in the future.

The Sweatt family brief lionizes the *Sweatt* decision, declaring,

> In *Sweatt*, this Court first recognized that in higher education, the interplay of ideas and exchange of views among students are critical. . . . It was in *Sweatt*—not *Bakke*—that the Court first found that diversity, including racial diversity, was a compelling component of effective higher education.[130]

What was most wrong with Heman Sweatt's exclusion at the University of Texas Law School, however, was not that it deprived him or others of "diversity." If the alternative law school for Negroes that the Texas authorities created overnight had offered *more* diversity than the University of Texas Law School, the arrangement would still have been outrageous and intolerable. The key deprivation was not pedagogical but an affront to basic human dignity by dint of an egregious policy based upon and expressive of the notion that blacks are a degraded caste that must be segregated from whites so as to avoid contaminating them.

Although the Sweatt family brief commendably relates Heman Sweatt's ordeal to the issues posed in *Fisher,* the brief stays within a framework that remains unduly narrow. It carefully avoids expressly justifying affirmative action on grounds of rectification. Seeking to invoke and replicate *Bakke* and *Grutter,* the brief champions "diversity" at every turn. Openly begging for Justice Kennedy's elusive favor, the brief ultimately accommodates itself to the ascendant currents of race relations law as it pleads with the Supreme Court to refrain from pruning Texas's admissions regime. I do not begrudge taking that tack to advance a cause. I do believe, though, that some advocates should be willing to voice arguments for reparatory justice, even if such arguments have previously been rejected by a majority of the justices. Things change. The composition of the Supreme Court evolves. Arguments that were once thought implausible become persuasive if backed with sufficient force. Ever since *Bakke,* the Supreme Court has wrongly rejected the rectification of "societal discrimination" as a basis for racial affirmative action. That is an argument, however, that should be preserved for the sake of future possibilities, notwithstanding current judicial disapproval.

It is widely expected that the Supreme Court will reverse the Court of Appeals ruling that upheld affirmative action at the University of Texas. One possibility is that the Court will use *Fisher* as an opportunity to relitigate *Grutter* and overrule it. *Grutter* was decided by a 5–4 majority. A key member of the majority coalition and the author of the opinion announcing the Court's judgment was Sandra Day O'Connor, now retired. She was replaced by Justice Samuel Alito, an ideologically hardened, intellectually confident conservative who seems to be hostile to affirmative action. Chief Justice William H. Rehnquist, who died in office, was replaced by Chief Justice John Roberts. But that transition changed nothing. The new chief justice is also an ardent opponent of affirmative action. Justice David Souter, who retired, was replaced by Justice Sonia Sotomayor. But that, too, changed little since both are supportive of affirmative action. Justice Elena Kagan (who replaced Justice John Paul Stevens) would almost certainly have voted, like her predeccesor, to uphold the Court of Appeals. But she recused herself, having taken a position in the litigation supporting the University of Texas as the United States solicitor general prior to her nomination by President Barack Obama. The anti–affirmative action bloc of justices would have to reach a bit to reverse *Grutter,* but they might well do so, fearing that time is running out, given the Supreme Court vacancies that are likely to open during President Obama's second term. Apprehensive about what a more liberal Court might do in the future, the conservative bloc could decide to strike now, surrounding future justices with precedents that will take time to erode, evade, or overrule.

Another possibility, more likely in my view, is that the Supreme Court will reverse the Court of Appeals on narrower grounds, ruling that explicitly racial affirmative action at the University of Texas is unnecessary and thus excessive in light of the racial diversity obtained through the Top Ten Percent Plan.

A Supreme Court ruling categorically barring race from admissions decisions—in other words, nationalizing Proposition 209 and *Hopwood v. Texas*—would have major consequences in higher education, since most colleges and universities have, for decades, relied upon Powellian diversity to guide their efforts to recruit and admit racial minorities who, absent special help, would lose out to better-prepared competitors. Such a ruling would directly affect all public universities. It would also affect most private institutions, inasmuch as their access to federal government funds is statutorily conditioned on their compliance with federal constitutional antidiscrimination standards. The protocols that colleges and universities have honed and relied upon over the past several decades, including the ritualistic, incantatory repetition of the terms "diversity" and "holistic," would presumably be rethought and reconfigured at considerable expense. Ostensibly "race-neutral" alternatives would likely take the place of explicit racial selectivity at many institutions. This has been the experience of colleges and universities in states in which racial affirmative action has been barred by voter initiatives. Still, as the *Fisher* litigation shows, there can be significant differences in the distributional effects of explicit racial selectivity versus race-neutral regimes. And there is some likelihood that at certain institutions, the discontinuation of old-style *Bakke-Grutter* racial selectivity will be superseded by nothing, as opposed to creative alternatives.

The ramifications will be more modest if the Court strikes down the Texas racial affirmative action program on account of the presence of the Top Ten Percent Plan. Officials and students in Texas will be affected, of course. At present, however, there are few if any other public universities that have pursued what officials in Texas have done in terms of layering racial-diversity affirmative action on top of a so-called race-neutral percentage plan.

Supreme Court decisions matter. But they are seldom, if ever, conclusive regarding deeply felt and sharply contested disputes. Decisions are not self-enforcing. They require interpretation and follow-up. They can inflect a conversation but not end it. No matter what the Court decides in *Fisher,* the affirmative action controversy will continue to reverberate.

5

Reflections on the Future
of the Affirmative Action Controversy

I conclude by offering three observations regarding the future of racial affirmative action in the United States. The first has to do with the likely fate of race-neutral but race-conscious measures such as the Texas ten percent law. The second concerns the trajectory of American race relations law against the backdrop of international developments. The third involves the question of a deadline for racial affirmative action.

Racial affirmative action will remain a substantial presence in American life for the foreseeable future, no matter how the Supreme Court resolves *Fisher*. The racial homogeneity in key institutions that was so prevalent and taken for granted prior to the 1960s—all-white presidential cabinets, all-white legislators, all-white firms, all-white university classes, all-white college faculties, all-white newsrooms, all-white police departments, all-white corps of military officers—is inconceivable today. Racial minorities are far less likely to confront the unyielding walls of prejudice that previous generations encountered. Larger numbers of racial minorities, moreover, hold their own in competitions with white peers, even though, as previously noted, whites still tend to outperform blacks and Latinos by a wide margin on standardized tests. Reflecting and reinforcing these changes is a sentiment, widely held, that reacts negatively to racial homogeneity in institutional life. Most Americans want to escape the gravitational pull of the country's ugly racial past. If affirmative action is required to effectuate that ambition, they will accept it, albeit in disguise.

Affirmative action disguised in plain sight includes "race-neutral" policies established for the purpose of elevating blacks and other marginalized groups but making no reference to race in their packaging.* Texas's Top Ten Percent Plan is such a policy. It is race neutral in that race plays no immediate explicit role in the criteria that determine eligibility for the plan's benefits. A student in the top 10 percent of a high school receives the benefit—automatic admission to the Texas public university system—whatever his or her race. The same rule applies evenly—neutrally—to all. On the other hand, the Top Ten Percent Plan is obviously race-conscious; one of its evident and articulated purposes was to increase the number of blacks and Latinos admitted to UT after the *Hopwood* decision invalidated the university's use of direct racial selectivity. That the Texas plan and similar programs are termed "race neutral" despite their clear purpose to assist racial minorities reflects a yearning to accommodate conflicting aims: an end to racially selective affirmative action and a simultaneous insistence that something be done to continue to advance the interests of racial minorities. The use of misleading or obfuscatory nomenclature to cover up racial realities is nothing new. The antebellum Constitution that supported slavery never used the term "slavery." And segregation was supposedly

---

* A percentage plan is not necessarily race conscious. State authorities could establish such a program with the authentic intention of preferring students on a geographical or class basis with changes in racial demographics an acknowledged but unsought collateral consequence. In fact, though, the most consequential percentage plans, those in Texas, Florida, and California, have been established primarily for racial reasons. See Michelle Adams, "Isn't It Ironic? The Central Paradox at the Heart of 'Percentage Plans,'" *Ohio State Law Journal*, 62 (2001): 1729.

equal. "Race neutral" policies that are actually race conscious are simply the latest in a long line of legal fictions in American race relations law.

Some opponents of racially selective affirmative action make much of the distinction between a law that is expressly race conscious on its face and one that is race conscious behind the scenes but raceless on its face. An example is the formidable scholar-activist Richard Kahlenberg, who writes in the aftermath of the oral argument in *Fisher*:

> In the minds of some commentators, [the race-neutral alternatives employed by UT] . . . aren't really race-neutral, because they are aimed at indirectly improving racial diversity. . . . But there is an enormous constitutional and policy difference between plans that treat individual students differently based on skin color and those that don't.[1]

Kahlenberg traces this "enormous" difference to what he sees as the "moral cost to employing racial preferences." Such decision making violates what he views as "the fundamental principle of nondiscrimination."[2]

There are several problems with Kahlenberg's formulation. First, he never answers the charge that there is little or no substantive difference between racially selective policies that openly seek to enlarge the numbers of racial minorities in key institutions and policies that seek to accomplish that purpose surreptitiously with no open reference to race. Surely Kahlenberg would accept that there is no substantive difference between laws that expressly exclude blacks from the ballot box and laws that purposely do so covertly. Both types of laws are unfairly racially discriminatory despite their difference in packaging. Packaging matters. But surely it should not be determinative. More important are the aims behind the packaging and the consequences that ensue.

Second, Kahlenberg never identifies concretely the "moral costs to employing racial preferences." There are, to be sure, moral costs that stem from employing racial preferences or dispreferences for evil reasons. But in what way are there moral costs that stem from employing racial preferences or dispreferences *for good reasons* such as assisting those hurt by past racial mistreatment? Kahlenberg doesn't say. He does say that his point would have been considered obvious by "mid-1960s liberals" and that his perspective was shared by the great Martin Luther King, Jr. But putting aside the accuracy of the historical observation,* what does it prove? Mid-1960s liberals, for all their virtues, were people limited (as are we all) by temporal circumstance. Some of them did not have the opportunity to see at close hand the sobering limits of mere antidiscrimination measures. Others did not have the wherewithal to put to optimal use the experiences they did have occasion to absorb. Why should we, better provisioned with experience than 1960s liberals, including Martin Luther King, Jr., not make use of that learning, even if the conclusions diverge from those reached by honorable ancestors?

Kahlenberg speaks reverentially of "the fundamental principle of nondiscrimination." Nondiscrimination, however, is better understood not as a "principle" but merely a tool. The pertinent principle should be racial justice. How one effectuates that principle is a matter that involves all manner of complex sociological and political judgments. Under certain circumstances, nondis-

---

* Previously I noted how opponents of racial affirmative action frequently, albeit inaccurately, invoke King for moral authority. See page 33. That misappropriation should cease.

crimination is probably the best vehicle available for attaining racial justice (or its closest practicable approximation). Under other conditions, however, racially selective affirmative action is a better vehicle.

Opponents of racial affirmative action have effectively grabbed the moral high ground by trumpeting nondiscrimination as a noble and transcendent "principle." A consequence is that supporters of affirmative action often adopt an apologetic defensive posture in which they concede that their position is morally flawed but plead for extenuation on the grounds that affirmative action will only be temporary and only be sharply limited in extent. Some advocates for affirmative action may not actually believe this but feel called upon to say it anyway, perceiving such a concession as necessary for the sake of seeming "sound" and gaining a hearing. I have felt this way in the past. No longer. The affirmative action ethos is not a necessary evil; it is a positive good.*

That is not to say that affirmative action is without risk and expense. As I have noted at some length, affirmative action does generate toxic side effects—like many useful medicines. If the side effects outpace the therapeutic benefit, the medicine should be discontinued (though, it is hoped, replaced by something more suitable). This is far from conceding, however, that affirmative action is burdened by a moral taint. Some observers who mistakenly believe that it is morally tainted somehow embrace guiltlessly so-called race-neutral, race-conscious measures. They delude themselves with thin formalism. I gain some solace, however, recognizing that they are at least moved to sup-

---

* I am aware of the delicious irony that this rhetoric was used by defenders of slavery in the nineteenth century to rehabilitate themselves.

port some intervention aimed at furthering the unfinished quest for racial justice.

The United States will have company as it continues fitfully to reform itself racially.[3] It is not the only divided society that has deployed programs that discriminate positively on behalf of marginalized groups. The Indian constitution expressly authorizes the reservation of places in favor of members of subordinate castes and other designated groups in certain jobs and in state-run educational institutions.*[4] The Canadian Charter of Rights and Freedoms authorizes "any law, program or activity that has as its object the amelioration of conditions of disadvantaged individuals or groups including those that are disadvantaged because of race, national or ethnic origin, colour, religion, sex, age, or mental or physical disability."[5] These and kindred authorizations in other nations have been acted upon and are consistent with the key provisions of international law regarding race relations.

There is arguably some tension between affirmative action and the text of the International Covenant on Civil and Political Rights (ICCPR). The covenant declares:

> All persons are equal before the law and are entitled without discrimination to the equal protection of the law. In this respect, the law shall prohibit any discrimination and guarantee to all per-

---

* The Indian constitution provides that "[t]he state shall not deny to any person equality before the law or the equal protection of the laws. . . ." It also provides that nothing in the constitution "shall prevent the State from making any special provision for the advancement of any socially and educationally backward classes of citizens or the Scheduled Castes and the Scheduled Tribes." See Constitution of India, Right to Equality, 14, 15(4).

sons equal and effective protection against discrimination on any ground such as race . . ."[6]

If "discrimination" was defined in the covenant in the unqualified fashion that color-blind immediatists advance, international law would condemn racial affirmative action. The color-blind interpretation was seen as sufficiently plausible by the American State Department to warrant the promulgation of an "Understanding" when the United States was in the process of ratifying the covenant. This Understanding set forth the United States' reading of the covenant's language. Under that reading, the covenant barred "discrimination," but permitted "distinctions" that are "at [a] minimum, rationally related to a legitimate governmental objective." In other words, during the affirmative action–friendly administration of President Clinton, the State Department made clear that, in its view, the only sort of racial "discrimination" barred by the covenant was the negative, exclusionary sort, not the positive, inclusive variety.[7]

Also pertinent to the status of racial affirmative action in international law is the International Convention on the Elimination of All Forms of Racial Discrimination. The convention outlaws racial "discrimination."* Exempted from this prohibition, however, are "special measures taken for the sole purpose of securing adequate advancement of certain racial or ethnic groups or individuals requiring such protection as may be necessary in order to ensure such groups or individuals equal enjoyment or exercise of human rights and fundamental freedoms. . . ."† Elsewhere

---

* The convention includes as "discrimination" any "distinction, exclusion, restriction or preference based on race . . . which has the purpose or effect of nullifying or impairing the recognition, enjoyment or exercise, on an equal footing, of human rights and fundamental freedoms in . . . public life."
† According to the convention these "special measures" shall not be continued "after the objectives for which they were taken have been achieved." International Convention on the Elimination of All Forms of Racial Discrimination, Art. I, Para. 4.

the convention reiterates the permissibility of affirmative action and adds that signatories "shall, when the circumstances so warrant, take, in social, economic, cultural and other fields, special and concrete measures to ensure the adequate development and protection of certain racial groups or individuals belonging to them. . . ."[8]

Although affirmative action of various sorts has been authorized by numerous countries, others have been resistant. Two with particularly close historical ties to the United States are Great Britain and France.

"The most fundamental thing to understand about [racial] affirmative action in Britain," Professor Steven M. Teles observes, "is that there is none," or at least none of the "hard" variety—racial preferences at the point of actually choosing someone for a job or a place in a university.[9] "In Britain, using differential standards to benefit minority groups [subsequent to the stage of recruitment or training] is called positive discrimination and is forbidden by the Race Relations Act of 1976 (RRA)."[10] British law does permit targeted recruitment and training for racial minorities. Hence, the British RRA expressly permits employers to encourage racial minorities to apply for job openings. For the most part, though, the RRA requires that persons be accorded the *same* treatment regardless of race. Under the RRA, "a person "discriminates" against another "if on racial grounds he treats [that person] less favorably than he treats or would treat other persons."*

The administration of the British RRA is consonant with its original intentions and legislative language. Courts, regulatory

---

* The British RRA, however, does feature a racial bona fide occupational qualification provision which permits race to be valued as a credential when it can be shown to be useful to the performance of a particular job. There is no such exception formally recognized in American antidiscrimination law.

agencies, and the ascendant sectors of British public opinion have provided little encouragement for American-style affirmative action. A paucity of racial-minority, particularly black, faces at leading universities in the United States generates major repercussions as we have seen. In Britain the conspicuous scarcity of racial minorities at Oxford and Cambridge has, thus far, caused little sustained controversy.

France, too, has pursued a course very different from the American model of affirmative action, though recently changes in both countries suggest the possibility of convergence.[11] The French constitution ensures "the equality of all citizens before the law, without distinction of origin, race, or religion."[12] This language has been interpreted as prohibiting all official racial boundary-making and thus all official race consciousness. Propounding something close to the color-blindness ideology that Ward Connerly sought to institute in California, administrators of the French census decline to elicit racial data, concerned that doing so will somehow undercut French transracial solidarity. Certain prominent figures have tentatively suggested taking race or national origin into account in selecting government officials and allocating opportunities for jobs and higher education. In 2004 President Jacques Chirac admitted that he had told his ministers to appoint someone of "immigrant origins" to head one of the country's regions. At the same time, Nicolas Sarkozy, then the minister of the interior, allowed as to how it might be necessary, given structural inequities, to take special steps to open up opportunities to France's immigrants. These moves, however, are outliers; for the most part, the French establishment has rejected affirmative action that is explicitly racial.

French authorities, however, have established programs that are silent as to race on their face (in that the criteria for eligibility say nothing explicitly about race) but race conscious in motivation and design (in that the criteria are chosen with the intention of assisting racial minorities). In allocating educational opportunities, for example, French authorities have quietly sought to influence the racial demographics of college admissions without saying so openly by using as criteria of eligibility for benefits the residential location and socio-economic class position of candidates—in other words "race neutral" affirmative action. French policy seems to be headed away from a determined indifference to racial outcomes toward an uneasy desire to assist racial minorities through means that are silent as to race albeit race conscious. American policy seems to be moving toward a similar destination but from a locus that, albeit conflicted, was previously more accepting of openly acknowledged racial affirmative action.

Other comparisons that usefully highlight important facets of the American experience with racial affirmative action involve Brazil and the Republic of South Africa.[13] Brazil received many times the number of African slaves that were shipped to British North America. Brazilian slavery, moreover, outlasted the American regime of human bondage. Whereas slavery in the United States was abolished in 1865, it was not abolished in Brazil until 1888. Slavery in the United States was followed by a long period during which blacks in the South were subjected to a dense array of segregation laws and officially sponsored (or required) discriminatory practices. Post-slavery Brazil, by contrast, was free of de jure segregation but pervaded by beliefs, customs, conditions, and practices that systematically subordinated blacks while favoring whites. The upshot was a Brazilian pigmentocracy in which light skin entailed opportunity and elevation while dark skin entailed deprivation and subordination. Notwithstanding this sobering reality, Brazilian intellectuals and policy makers created a concept of "racial democracy" that celebrated Brazil's supposed freedom from American-style bigotry.

Proponents of racial democracy frowned on attempts to understand Brazilian social stratification in racial terms or to organize racially to advance Afro-Brazilians. Hence, when activists first broached the idea of racial affirmative action in Brazil's colleges and universities, racial democracy was deployed in opposition from a wide range of ideological vantages from right to left.

For a while, the status of racial affirmative action in Brazil was stuck, as in the United States, in a stalemate. On the one hand, local authorities intermittently generated affirmative action initiatives. In 1999, for example, the city of Porto Alegre required that firms doing business with the municipality have workforces in which blacks constituted at least 5 percent of the employees.[14] That same year, the state of Bahia required that in official publicity releases at least one-third of all models or actors must be black.[15] On the other hand, opposition delayed or otherwise stymied all sorts of proposed affirmative action plans.

Recently, however, the stalemate in Brazil seems to have been decisively breached by affirmative action measures undertaken or approved by authorities at all levels of Brazilian politics and law. The Brazilian Supreme Court upheld a 2004 law that requires the University of Brasília to reserve 20 percent of its seats for black Brazilians. Still more recently, the president of Brazil signed the Law of Social Quotas that mandates that public universities allocate admissions in accordance with the racial make-up of the state in which a college or university is located. Explaining his support for the new quotas, Brazil's former president Luis Inácio Lula da Silva remarked: "Try finding a black doctor, a black dentist, a black bank manager, and you will encounter great difficulty. It's important, at least for a span of time, to guarantee that blacks in Brazilian society can make up for lost time."[16]

Another racially divided country that has used affirmative action as a means of addressing multiple pressing problems is the Republic of South Africa. Its post-apartheid constitution echoes India's. The South African constitution declares that "everyone is equal before the law and has the right to equal protection of the law." It then asserts that "[t]o promote the achievement of equality, legislative, and other measures designed to protect or advance persons, or categories of persons, disadvantaged by unfair discrimination may be taken." Political authorities have made use of this constitutional authorization, enacting legislation such as the Higher Education Act that commands all South African universities to generate "appropriate measures for the redress of past inequalities." A consequence is university admission policies that openly favor colored, Indian, and black applicants, admitting them with test scores and other indicia of achievement that are lower than those of white competitors.

The dominant political force in the Republic of South Africa, the African National Congress (ANC), enthusiastically and unequivocally supports affirmative action. Hence, for the foreseeable future, legally authorized racial selectivity in the distribution of scarce and valued resources, including seats in institutions of higher education, will be an important feature of South African life. Behind the support is a sense, on the part of leading figures, that in the South African context, affirmative action is not merely permissible but morally and legally obligatory. In the words of Nelson Mandela, the founding father of post-apartheid South Africa,

> Affirmative action is a principal means of dealing in as just and realistic a manner as possible with the progressive eradication of the guilt created by the past discrimination. It must be seen as an

alternative . . . to waiting for centuries for the market on its own to eliminate the massive inequalities left by apartheid.[17]

South Africa offers a setting for affirmative action that is less problematic in important respects than that which obtains in the United States. For one thing, South African affirmative action followed right on the heels of apartheid. Its racial beneficiaries were categorically oppressed within recent memory and those whom it collaterally disadvantages are obviously the beneficiaries of the old white supremacist regime. Remarkably, though, virtually all of the anti–affirmative action arguments that surface in America also surface in South Africa. Professor R. W. Johnson asserts, for example, that "[t]he decision to press ahead . . . with affirmative action . . . was the greatest single disaster to overtake the new South Africa."[18] In his view, affirmative action amounted to a replication of apartheid, albeit with different racial winners and losers. It lowered economic efficiency. It redistributed resources "away from the poor towards the middle classes." It mocked meritocracy since "whether a person or an institution has been 'historically disadvantaged' . . . now determined who got which job, contract, or grant." Affirmative action, Johnson writes, "offered nothing to the black majority other than worse services." Johnson is a centrist liberal. But his disdain for racial affirmative action is shared by others, including some far to his left. Hence the Marxist sociologist Neville Alexander portrays racial affirmative action in South Africa as a disappointing compromise that is a betrayal of socialist and nonracialist aspirations. "The real beneficiaries of the deal," Alexander complains, "have been the bourgeoisie and the rising black and established white middle and professional classes."[19]

I do not propound a universal assessment of racial affirmative action. Whether it is good or bad depends on local conditions—the character of the society's needs, the relative strength of those benefited and disadvantaged, the plausibility of alternative vehicles for reform. One thing clarified, though, by comparative study of affirmative action internationally is that virtually everywhere, no matter what the design of the program at issue, opposition will arise against efforts to redistribute resources regardless of the privations endured by marginalized groups or the lineage of the injustices sought to be remedied. I draw attention to the ubiquity of opposition to reform not to damn criticism of affirmative action. Criticism is essential. Specific affirmative action programs can be stupid, corrupt, counterproductive, exploitative. The ubiquity of opposition, however, should counsel against undue squeamishness in the face of criticism or an excessive concern with crafting a program free of shortcomings. Racial affirmative action in contemporary America is by no means perfect. It is riddled with problems. But it is a better response to daunting challenges than available alternatives.

As affirmative action enters a fourth decade of controversial existence in the United States, an important issue shadowing it is the matter of an endpoint. Color-blind immediatists contend that it should end now. Many who support the continuation of affirmative action contend that it should end at some point in the foreseeable future. In *Grutter,* Justice O'Connor voiced a hope for a quarter-century sunset. Writing in 2003 she averred:

It has been 25 years since Justice Powell first approved the use of race to further an interest in student body diversity in the context of public higher education. Since that time, the number of minority applicants with high grades and test scores has indeed increased. We expect that 25 years from now, the use of racial preferences will

no longer be necessary to further [the compelling interest identified by the Court].[20]

While there is nothing wrong with expressing a hope that one
day special measures on behalf of marginalized groups will no
longer be essential, anxiety about an endpoint should not be
allowed to stymie the continued deployment of affirmative
action for as long as it is needed to accomplish the wide variety
of important missions that it serves.

Throughout American history there has surfaced repeatedly
a regrettable tendency to underestimate the power of racism's
influence and to bring to an end too soon promising interventions. From differing ideological vantage points both Justices
Ginsburg and Thomas offer support to my cautionary point in
their responses to Justice O'Connor's invocation of a quarter-
century timeline. Justice Thomas observes that O'Connor

> cannot rest [her] time limitations on evidence that the gap in cre-
> dentials between black and white students is shrinking or will be
> gone in that timeframe. . . . No one can seriously contend . . . that
> the racial gap in academic credentials will disappear in 25 years.[21]

Justice Ginsburg also offered sobering reflections, stressing the
stubborn persistence of racism. "It is well documented," she
related, "that conscious and unconscious race bias, even rank
discrimination based on race, remain alive and well in our
land. . . ." Largely because of the consequences wrought by
biases "one may hope, but not firmly forecast, that over the next
generation's span, progress toward nondiscrimination and genuinely equal opportunity will make it safe to sunset affirmative
action."[22] Ending it prematurely would be a calamity.

Acknowledgments

Many people have assisted me with this book. The following read early drafts and offered useful corrections and suggestions: Michelle Adams; Gary Bell; Thaddeus Bell; Betsey Boutelle; Scott Brewer; Jonathan Bruno; Sherry Colb; Jared English; Brian Fitzpatrick; Eric Foner; Matthew Giffin; Anne Hudson-Price, Samuel Issacharoff; Henry H. Kennedy Jr.; Laura King; Michael Klarman; Amanda Korber; Sherilyn Ifill; Sanford Levinson; Patrick Llewellyn; Anthony W. Mariano; Frank Michelman; Angela Onwuachi-Willig; Richard Primus; Ronni Sadovsky; Tommie Shelby; Girardeau Spann; Marc Spindleman and Julie K. Suk. Professor Ilya Somin ventured way beyond collegial courtesy to provide a close reading of the manuscript. I am deeply grateful.

I developed many of my ideas in a seminar I taught at the University of Pennsylvania Law School as the Raymond Pace and Sadie Tanner Mossell Alexander Visiting Professor of Civil Rights. My thanks go to Dean Michael Fitts and his colleagues and students for their exemplary hospitality. I also had an opportunity to try out portions of the book at a symposium on affirmative action at the Pontifical Catholic University of Rio de Janeiro (under the auspices of Professor Angela Randolpho Paiva), at a Constitution Day lecture at Northeastern University (under the auspices of Professor Michael Tolley), at the James Fraser Smith Lecture at the University of Iowa College of Law (under the auspices of Dean Gail B. Agrawal), and at the Robert L. Levine Lecture at the Fordham Law School (under the auspices of Dean Michael B. Martin).

People who gave me a good push when I needed it include my editor, Erroll McDonald; my other friends at Pantheon Books, especially Altie Karper and Michiko Clark; my agent, Andrew Wylie; and my assistant, Benjamin Sears.

The dean of Harvard Law School, Martha Minow, has been unreservedly helpful, as have been other colleagues, particularly a remarkable cadre of people in the Harvard Law Library: Jennifer Allison, Aslihan Bulut, Claire DeMarco, Lisa Junghahn, Josh Kantor, Janet Katz, Mindy Kent, Meg Kribble, Karen Storin Linitz, Michelle Pearse, Terri Saint-Amour, Craig Smith, Carli Spina, George Taoultsides, Anne-Marie Taylor, Stephen Wiles, Selina Ahad, Route Asefa, Margery Brothers, Kristin Bruner, June Casey, Kyle K. Courtney, Tanya Flink, Larry McCarthy, Shahrzad Mirshamsy, Ashley Pierce, Heather Pierce, Louise Ragno, Jessica Rios, Samantha Sullivan.

Notes

INTRODUCTION

1. See Randall Kennedy, "Neil Rudenstine and Blacks at Harvard," *Journal of Blacks in Higher Education,* January 31, 2002. A classic scholarly embodiment of the affirmative action ethos is William G. Bowen and Derek Bok, *The Shape of the River: Long-Term Consequences of Considering Race in College and University Admissions* (1998).

2. See, e.g., Ruth Marcus, "Minority Groups Assail Course at Harvard Law," *Washington Post,* July 26, 1982; Christopher Edley, Jr., "The Boycott at Harvard: Should Teaching Be Colorblind?" *Washington Post,* August 18, 1982; Carl Rowan, "Harvard's Closed Circle," *Washington Post,* August 27, 1982; Nick King, "Minority-Hiring Fight at Harvard," *Boston Globe,* November 17, 1982.

3. Eric Foner, "Hiring Quotas for White Males Only," *The Nation,* June 26, 1995.

4. For elucidations of this point, see Elizabeth Anderson, *The Imperative of Integration* (2010), 144–48; Michael J. Yelnosky, "The Prevention Justification for Affirmative Action," *Ohio State Law Journal* 64 (2003): 1385; David A. Strauss, "The Law and Economics of Racial Discrimination in Employment: The Case for Numerical Standards," *Georgetown Law Journal* 79 (1991): 1619. See also Michael H. Gottesman, "Twelve Topics to Consider Before Opting for Racial Quotas," *Georgetown Law Journal* 79 (1991): 1737; John J. Donohue III and James Hackman, "Re-Evaluating Federal Civil Rights Policy," *Georgetown Law Journal* 79 (1991): 1713.

5. Anderson, *The Imperative of Integration,* 10.

6. See *Personnel Administrator of Massachusetts v. Feeney,* 442 U.S. 256 (1979).

7. Glenn C. Loury, "Democracy and the Choosing of Elites," in David L. Featherman, Martin Hall, and Marvin Krislov, eds., *The Next Twenty-five Years: Affirmative Action in Higher Education in the United States and South Africa* (2010), 317.

8. The image of the wounded bear echoes a memorable metaphor created by the distinguished historian Richard Hofstadter. What he said of the United States, I apply to affirmative action. See Richard Hofstadter and Michael Wallace, eds., *American Violence: A Documentary History* (1970), 43.

9. *Dawn v. State Personnel Board,* 91 Cal. App. 3d 588, 593 (1979).

10. *Lungren v. Superior Court,* 48 Cal. App. 4th 435 (1996).

11. See Lydia Chavez, *The Color Bind: California's Battle to End Affirmative Action* (1998).

12. See Lino Graglia, "Affirmative Action: Today and Tomorrow," *Ohio Northern University Law Review* 22 (1995); Brian Fitzpatrick, "The Diversity Lie," *Harvard Journal of Law and Public Policy* 27 (2003): 385.

13. 1945 N.Y. Laws 457. See also Morroe Berger, *Equality by Statute: The Revolution in Civil Rights* (1967); David Freeman Engstrom, "The Lost Origins of American Fair Employment Law: Regulatory Choice and the Making of Modern Civil Rights, 1943–1972," *Stanford Law Review* 63 (2011): 1071; David J. Garrow, "The Evolution of Affirmative Action and the Necessity of Truly Individualized Admissions Decisions," *Journal of College and University Law* 34 (2007): 1–3.

14. Exec. Order No. 10, 925, 26 C.F.R. 1977 (1961).

15. See, e.g., Morris B. Abram, "Affirmative Action: Fair Shakes and Social Engineers," *Harvard Law Review* 99 (1986): 1312; Nathan Glazer, *Affirmative Discrimination: Ethnic Inequality and Public Policy* (1975, 1978).

16. Barack Obama, *The Audacity of Hope: Thoughts on Reclaiming the American Dream* (2006), 246.

17. See Randall Kennedy, *The Persistence of the Color Line: Racial Politics and the Obama Presidency* (2011), 266.

18. See Randall Kennedy, "Persuasion and Distrust: A Comment on the Affirmative Action Debate," *Harvard Law Review* 99 (1986): 1327, n.1.

19. See Richard Primus, "The Future of Disparate Impact," *Michigan Law Review* 108 (2010): 1341; Randall Kennedy, "Competing Conceptions of 'Racial Discrimination,'" *Harvard Journal of Law and Public Policy* 14 (1991): 93.

1. Affirmative Action in the History of American Race Relations

1. See Ira Berlin, *Slaves Without Masters: The Free Negro in the Antebellum South* (1974); Leon F. Litwack, *North of Slavery: The Negro in the Free States, 1790–1860* (1961); Stephen A. Siegel, "The Federal Government's Power to Enact Color-Conscious Laws: An Original-

ist Inquiry," *Northwestern University Law Review* 92 (1997): 477; Paul Finkelman, "Prelude to the Fourteenth Amendment: Black Legal Rights in the Antebellum North," *Rutgers Law Journal* 17 (1986): 415.

2. President Andrew Johnson, Veto of the Civil Rights Act, March 27, 1866.

3. See David A. Strauss, "The Myth of Color Blindness," *Supreme Court Review* 1986 (1986): 99; Jack Balkin, "Obscured Vision About Color-blindness?" *Balkanization,* January 8, 2003.

4. Quoted in James Oakes, *The Ruling Race: A History of American Slave-holders* (1998), 233. See also Bruce Levine, *Confederate Emancipation: Southern Plans to Free and Arm Slaves During the Civil War* (2006), 7.

5. Quoted in Heather Cox Richardson, *The Depth of Reconstruction: Race, Labor and Politics in the Post-Civil War North, 1865–1901* (2004).

6. *Civil Rights Cases,* 109 U.S. 3, 25 (1883).

7. See Andrew Kull, *The Color-Blind Constitution* (1992), 62.

8. Arval A. Morris, "Constitutional Alternatives to Racial Preferences in Higher Education Admissions," *Santa Clara Law Review* 17 (1977): 279, 292.

9. See Jed Rubenfeld, "Affirmative Action," *Yale Law Journal* 107 (1997): 427, 430–32. See also Siegel, "The Federal Government's Power."

10. See Ilya Somin, "Originalism and Affirmative Action," The Volokh Conspiracy blog, September 7, 2012.

11. See Siegel, "The Federal Government's Power," 549–55.

12. Quoted in Anthony S. Chen, "The Hitlerian Rule of Quotas: Racial Conservatism and the Politics of Fair Employment Legislation in New York State, 1941–1945," *Journal of American History* 92 (2006): 1238, 1246.

13. Quoted in ibid., 1256.

14. Quoted in ibid., 1257.

15. Fair Employment Practice Act: Hearings Before a Subcommittee of the Committee on Education and Labor on S. 101 and S. 459, 79th Congress 171 (1945) (statement of William H. Hastie). See also Engstrom, "The Lost Origins of American Fair Employment Law," 1127–28.

16. See George S. Schuyler, "A Dangerous Boomerang," *Crisis* 41 (1934), 259; "The Fallacy of Racial Proportionalism," *Pittsburgh Courier,* June 6, 1942.

17. See Paul D. Moreno, *From Direct Action to Affirmative Action: Fair Employment Law and Policy in America, 1933–1972* (1997), 30–65, 84–106; Mark Tushnet, "Change and Continuity in the Concept of Civil Rights: Thurgood Marshall and Affirmative Action," in Ellen Frankel

Paul, Fred D. Miller, Jr., and Jeffrey Paul, eds., *Reassessing Civil Rights* (1991).

18. See "A Sane Approach to Job Seniority," *Chicago Defender*, December 16, 1944; Ralph E. Koger, "CIO Advisor Says: 'Negroes Must Not Seek Special Treatment When Layoffs Come,'" *Pittsburgh Courier*, August 11, 1945. See also Engstrom, "The Lost Origins of American Fair Employment Law," 1127.

19. The term seems to have been coined by Paul Moreno. See Moreno, *From Direct Action to Affirmative Action*.

20. *Hughes v. Superior Court,* 339 U.S. 460 (1950).

21. *Hughes v. Superior Court,* 198 P.2d 885 (1948).

22. *Hughes v. Superior Court,* 339 U.S. 464 (1950).

23. See Tushnet, "Change and Continuity," 151.

24. Quoted in ibid., 151–52.

25. *Hughes v. Supreme Court,* 198 P.2d 895 (Traynor, C.J., dissenting).

26. Quoted in Hugh Davis Graham, *The Civil Rights Era: Origins and Development of National Policy 1960–1972* (1990), 105.

27. Ibid.

28. Quoted in Terry H. Anderson, *The Pursuit of Fairness: A History of Affirmative Action* (2004), 86.

29. Martin Luther King, Jr., *Why We Can't Wait* (1963), 124.

30. Ibid., 127–28.

31. Lyndon B. Johnson, Commencement Address at Howard University, "To Fulfill These Rights," June 4, 1965.

32. See Matthew J. Countryman, *Up South: Civil Rights and Black Power in Philadelphia* (2006); Thomas J. Sugrue, *Sweet Land of Liberty: The Forgotten Struggle for Civil Rights in the North* (2008); Thomas J. Sugrue, "Affirmative Action from Below: Civil Rights, the Building Trades, and the Politics of Racial Equality in the Urban North, 1945–1969," *Journal of American History* 91 (2004): 145; Thomas J. Sugrue, *The Origins of the Urban Crisis: Race and Inequality in Postwar Detroit* (1996). See also Jim Sidanius, Pam Singh, John J. Hetts, and Chris Federico, "It's Not Affirmative Action, It's the Blacks: The Continuing Relevance of Race in American Politics," in David O. Sears, Jim Sedanius, and Lawrence Bobo, eds., *Racialized Politics: The Debate About Racism in America* (2000).

33. Cited in Graham, *The Civil Rights Era,* 106.

34. See Kyle Heselden, "Should There Be 'Compensation' for Negroes?" *The New York Times Magazine,* October 1963; Graham, *The Civil Rights Era,* 113.

35. Quoted in Anderson, *The Pursuit of Fairness,* 87.

36. Graham, *The Civil Rights Era,* 120.

37. Quoted in *United Steelworkers v. Weber,* 443 U.S. 193, 238 (1979) (Rehnquist, J., dissenting).

38. Quoted in ibid., 243.

39. Quoted in ibid., 240.

40. See Daniel A. Farber and Philip P. Frickery, "Is Carolene Products Dead? Reflections on Affirmative Action and the Dynamics of Civil Rights Legislation," *California Law Review* 79 (1991): 685.

41. *Green v. County School Board,* 391 U.S. 430 (1968).

42. *Swann v. Charlotte-Mecklenburg Board of Education,* 402 U.S. 1 (1971).

43. See Johnson, Commencement Address at Howard University.

44. Quoted in Anderson, *The Pursuit of Fairness,* 99.

45. Quoted in Dennis A. Deslippe, "Do Whites Have Rights? White Detroit Policemen and 'Reverse Discrimination' Protests in the 1970s," *Journal of American History* 91 (2004), 932.

46. Key interventions that nourished this important process of reconsideration and revision include Winthrop Jordan, *White Over Black: American Attitudes Toward the Negro, 1550–1812* (1968); Kenneth Stampp, *The Peculiar Institution* (1956); Kenneth Stampp, *The Era of Reconstruction, 1965–1877* (1965); Robert Blauer, *Racial Oppression in America* (1972); and Derrick Bell, *Race, Racism and American Law* (1973).

47. Kaplan, "Equality in an Unequal World," *Northwestern University Law Review* 61 (1966): 363, 367. See also D. Bell, "Black Students in White Schools: The Ordeal and the Opportunity," *University of Toledo Law Review* 2 (1970): 539, 543 (one of the aims and functions of affirmative action was "ghetto calming"); Graham Hughes, "Reparations for Blacks?" *New York University Law Review* 43 (1968): 1063–64 ("the still half-submerged position of black people causes discontent amongst them and leads to social unrest with the prospect of episodic violent disturbances . . . Ordinary political wisdom dictates the adoption of a program to alleviate and ultimately remove the resentment by demonstrating to the minority groups that the fullest benefits of life in that society are open to them").

48. Quoted in Anderson, *The Pursuit of Fairness,* 105.

49. Quoted in Kevin L. Yuill, *Richard Nixon and the Rise of Affirmative Action: The Pursuit of Racial Equality in an Era of Limits* (2006), 98.

50. See John David Skrentny, *The Ironies of Affirmative Action: Politics, Culture, and Justice in America* (1996); Yuill, *Richard Nixon and the Rise of Affirmative Action.*

51. See Yuill, *Richard Nixon and the Rise of Affirmative Action;* Dean J. Kotlowksi, *Nixon's Civil Rights: Politics, Principle, and Policy* (2001).

52. Quoted in Graham, *The Civil Rights Era,* 323.

53. On the Philadelphia Plan, see James E. Jones, Jr., "The Bugaboo of Employment Quotas," *Wisconsin Law Review* 2 (1970): 371. See also Robert D. Schuwerk, "The Philadelphia Plan: A Study in the Dynamics of Executive Power," *University of Chicago Law Review* 39 (1972): 732; Paul Marcus, "The Philadelphia Plan and Strict Racial Quotas on Federal Contracts," *UCLA Law Review* 17 (1970): 817.

54. Quoted in Kotlowski, *Nixon's Civil Rights,* 531.

55. Graham, *The Civil Rights Era,* 325.

56. Quoted in Kotlowski, *Nixon's Civil Rights,* 533–34. See also "Nixon Gives View on Aid to Negroes and the Poor," *New York Times,* December 20, 1967.

57. Ibid., 534.

58. Ibid., 536.

59. Ibid., 532.

60. See Herbert Hill, "Black Labor and Affirmative Action: An Historical Perspective," in Steven Shulman and William Derrity, Jr., eds., *The Question of Discrimination* (1998).

61. *DeFunis v. Odegaard,* 507 P.2d 1169, 1175 (Wash. 1973).

62. *Regents of the University of California v. Bakke,* 438 U.S. 265, 274–275 (1978).

63. See *Steelworkers v. Weber,* 443 U.S. 193 (1979).

64. Quoted in Anderson, *The Pursuit of Fairness,* 139.

65. Ibid., 147.

66. Quoted in Joan Biskupic, *Sandra Day O'Connor* (2005), 71.

67. President William Jefferson Clinton, Address on Affirmative Action, July 19, 1995.

68. Quoted in Nicholas Laham, *The Reagan Presidency and the Politics of Race: In Pursuit of Colorblind Justice and Limited Government* (1998), 20.

69. *Wygant v. Jackson Board of Education,* 476 U.S. 267, n. 2 (1986).

70. Ibid., 270.

71. Ibid., 276.

72. Ibid., 283.

73. Quoted in *City of Richmond v. J. A. Croson,* 488 U.S. 478 (1989).

74. Quoted in ibid., 480.

75. Ibid.

76. Ibid., 494.

77. Ibid., 504.

78. Ibid., 504.

79. Ibid., 504–506.

80. Ibid., 526 (Marshall, J., dissenting).

81. Ibid., 559 (Blackmun, J., dissenting).

82. Ibid., 559 (Marshall, J., dissenting).

83. *Metro Broadcasting Inc. v. Federal Communications Commission,* 497 U.S. 547, 612 (1990) (O'Connor, J., dissenting).

84. Ibid., 615.

85. *Adarand Constructors v. Peña,* 515 U.S. 200 (1995).

86. Ibid., 240 (Thomas, J., concurring).

87. See Laham, *The Reagan Presidency;* Raymond Walters, *Right Turn: William Bradford Reynolds, the Reagan Administration and Black Civil Rights* (1996).

88. *Griggs v. Duke Power Co.,* 401 U.S. 424 (1971).

89. Office of Legal Policy, U.S. Department of Justice, Report to the Attorney General: "Redefining Discrimination: Disparate Impact and the Institutionalization of Affirmative Action," November 4, 1987.

90. *Wards Cove Packing Co. v. Atonio,* 490 U.S. 642 (1989).

91. Ibid., 662 (Blackmun, J., dissenting).

92. Civil Rights Act of 1991, Pub. L. No. 102–166, 105 Stat. 1071.

93. See, generally, "The Civil Rights Act of 1991: The Business Necessity Standard," *Harvard Law Review* 106 (1993): 896.

94. California Constitution, Article I § 31(a).

95. See Eugene Volokh, "The California Civil Rights Initiative: An Interpretive Guide," *UCLA Law Review* 44 (1997): 1335.

96. *Coalition for Economic Equality v. Wilson,* 946 F.Supp. 1480, n. 12 (N.D. Cal. 1996).

97. See Chavez, *The Color Bind.*

98. Quoted in ibid., 50.

99. Quoted in ibid., 52.

100. See Ward Connerly, *Creating Equal: My Fight Against Racial Preferences* (2000); Chavez, *The Color Bind.*

101. Quoted in Chavez, *The Color Bind,* 74.

102. See *Anti–Affirmative Action Ballot Initiatives,* Kirwan Institute for the Study of Race and Ethnicity, December 2008. http://kirwaninstitute .osu.edu/anti-affirmative-action-ballot-initiatives.

2. The Affirmative Action Policy Debate

1. See, e.g., Paul Brest and Miranda Oshige, "Affirmative Action for Whom?" *Stanford Law Review* 47 (1994): 855, 866 n. 33 (reparations "has been the implicit rationale for most affirmative action programs"); Richard Posner and Adrian Vermeule, "Reparations for Slavery and Other Historical Injustices," *Columbia Law Review* 103 (2003): 689, 727 ("The leading mode of in-kind reparative payment [in the United States] is remedial affirmative action").

2. Kim Forde-Mazrui, "Taking Conservatives Seriously: A Moral Jus-

tification for Affirmative Action and Reparations," *California Law Review* 92 (2004): 683, 709.

3. See, e.g., Charles Lawrence III, "Two Views of the River: A Critique of the Liberal Defense of Affirmative Action," *Columbia Law Review* 101 (2001): 928.

4. Bernard A. Boxill, *Blacks and Social Justice,* rev. ed. (1992), 147. See also Kenneth Karst, "The Revival of Forward-Looking Affirmative Action," *Columbia Law Review* 104 (2004): 60; Kathleen M. Sullivan, "Sins of Discrimination: Last Term's Affirmative Action Cases," *Harvard Law Review* 101 (1986): 78.

5. See, e.g., Kenneth Karst and Harold Horowitz, "Affirmative Action and Equal Protection," *Virginia Law Review* 60 (1974): 955, 964.

6. See Michelle Alexander, *The New Jim Crow: Mass Incarceration in the Age of Colorblindness* (2010).

7. See Thomas Ross, "Innocence and Affirmative Action," *Vanderbilt Law Review* 43 (1990): 297; Antonin Scalia, "The Disease as Cure: In Order to Get Beyond Racism, We Must First Take Account of Race," *Washington University Law Quarterly* 1979 (1979): 147.

8. See, generally, "Symposium: After Disaster: The September 11th Compensation Fund and the Future of Civil Justice," *DePaul Law Review* 53 (2001): 209.

9. Kwame Anthony Appiah, " 'Group Rights' and Racial Affirmative Action," *Journal of Ethics* 15 (2011): 265, 275.

10. See Boris Bittker, *The Case for Black Reparations* (1973).

11. See Dalton Conley, *Being Black, Living in the Red: Race, Wealth and Social Policy in America* (1999); Melvin L. Oliver and Thomas M. Shapiro, *Black Wealth/White Wealth: A New Perspective on Racial Inequality* (1995).

12. See, e.g., Eugene Robinson, *Disintegration: The Splintering of Black America* (2010), 208–17; Richard D. Kahlenberg, *The Remedy: Class, Race, and Affirmative Action* (1996), 42, 46–47; Derrick Bell, *And We Are Not Saved: The Elusive Quest for Racial Justice* (1991), 140–61; Norman Vieira, "Racial Imbalance, Black Separatism, and Permissible Classification by Race," *Michigan Law Review* 67 (1968–1969): 1613. For judicial voicings of this complaint, see *Fullilove v. Klutznick,* 448 U.S. 448, 538 (1980) (Stevens, J., dissenting).

13. See Kenneth W. Mack, *Representing the Race: The Creation of the Civil Rights Lawyer* (2012); David Levering Lewis, *W. E. B. DuBois, 1919–1963: The Fight for Equality and the American Century* (2001).

14. Hughes, "Reparations for Blacks?" 1063, 1073 ("Even if a black person has been personally lucky enough to escape the prevalent racial

burdens that weigh upon many or most blacks, the question of social justice is . . . a question of group advancement and we may legitimately use [the privileged black] for the benefit of his group"); Amy Gutmann, "How Affirmative Action Can (and Cannot) Work Well," in Robert Post and Michael Rogin, eds., *Race and Representation: Affirmative Action* (1998), 345.

15. See Deborah Malamud, "Affirmative Action, Diversity, and the Black Middle Class," *University of Colorado Law Review* 68 (1997): 939.

16. See, e.g., Neville Alexander, "The Struggle for National Liberation and the Attainment of Human Rights in South Africa," in David L. Featherman, Martin Hall, and Marvin Krislov, eds., *The Next Twenty-five Years: Affirmative Action in Higher Education in the United States and South Africa* (2010) ("the real beneficiaries of the [affirmative action] deal have been the bourgeoisie and the rising black and established white middle and professional classes"; Pradipta Chaudhury, "The 'Creamy Layer': Political Economy of Reservations," *Economic and Political Weekly,* May 15, 2004.

17. See, e.g., Clarence Thomas in *Grutter v. Bollinger,* 539 U.S. 306, 354, n. 3 (2003); Dinesh D'Souza, *Illiberal Education: The Politics of Race and Sex on Campus* (1991), 251–53.

18. See, e.g., *United Steelworkers of America, AFL-CIO v. Weber,* 443 U.S. 193 (1979); *Petit v. City of Chicago,* 352 F.3d 1111 (7th Cir. 2003); *Wittmer v. Peters,* 87 F.3d 916 (7th Cir. 1996); *University Community College System of Nevada v. Farmer,* 930 P.2d 730 (Nev. 197); *Maryland Troopers Ass'n., Inc. v. Evans,* 993 F.2d 1072 (4th Cir. 1993); *Middleton v. City of Flint,* 92 F.3d 396 (6th Cir. 1996). See also Jonathan Leonard, "The Impact of Affirmative Action in Employment," *Journal of Labor Economics* 2 (1984): 439.

19. Anne Hudson-Price, final paper for "Race Relations Law: 1877–Present," February 6, 2013. Unpublished. On file at the Harvard Law School library.

20. Thomas M. Shapiro and Melvin L. Oliver, *Black Wealth/White Wealth: A New Perspective on Racial Inequality* (1995).

21. Deborah C. Malamud, "Affirmative Action, Diversity, and the Black Middle Class," *University of Colorado Law Review* 68 (1997): 939.

22. Richard Sander and Stuart Taylor, Jr., *Mismatch* (2012), 255.

23. William Julius Wilson, *More Than Just Race: Being Black and Poor in the Inner City* (2009), 141.

24. William Julius Wilson, *The Truly Disadvantaged: The Inner City, the Underclass, and Public Policy* (1987).

25. Ibid., 163.

26. See, e.g., Martin Gilens, *Why Americans Hate Welfare: Race, Media, and the Politics of Antipoverty Policy* (2000).

27. Brief for Amici Curiae 65, Leading American Businesses in Support of Respondents, *Grutter v. Bollinger*, Gerhard Casper and Kathleen M. Sullivan, eds., Supreme Court of the United States (2003) in *Landmark Briefs and Arguments of the Supreme Court of the United States: Constitutional Law*, vol. 321 (2004), 921, 935.

28. Brief of Amici Curiae Lt. General Julius W. Becton, Jr., et al., Ibid, 86, 99.

29. Brief of Dean Robert Post and Dean Martha Minow as Amici Curiae in Support of Respondents, *Fisher v. University of Texas at Austin*, Supreme Court of the United States (2012).

30. Samuel Issacharoff, "*Bakke* in the Admissions Office and the Courts: Can Affirmative Action Be Defended?" *Ohio State Law Journal* 59 (1998): 669, 677 ("One of the clear legacies of *Bakke* has been to enshrine the term 'diversity' within the legal lexicon"); Malamud, "Affirmative Action, Diversity, and the Black Middle Class," 943 ("Proponents of affirmative action have every incentive to rely solely upon justifications that they know will pass judicial muster. Thus, the Court has the unique power to control not only what institutions do on the affirmative action front, but also what they say—and thus the Court directly affects the arguments the public will hear from government officials.")

31. See Peter Wood, *Diversity: The Invention of a Concept* (2003) 135 ("*diversity* offers a language for promoting racial togetherness that, on its face, is grievance-free").

32. Brief for the United States as Amicus Curiae Supporting Petitioner, *Grutter v. Bollinger,* 539 U.S. (2003).

33. See "Bush and Affirmative Action; Bush's Remarks on Michigan Admissions Policies," *New York Times,* January 16, 2003.

34. *Grutter v. Bollinger,* 539 U.S. 306, 354 n.3 (2003) (Thomas, J., dissenting).

35. Shelby Steele, e-mail message to author.

36. Wood, *Diversity: The Invention of a Concept,* 1.

37. Walter Benn Michaels, *The Trouble With Diversity: How We Learned to Love Identity and Ignore Inequality* (2006) 16.

38. Ibid., 12.

39. Kingsley Brown, "Affirmative Action: Policy-Making by Deception," *Ohio Northern University Law Review* 22 (1995): 1291 ("affirmative action has been characterized by deception and denial").

40. Graglia, "Affirmative Action: Today and Tomorrow," 1535, 1539.

41. Brief of Amici Curiae Law Professor Alexander et al. in Support of Petitioner, *Grutter v. Bollinger*, Supreme Court of the United States (2003).

42. See *Grutter v. Bollinger*, 539 U.S. 347 (2003) (Scalia, J., dissenting) and 383 (Rehnquist, C.J., dissenting).

43. See, e.g., Brief of Amici Curiae California Association of Scholars, et al., *Fisher v. University of Texas at Austin*, 644 F.3d 301 (2011), 13–18.

44. Sanford Levinson, *Wrestling with Diversity* (2003), 56.

45. Samuel Issacharoff, "Law and Misdirection in the Debate Over Affirmative Action," *University of Chicago Law Forum* 2002 (2002): 11, 18. See also John H. McWhorter, "The Campus Diversity Fraud," *City Journal* (2002) ("Mormons, paraplegics, people from Alaska, lesbians, Ayn Randians, and poor whites exert little pull on the heartstrings of admissions committees so committed to making campuses 'look like America.' The diversity that counts is brown-skinned minorities, particularly African Americans").

46. See Rubenfeld, "Affirmative Action," 427, 471.

47. Guido Calabresi, "Bakke as Pseudo-Tragedy," *Catholic University Law Review* (1978): 427, 429.

48. See Michael J. Klarman, "Brown, Originalism, and Constitutional Theory: A Reply to Professor McConnell," *Virginia Law Review* 81 (1995): 1881.

49. See Christopher W. Schmidt, "The Sit-Ins and the State Action Doctrine," *William & Mary Bill of Rights Journal* 18 (2010): 767, 810-811.

50. Calabresi, "Bakke as Pseudo-Tragedy," 431.

51. See Anderson, *The Imperative of Integration*.

52. *Grutter v. Bollinger*, 539 U.S. 334 (2003).

53. Anderson, *The Imperative of Integration*, 148.

54. See Michael J. Yelnosky, "The Prevention Justification for Affirmative Action," *Ohio State Law Journal* 64 (2003): 1385. See also Christopher Edley, Jr., *Not All Black and White* (1996), 113–14; Michael Selmi, "Testing for Equality: Merit, Efficiency and the Affirmative Action Debate," *UCLA Law Review* 42 (1995): 1251, 1277–1314.

55. Clinton, Address on Affirmative Action, July 19, 1995.

56. *Grutter v. Bollinger*, 539 U.S. 306, 345 (2003) (Ginsburg, J., concurring).

57. See Paul M. Sniderman and Thomas Piazza, *The Scar of Race* (1993).

58. See Thomas Ross, "Innocence and Affirmative Action," *Vanderbilt Law Review* 43 (1990): 297.

59. Cf. Rhoda E. Howard-Hassmann, "Getting to Reparations: Japanese Americans and African Americans," *Social Forces* 83 (2004): 823; Eric

K. Yamamoto, "Racial Reparations: Japanese American Redress and African American Claims," *Boston College Third World Law Journal* 19 (1998): 477. See also Eric K. Yamamoto, Margeret Chon, Carol L. Izumi, and Frank H. Wu, *Race, Rights, and Reparation: Law of the Japanese American Internment* (2001).

60. See John Hart Ely, "The Constitutionality of Reverse Racial Discrimination," *University of Chicago Law Review* 41 (1974): 723.

61. Ronald Dworkin, *Taking Rights Seriously* (1977).

62. For an illuminating discussion of "merit" see Richard Fallon, Jr., "To Each According to His Ability, from None According to His Race: The Concept of Merit in the Law of Antidiscrimination," *Boston University Law Review* 60 (1980): 815.

63. Michael J. Sandel, *Justice: What's the Right Thing to Do?* (2009), 178.

64. Quoted in ibid.

65. Sandel, *Justice,* 178.

66. Goodwin Liu, "The Causation Fallacy: *Bakke* and the Basic Arithmetic of Selective Admissions," *Michigan Law Review* 100 (2001): 1045.

67. Ibid., 1049.

68. Barbara Bergman, *In Defense of Affirmative Action* (1997), 132.

69. See, generally, Andrew F. Halaby and Stephen R. McAllister, "An Analysis of the Supreme Court's Reliance on Racial 'Stigma' as a Constitutional Concept in Affirmative Action Cases," *Michigan Journal of Race & Law* 2 (1997): 235; Ashley Hibbett, "The Enigma of the Stigma: A Case Study of the Validity of the Stigma Arguments Made in Opposition to Affirmative Action Programs in Higher Education," *Harvard BlackLetter Law Journal* 21 (2005): 75; Angela Onwuachi-Willig, Emily Hough, and Mary Campbell, "Which Came First—Stigma or Affirmative Action?" *California Law Review* 96 (2008): 1299.

70. *Bakke,* 438 U.S. 298 (1978).

71. *City of Richmond v. J. A. Croson,* 488 U.S. 469, 493 (1989).

72. *Metro Broadcasting,* 497 U.S. 635 (1990).

73. *Adarand v. Peña,* 515 U.S. 200, 241 (1995) (Thomas, J., concurring).

74. See Christopher Edley, Jr., "Doubting Thomas: Law Politics and Hypocrisy," *Washington Post,* July 17, 1991.

75. See Rupert W. Nacoste, "Policy Schemas for Affirmative Action," in Linda Heath et al., eds., *Application of Heuristics and Biases to Social Issues* (1993), 205; Madeline E. Heilman et al., "Presumed Incompetent? Stigmatization and Affirmative Action Efforts," *Journal of Applied Psychology* 77 (1992): 536; Luis T. Garcia et al., "The Effect of Affirmative Action on Attributions About Minority Group Members," *Journal of Personality* 49 (1981): 427.

76. See Gregory B. Northcraft and Joanne Martin, "Double Jeopardy: Resistance to Affirmative Action from Potential Beneficiaries," in Barbara A. Gutek, ed., *Sex Role Stereotyping and Affirmative Action Policy* (1982), 81.

77. See Linda Hamilton Krieger, "Civil Rights Perestroika: Intergroup Relations After Affirmative Action," *California Law Review* 86 (1998): 1251, 1265.

78. Midge Decter, "On Affirmative Action and Lost Self-Respect," *New York Times*, July 6, 1980.

79. Stephen C. Carter, *Reflections of an Affirmative Action Baby* (1991), 47.

80. Ibid., 49.

81. Ibid., 5.

82. Ibid., 12–14 ("prickly sensitivity is the best evidence . . . of one of the principal costs of racial preferences. . . . The terrible psychological pressure that racial preferences put on their beneficiaries").

83. Quoted in Carl Cohen and James P. Sterba, *Affirmative Action and Racial Preference: A Debate* (2003), 118.

84. James Blanton, "A Limit to Affirmative Action?" *Commentary,* June 1989.

85. See, e.g., Lani Guinier and Susan Sturm, *Who's Qualified?* (2001).

86. Susan Sturm and Lani Guinier, "The Future of Affirmative Action: Reclaiming the Innovative Ideal," *California Law Review* 84 (1996): 953, 956.

87. See Russell Jacoby and Naomi Glauberman, eds., *The Bell Curve Debate* (1995); Steven Fraser, ed., *The Bell Curve Wars: Race, Intelligence, and the Future of America* (1995).

88. See, e.g., Myron Magnet, *The Dream and the Nightmares: The Sixties' Legacy to the Underclass* (2000); Dinesh D'Souza, *The End of Racism: Principles for a Multicultural Society* (2005); Charles Murray, *Losing Ground: American Social Policy 1950–1980* (1984).

89. Bowen and Bok, *The Shape of the River,* 265.

90. See *Spurlock v. United Airlines,* 330 F.Supp. 228 (D. Colo.) aff'd 475 F.2d 216 (1972).

91. Mary C. Curtis, "Opinion: Chelsea Clinton's Affirmative Action TV Job," *Washington Post*, December 15, 2011.

92. Quoted in Emily Houth, Angela Onwuachi-Willig, Mary Campbell, "Cracking the Egg: Which Came First—Stigma or Affirmative Action," *California Law Review* 96 (2008): 1343.

93. Letter to the Editor, *New York Times*, July 26, 1980.

94. Bowen and Bok, *The Shape of the River,* 265.

95. See Jill Elaine Hadey, "Protecting Them from Themselves: The Per-

sistence of Mutual Benefits Arguments for Sex and Race Inequality," *New York University Law Review* 84 (2009): 1464.

96. See Sander and Taylor, *Mismatch;* Richard H. Sander, "A Systemic Analysis of Affirmative Action in American Law Schools," *Stanford Law Review* 57 (2004): 367. See also Thomas Sowell, "The Plight of Black Students in the United States," *Daedalus* 103 (Spring 1974); Clyde Summers, "Preferential Admissions: An Unreal Solution to a Real Problem," *University of Toledo Law Review* 2 (1970): 377.

97. Sander, "A Systemic Analysis," 481.

98. Ibid., 372.

99. See Adam Liptak, "For Blacks in Law School, Can Less Be More?" *New York Times,* February 13, 2005 (Sander "has found a new way to influence the debate"); Emily Bazelon, "Sanding Down Sander," *Slate,* April 29, 2005.

100. See Ian Ayres and Richard Brooks, "Does Affirmative Action Reduce the Number of Black Lawyers?" *Stanford Law Review* 57 (2005): 1807; David L. Chambers, Timothy T. Clydesdale, William C. Kidder, and Richard O. Lempert, "The Real Impact of Eliminating Affirmative Action in American Law Schools: An Empirical Critique of Richard Sander's Study," *Stanford Law Review* 57 (2005): 1855; David B. Wilkins, "A Systematic Response to Systemic Disadvantage: A Response to Sander," *Stanford Law Review* 57 (2005): 1915.

101. Ayres and Brooks, "Does Affirmative Action Reduce," 1807, 1824.

102. Ibid., 1825.

103. Wilkins, "A Systematic Response to Systemic Disadvantage," 1915.

104. Ibid., 1931.

105. Ibid.

106. Ibid., 1932.

107. See Chambers et al., "The Real Impact of Eliminating Affirmative Action," 1893.

108. See Kennedy, "Persuasion and Distrust," 1327.

109. See Sander, "A Systemic Analysis," 370.

110. Sander and Taylor, *Mismatch,* 61.

111. See W. E. B. DuBois, "The Talented Tenth," in Andrew Paschal, ed., *A W. E. B. DuBois Reader* (1971), 31.

112. See, generally, Kenneth W. Mack, *Representing the Race: The Creation of the Civil Rights Lawyer* (2012).

113. See, generally, Tseming Yang, "Choice and Fraud in Racial Identification: The Dilemma of Policing Race in Affirmative Action, the Census, and a Color-Blind Society," *Michigan Journal of Race and Law* 11 (2006): 367; Christopher A. Ford, "Administering Identity: The Determination of 'Race' in Race-Conscious Law," *California*

Law Review 82 (1994): 1231; Christopher A. Ford, "Challenges and Dilemmas of Racial and Ethnic Identity in American and Post-Apartheid South African Affirmative Action," *UCLA Law Review* 43 (1996): 1953; John Martinez, "Trivializing Diversity: The Problem of Overinclusion in Affirmative Action Programs," *Harvard BlackLetter Law Journal* 12 (1995): 49; Luther Wright, Jr., "Who's Black, Who's White, and Who Cares: Reconceptualizing the United States' Definition of Race and Racial Classification," *Vanderbilt Law Review* 48 (1995): 513.

114. *Fisher v. University of Texas,* 644 F.3d 301 (2011), Oral Argument Transcript, October 10, 2012.

115. Edward E. Telles, *Race in Another America: The Significance of Skin Color in Brazil* (2004), 264.

116. See Marion Lloyd, "Affirmative Action, Brazilian-Style," *Chronicle of Higher Education,* October 11, 2009; Raymond Colitt and Stuart Grudings, "Brazil Pushes Quotas for Blacks Despite Criticism," Reuters News, May 13, 2008.

117. See *Malone v. Haley,* No. 88–339 (Sup. Jd. Ct., Suffolk County, Mass., 1989). See also Peggy Hernandez, "Firemen Who Claimed to Be Black Lose Appeal," *Boston Globe,* July 26, 1989; Ford, "Administering Identity" 1231, 1232–34; Charlie Gerstein, "What Can the Brothers Malone Teach Us About *Fisher v. University of Texas?*" *Michigan Law Review* 111 (2012): 1; http://www.michiganlawreview.org/articles/what-can-the-brothers-malone-teach-us-about-em-fisher-v-university-of-texas-em.

118. See Ariela Gross, *What Blood Won't Tell: A History of Race on Trial in America* (2008).

119. See Christine B. Hickman, "The Devil and the One Drop Rule: Racial Categories, African Americans, and the U.S. Census," *Michigan Law Review* 95 (1997): 1161.

120. See, e.g., Thomas Sowell, *Affirmative Action Around the World: An Empirical Study* (2005).

121. *City of Richmond v. J. A. Croson Co.,* 488 U.S. 469, 506 (1989).

122. See *Podberesky v. Kirwan,* 38 F.3d 147 (4th Cir. 1994).

123. See Sharon S. Lee, "De-Minoritization of Asian Americans: A Historical Examination of the Representations of Asian Americans in Affirmative Action Admissions Policies at the University of California," *Asian American Law Journal* 15 (2008): 129; Nancy Chung Allred, "Asian Americans and Affirmative Action: From Yellow Peril to Model Minority and Back Again," *Asian American Law Journal* 14 (2007): 57; Frank Wu, "Neither Black nor White: Asian Americans and Affirmative Action," *Boston College Third World Journal* 15 (1995): 225; Selene Dong, "Too Many Asians: The Challenges of Fighting Discrimination

Against Asian-Americans and Preserving Affirmative Action," *Stanford Law Review* 47 (1995): 1027.

124. Kevin Brown and Jeannine Bell, "Demise of the Talented Tenth: Affirmative Action and the Increasing Underrepresentation of Ascendant Blacks at Selective Higher Education Institutions," *Ohio State Law Journal* 69 (2008): 1229.

125. Ronald C. Roach, "Drawing Upon the Diaspora," *Diverse: Issues in Higher Education,* August 15, 2005. http://diverseeducation.com/article/4558.

126. Brown and Bell, "Demise of the Talented Tenth," 1281.

3. THE COLOR-BLIND CHALLENGE TO AFFIRMATIVE ACTION

1. *Bakke,* 438 U.S. 265,407 (1978) (Blackmun, J., concurring and dissenting).

2. *Parents Involved in Community Schools v. Seattle School District No. 1,* 551 U.S. 701, 748 (2007).

3. William Van Alstyne, "Rites of Passage: Race, the Supreme Court, and the Constitution," *University of Chicago Law Review* 46 (1979): 775, 809–810.

4. *Plessy v. Ferguson,* 163 U.S. 537, 554–559 (1896) (Harlan, J., dissenting).

5. Ibid., 557.

6. Quoted in Kull, *The Color-Blind Constitution,* 22.

7. Brief for Plaintiff in Error, *Plessy v. Ferguson* (1896), Supreme Court of the United States, Philip B. Kurland, Gerhard Casper, eds., *Landmark Briefs and Arguments of the Supreme Court of the United States: Constitutional Law,* Volume 13, (1975), 46.

8. Quoted in Kull, *The Color-Blind Constitution,* 62.

9. *Pace v. Alabama,* 106 U.S. 583 (1883).

10. See, e.g., *Burns v. State,* 48 Ala. 195 (1872) (invalidating Alabama miscegenation law). See, generally, Peter Wallenstein, *Tell the Court I Love My Wife: Race, Marriage, and the Law—An American History* (2002), 73.

11. On the status of racial distinctions in state and federal statutes around the time of the framing and ratification of the Fourteenth Amendment see Randall Kennedy, *Interracial Intimacies: Sex, Marriage Identity, and Adoption* (2003), 249–54; Andrew Kull, *The Color-Blind Constitution* (1994); Stephen A. Siegel, "The Federal Government's Power to Enact Color-Conscious Laws: An Originalist Inquiry," *Northwestern University Law Review* 92 (1998): 478; Jed Rubenfeld, "Affirmative Action," *Yale Law Journal* 107 (1997): 427; Micheal W. McConnell, "Originalism and the Desegregation Decision," *Virginia Law Review* 81 (1995):

947; Michael J. Klarman, "*Brown,* Originalism and Constitutional Theory: A Response to Professor McConnell," *Virginia Law Review* 81 (1995): 1881; Alexander M. Bickel, "The Original Understanding and the Segregation Decision," *Harvard Law Review* 69 (1955): 1. For a defense of Fourteenth Amendment originalism that condemns racial affirmative action see Michael B. Rappaport, "Originalism and the Colorblind Constitution," *Social Science Research Network* (SSRN, April 3, 2013).

12. *Plessy,* 163 U.S. 559 (Harlan, J., dissenting).

13. See Earl M. Maltz, "Only Partially Color-Blind: John Marshall Harlan's View of Race and the Constitution," *Georgia State University Law Review* 12 (1996): 973.

14. *Garner v. Louisiana,* 368 U.S. 157 (1961). See the excellent discussion of the history of the Harlan declaration in the Supreme Court by Richard A. Primus, "Canon, Anti-Canon, and Judicial Dissent," *Duke Law Journal* 48 (1998): 243, 245–47.

15. *Fullilove v. Klutznick,* 448 U.S. 448, 523 (1980).

16. *City of Richmond v. J. A. Croson Co.,* 488 U.S. 469, 520–21 (1989) (Scalia, J., concurring).

17. *Parents Involved in Community Schools v. Seattle School District No. 1,* 551 U.S. 701 (2007).

18. Michael Kinsley, "The Spoils of Victimhood: The Case Against the Case Against Affirmative Action," *The New Yorker,* March 27, 1995.

19. "Churchmen Urge Full Negro Rights," *New York Times,* December 26, 1942.

20. "Democracy Is Color-Blind," *New York Times,* January 28, 1951.

21. Quoted in *Parents Involved,* 551 U.S. 770 (2007).

22. Ibid., 772.

23. Ibid., 772.

24. See Gary Peller, *Critical Race Consciousness: Reconsidering American Ideologies of Racial Justice* (2011).

25. See Peter Irons, *Justice at War: The Story of the Japanese Internment Cases* (1983).

26. *Swain v. Alabama,* 380 U.S. 202 (1965).

27. See Randall Kennedy, *Race, Crime, and the Law* (1997), 193–203.

28. *Batson v. Kentucky,* 476 U.S. 79 (1986).

29. See Kennedy, *Race, Crime, and the Law,* 136–167.

30. See Stuart Taylor, Jr., "The Case for Using Racial Profiling at Airports, *National Journal,* September 22, 2001.

31. See Randall Kennedy, "Blind Spot: Racial Profiling, Meet Your Alter Ego: Affirmative Action," *Atlantic Monthly,* April 2002.

32. See Bruce S. Gelber, "Race-Conscious Approaches to Ending Segrega-

tion in Housing: Some Pitfalls on the Road to Integration," *Rutgers Law Review* 37 (1985): 921; Rodney A. Smolla, "Integration Mainte-nance: The Unconstitutionality of Benign Programs That Discour-age Black Entry to Prevent White Flight," *Duke Law Journal* (1981): 891; Bruce L. Ackerman, "Integration for Subsidized Housing and the Question of Racial Occupancy Controls," *Stanford Law Review* 26 (1973): 245; Boris I. Bittker, "The Case of the Checker-Board Ordi-nance: An Experiment in Race Relations," *Yale Law Journal* 71 (1962): 1387; Victor Navasky, "The Benevolent Housing Quota," *Howard Law Journal* 6 (1960): 30.

33. See Randall Kennedy, *Interracial Intimacies: Sex, Marriage, Identity and Adoption* (2003), 367–401; Elizabeth Bartholet, "Where Do Black Children Belong? The Politics of Race Matching in Adoption," *Uni-versity of Pennsylvania Law Review* 139 (1991): 1163.

34. Kull, *The Color-Blind Constitution*, 5.

35. *Adarand v. Peña*, 515 U.S. 240 (Thomas, J., concurring).

36. *Johnson v. California*, 543 U.S. 499 (2005).

37. Nathan Glazer, *The Social Basis of American Communism* (1961), 181–82.

38. See Brad Snyder, "How the Conservatives Canonized *Brown v. Board of Education*," *Rutgers Law Review* 52 (2000): 383.

39. See Keith M. Finley, *Delaying the Dream: Southern Senators and the Fight Against Civil Rights, 1938–1965* (2008); William A. Link, *Righteous Warrior: Jesse Helms and the Rise of Modern Conservatism* (2008).

40. See Richard Kluger, *Simple Justice: The History of* Brown v. Board of Education *and Black America's Struggle for Equality* (1976), 606–609; Brad Snyder and John Q. Barrett, "Rehnquist's Missing Letter: A For-mer Law Clerk's 1955 Thoughts on Justice Jackson and *Brown*," *Boston College Law Review* 53 (2012): 631.

41. See *Batson v. Kentucky*, 476 U.S. 79 (1986) (Rehnquist, J., dissenting).

42. An exception was *Hunter v. Underwood*, 471 U.S. 222 (1985).

43. See Jerome Cristal Culp, Jr., "Understanding the Racial Discourse of Justice Rehnquist," *Rutgers Law Journal* 25 (1993): 597; Alan Dersho-witz, "Telling the Truth About Chief Justice Rehnquist," *Huffington Post*, September 4, 2005.

44. *Adarand v. Peña*, 515 U.S. 200, 240–41 (1995) (Thomas, J., concurring) (internal quotation marks omitted).

45. Stanley Fish, "Reverse Racism, or How the Pot Got to Call the Kettle Black," *The Atlantic Monthly*, November 1993.

46. See *Weber v. Kaiser Aluminum Chemical Corp.*, 611 F.2d 139 (5th Cir. 1980).

47. *Adarand v. Peña,* 515 U.S. 200, 243–47 (1995).
48. *Griggs v. Duke Power Co.,* 401 U.S. 424 (1971).
49. Ibid., 431.
50. Ibid.
51. See the decisions disapprovingly cited by the Supreme Court in *Washington v. Davis,* 426 U.S. 229, 244 n.12 (1976).
52. *Washington v. Davis,* 426 U.S. 229 (1976).
53. See, e.g., *Personnel Administration v. Feeney,* 442 U.S. 256 (1979).
54. Office of Legal Policy, U.S. Department of Justice, Report to the Attorney General Redefining Discrimination: Disparate Impact and the Institutionalization of Affirmative Action (November, 1987), 1.
55. See *Ricci v. Stefano,* 557 U.S. 557–594 (2009) (Scalia, J., concurring).
56. Ibid., 594–595.
57. See Primus Richard, "Equal Protection and Disparate Impact: Round Three," *Harvard Law Review* 117 (2003): 493, 526 ("criticism of facially neutral antidiscrimination laws seems tendentious and farfetched. Such laws are now deeply entrenched within a normative consensus").
58. See J. Morgan Kousser, *The Shaping of Southern Politics: Suffrage Restrictions and the Establishment of the One-Party South 1880–1910* (1974): 58–59; *Guinn v. United,* 238 U.S. 347 (1915) (Supreme Court invalidates grandfather clauses in constitution of Oklahoma).
59. See, e.g., *Hunter v. Underwood,* 471 U.S. 222 (1985).
60. Brief for the United States as Amicus Curiae Supporting Petitioner, *Grutter v. Bollinger,* Supreme Court of the United States (2003) in Gerhard Casper and Kathleen M. Sullivan, eds., *Landmark Briefs and Arguments of the Supreme Court of the United States: Constitutional Law 2002 Term Supplement* (2004), 452–457.
61. *City of Richmond,* 488 U.S. (1989), 507.
62. *Grutter v. Bollinger,* 539 U.S. (2003), 339.
63. *Parents Involved v. Seattle School Dist. No. 1,* 551 U.S. 700, 735 (2007).
64. Brian T. Fitzpatrick, "Can Michigan Universities Use Proxies for Race After the Ban on Racial Preferences?" *Michigan Journal of Race and Law* 19 (2007): 277. See also Brian T. Fitzpatrick, "Strict Scrutiny of Facially Race-Neutral State Action and the Texas Ten Percent Plan," *Baylor Law Review* 53 (2001): 289.
65. Ward Connerly, " 'No Place in Life or Law': Racial Preferences Deserve No Federal Support," *Washington Times,* January 21, 2003.
66. Roger Clegg, "Preferences by Any Other Name," *Legal Times,* February 10, 2003.
67. See Randall Kennedy, *The Persistence of the Color Line,* 263–64.
68. *Grutter v. Bollinger,* 539 U.S. 306, 349–350 (2003) (Thomas, J., concurring and dissenting).

69. See Paul Freund, "Constitutional Dilemmas," *Boston University Law Review* 45 (1965): 13, 20.

4. THE SUPREME COURT AND AFFIRMATIVE ACTION

1. *Bakke v. Regents of the University of California,* 553 P. 2d 1152, 1170 (Cal. 1976).
2. Ibid., 1171.
3. See Howard Ball, *The Bakke Case: Race, Education, and Affirmative Action* (2000); Bernard Schwartz, *Behind Bakke: Affirmative Action and the Supreme Court* (1988); Joel Dreyfuss and Charles Lawrence III, *The Bakke Case: The Politics of Inequality* (1979).
4. Harry T. Edwards, "Preferential Remedies and Affirmative Action in Employment in the Wake of *Bakke,*" *Washington University Law Quarterly* 1979 (1979): 113–14.
5. Guido Calabresi, "*Bakke* as Pseudo-Tragedy," *Catholic University Law Review* 28 (1979): 427.
6. Vincent Blasi, "*Bakke* as Precedent: Does Mr. Justice Powell Have a Theory?" *California Law Review* 67 (1979): 21.
7. Ronald Dworkin, "The *Bakke* Decision: Did It Decide Anything?" *New York Review of Books,* August 17, 1978.
8. Quoted in Michael Selmi, "The Life of *Bakke*: An Affirmative Action Retrospective," *Georgetown Law Journal* 87 (1999): 981, 1005.
9. Quoted in ibid.
10. Quoted in Charles R. Babcock and Loretta Tofani, "The Reaction: All Sides Optimistic, a Ruling with Something for Everyone," *Washington Post,* June 29, 1978.
11. Ibid.
12. Scalia, "The Disease as Cure," 148.
13. See, e.g., Anthony Lewis, "A Solomonic Decision," *New York Times,* June 29, 1978.
14. Kenneth L. Karst and Harold W. Horowitz, "The *Bakke* Opinions and Equal Protection Doctrine," *Harvard Civil Rights–Civil Liberties Law Review* 14 (1979): 7.
15. Paul J. Mishkin, "The Uses of Ambivalence: Reflections on the Supreme Court and the Constitutionality of Affirmative Action," *University of Pennsylvania Law Review* 131 (1983): 907, 929.
16. *Regents of the University of California v. Bakke,* 438 U.S. 265, 291 (1978).
17. Ibid., 293.
18. Ibid.
19. Ibid.
20. Ibid., 292.

21. Ibid., 295.

22. Ibid.

23. See John Hart Ely, "The Constitutionality of Reverse Discrimination," *University of Chicago Law Review* 41 (1974): 723.

24. *Regents of the University of California*, 438 U.S. 295 (1978).

25. Ibid., 297–98.

26. Brief for Petitioner, *Regents of the University of California v. Bakke*, 438 U.S. 265 (1978). See Philip B. Kurland and Gerhard Casper, eds., *Landmark Briefs and Arguments of the Supreme Court of the United States: Constitutional Law 1977 Term Supplement*, vol. 99 (1978): 98.

27. Brief for the United States as Amicus Curiae, *Regents of the University of California v. Bakke*, 438 U.S. 265 (1978). See Kurland and Casper, eds., *Landmark Briefs and Arguments*, vol. 99, 294–295.

28. *Regents of the University of California*, 438 U.S. 307 (1978).

29. Ibid.

30. Ibid.

31. Ibid.

32. Ibid., 311.

33. Ibid., 314.

34. Ibid.

35. Ibid., 313.

36. Ibid.

37. Ibid., 314.

38. Ibid.

39. Ibid., 315.

40. Ibid., 322–23.

41. Ibid., 317.

42. Ibid., 318.

43. Ibid., 294.

44. Ibid., 389.

45. Ibid., 390.

46. Ibid., 396.

47. Vincent Blasi, "*Bakke* as Precedent: Does Mr. Justice Powell Have a Theory?" *California Law Review* 67 (1979): 21.

48. *Regents of the University of California*, 438 U.S. 312 n.48 (1978).

49. Ibid.

50. Karst and Horowitz, "The *Bakke* Opinions and Equal Protection Doctrine," 16.

51. Ibid., 16.

52. Ibid., 17.

53. John C. Jeffries, Jr., "*Bakke* Revisited," *The Supreme Court Review* (2003): 1, 7.

54. George Will, "The Unintended Consequences of Racial Preferences," *Washington Post,* November 30, 2011.
55. Jeffries, "*Bakke* Revisited," 8.
56. *Regents of the University of California,* 438 U.S. 318 (1978).
57. Ibid., 406.
58. Ibid., 319.
59. *Hopwood v. Texas,* 78 F.3d 932 (5th Cir. 1996).
60. *Metro Broadcasting,* 497 U.S. 547 (1990).
61. *Adarand v. Peña,* 515 U.S. 200 (1995).
62. *Hopwood v. Texas,* 78 F.3d 948 (5th Cir. 1996).
63. Ibid. (quoting Richard A. Posner, "The *DeFunis* Case and the Constitutionality of Preferential Treatment of Racial Minorities," *Supreme Court Review* 1974 [1974]: 12).
64. *Grutter v. Bollinger,* 288 F.3d732, 772 (6th Cir. 2002).
65. Ibid., 752–753.
66. *Metro Broadcasting,* 497 U.S. 547, 568 (1990).
67. Ibid., 612.
68. *Grutter v. Bollinger,* 539 U.S. 325 (2003).
69. Ibid., 330.
70. Ibid., 330 (citing Brief for American Educational Research Association et al. as Amici Curiae).
71. Ibid., 330–31 (citing Brief for 3M et al. as Amici Curiae and Brief for General Motors as Amicus Curiae).
72. *Grutter v. Bollinger,* 539 U.S. 331 (2003) (quoting Brief for Julius W. Becton, Jr., et al. as Amici Curiae).
73. Ibid.
74. *Grutter v. Bollinger,* 539 U.S. 331 (2003).
75. Ibid., 332.
76. Ibid., 314.
77. Ibid., 315.
78. Ibid., 316.
79. Ibid., 334.
80. Ibid., 335.
81. Ibid., 336.
82. Ibid., 298.
83. Ibid.
84. Ibid.
85. See Justin Pidot, "Intuition or Proof: The Social Science Justification for the Diversity Rationale in *Grutter v. Bollinger* and *Gratz v. Bollinger,*" *Stanford Law Review* 59 (2007): 761.
86. *Grutter v. Bollinger,* 539 U.S. 384–386 (2003).
87. Ibid., 389.

88. See Brian T. Fitzpatrick, "The Diversity Lie," *Harvard Journal of Law and Public Policy* 27 (2003): 384; Peter H. Schuck, "Affirmative Action: Past, Present, and Future," *Yale Law & Policy Review* 20 (2002): 1, 34.

89. *Grutter v. Bollinger,* 539 U.S. 304 (2003).

90. *Grutter v. Bollinger,* 539 U.S. 354 n.3 (2003).

91. See Albert O. Hirschman, *The Rhetoric of Reaction* (1991).

92. *Grutter v. Bollinger,* 539 U.S. 332 (2003).

93. Jack Balkin, "*Plessy, Brown,* and *Grutter*: A Play in Three Acts," *Cardozo Law Review* 26 (2005): 1689; Cynthia Estlund, "Putting *Grutter* to Work: Diversity, Integration, and Affirmative Action in the Workplace," *Berkeley Journal of Employment and Labor Law* 14 (2005): 1; Robert Post, "Foreword: Fashioning the Legal Constitution: Culture, Courts, and Law," *Harvard Law Review* 117 (2003): 4.

94. *Fisher v. University of Texas at Austin,* 631 F.3d 213, 225 (5th Cir. 2011).

95. Ibid., 217.

96. Ibid., 242.

97. Ibid., 247.

98. See *Fisher v. University of Texas,* 644 F.3d 301 (5th Cir. 2011).

99. Ibid., 303.

100. Ibid.

101. Brief of the Petitioner, *Fisher v. University of Texas at Austin,* Supreme Court of the United States (2012), 19.

102. Ibid., 20.

103. Ibid., 23.

104. Brief of Amicus Curiae California Association of Scholars, Center for Constitutional Jurisprudence, Reason Foundation, Individual Rights Foundation, and American Civil Rights Foundation in Support of Petitioner in *Fisher v. University of Texas at Austin,* Supreme Court of the United States (2012), 2.

105. Brief of Abigail Thernstrom, Stephen Thernstrom, and Russell Nieli as Amici Curiae in Support of Petitioner, *Fisher v. University of Texas at Austin,* Supreme Court of the United States (2012), 4.

106. Brief for respondent, *Fisher v. University of Texas at Austin,* Supreme Court of the United States (2012), 1.

107. Ibid., 2–3.

108. Ibid., 30.

109. Ibid., 31.

110. Ibid., 32.

111. Ibid., 32.

112. Ibid., 33.

113. Ibid., 34.

114. Brief of Lt. Gen. Julius W. Becton, et al., as Amici Curiae in Support

of Respondent, *Fisher v. University of Texas at Austin,* Supreme Court of the United States (2012), 1.

115. Ibid., 2.
116. Ibid., 3.
117. Brief for Amici Curiae Fortune-100 and Other Leading American Businesses in Support of Respondents, *Fisher v. University of Texas at Austin,* Supreme Court of the United States (2012), 2.
118. Ibid., 2–3.
119. *Sweatt v. Painter,* 339 U.S. 629, 634 (1950).
120. *Hopwood v. Texas,* 861 F.Supp 551, 554 (W.D. Tex. 1994).
121. Ibid., 553.
122. Ibid., 554.
123. Ibid., 583.
124. Ibid., 572.
125. Ibid., 577.
126. *Hopwood v. Texas,* 78 F.3d 932 (5th Cir. 1996).
127. Ibid., 953, quoting *Maryland Troopers Ass'n. v. Evans,* 993 F.2d 1072, 1079 (4th Cir. 1993).
128. Ibid.
129. Ibid.
130. The Sweatt Family Brief in support of respondent, *Fisher v. University of Texas at Austin,* Supreme Court of the United States (2012), 1.

5. Reflections on the Future of the Affirmative Action Controversy

1. Richard Kahlenberg, Online Fister Symposium: In Defense of Race-Neutral Alternative Jurisprudence, Scotusblog, September 11, 2012.
2. Ibid.
3. See, generally, Zoya Hasan and Martha C. Nussbaum, eds., *Equalizing Access: Affirmative Action in Higher Education in India, United States, and South Africa* (2012); Thomas Sowell, *Affirmative Action around the World; An Empirical Study* (2004); Thomas Sowell, *Preferential Policies: An International Perspective* (1990); George M. Fredrickson, *Diverse Nations: Exploration in the History of Racial and Ethnic Pluralism* (2001); James P. Sterba, "Completing Thomas Sowell's Study of Affirmative Action and then Drawing Different Conclusions," *Stanford Law Review* 57 (2004): 657.
4. See Zoya Hasan, *Politics of Inclusion: Castes, Minorities, and Affirmative Action* (2009); Marc Galanter, *Competing Equalities: Law and the Backward Classes in India* (1984).

5. See Canadian Charter of Rights and Freedoms, Section 15(2).

6. International Covenant on Civil and Political Rights, Article 26 (1976).

7. See Statement of May 11, 1994, of Legal Advisor Conrad Harper to the Senate Committee on Foreign Relations, reprinted in *American Journal of International Law* 88 (1994): 721.

8. International Convention on the Elimination of All Forms of Racial Discrimination, Art. 2, para. 2 (1969).

9. Steven M. Teles, "Positive Action or Affirmative Action? The Persistence of Britain's Antidiscrimination Regime," in *Color Lines: Affirmative Action, Immigration, and Civil Rights Options for America*, John David Skrentny, ed. (1998), 241.

10. Ibid.

11. See Daniel Sabbagh, "The Rise of Indirect Affirmative Action: Converging Strategies for Promoting 'Diversity' in Selective Institutions of Higher Education in the United States and France," *World Politics* 63 (2011): 470; "Color-Blind Affirmative Action: The Case for France," unpublished paper, June 2012.

12. French constitution of October 4, 1958.

13. See, generally, Anthony W. Marx, *Making Race and Nation: A Comparison of the United States, South Africa, and Brazil* (1998).

14. Edward E. Telles, *Race in Another America: The Significance of Skin Color in Brazil* (2006), 59.

15. Ibid., 60.

16. Quoted in Simon Romero, "Brazil Enacts Affirmative Action for Universities," *New York Times,* August 30, 2012.

17. Quoted in Judith February, "From Redress to Empowerment: The New South African Constitution and Its Implementation," in *The Next Twenty-five Years: Affirmative Action in Higher Education in the United States and South Africa,* David L. Featherman, Martin Hall, and Marvin Krislow, eds. (2010), 75.

18. R. W. Johnson, *South Africa's Brave New World: The Beloved Country Since the End of Apartheid* (2013), 112.

19. Neville Alexander, "The Struggle for National Liberation and the Attainment of Human Rights in South Africa," in *The Next Twenty-five Years: Affirmative Action in Higher Education in the United States and South Africa,* David L. Featherman, Martin Hall, and Marvin Kirslov, eds. (2010), 55.

20. *Grutter v. Bollinger,* 539 U.S. 306, 343 (2003).

21. Ibid., 376 (Thomas, J., dissenting).

22. Ibid., 345 (Ginsburg, J., concurring).

Index

ALSO BY

RANDALL KENNEDY

THE PERSISTENCE OF THE COLOR LINE
Racial Politics and the Obama Presidency

Renowned for his insightful, common-sense critiques of
racial politics, Randall Kennedy gives us a shrewd and penetrating analysis of the complex relationship between the
first black president and his African-American constituency.
Kennedy tackles such hot-button issues as the nature of
racial opposition to Barack Obama; whether Obama has
a singular responsibility to African Americans; the differences in Obama's presentation of himself to blacks and
to whites; the increasing irrelevance of a certain kind of
racial politics and its consequences; the complex symbolism of Obama's achievement and his own obfuscations
and evasions regarding racial justice. Eschewing the critical excesses of both the left and the right, Kennedy offers
an incisive view of Obama's triumphs and travails, his
strengths and weaknesses, as they pertain to the troubled
history of race in America.

Current Affairs/Politics

ALSO AVAILABLE

Interracial Intimacies
Nigger
Race, Crime, and the Law
Sellout

VINTAGE BOOKS
Available wherever books are sold.
www.vintagebooks.com

Printed in the United States
by Baker & Taylor Publisher Services